Fashion Illustrator

Bethan Morris

LAURENCE KING

Introduction

Who this book is for **6** / What is in the book **7** /

1. Inspiration

Discovering sources of inspiration **10** / Researching themes **13** /
Working sketchbooks **16** / From inspiration to illustration **22**

2. The Figure

Drawing from life **30** / Life drawing **34** / Observational drawing and intuitive
exercises **36** / Body proportions: theory and practice **40** / Templates **46** /
Hot spots **50**

3. Artistic Techniques

Art materials and equipment **62** / Colour **78** / Fabric rendering and pattern
reproduction **83**

4. Tutorials

Mixed media **94** / Illustrator **98** / Embroidery **102** /
Photomontage **106** / Drawing **109** / Photoshop **113** / Ink **118**

5. Presentation for Fashion Design

Mood boards and portfolio presentation **122** / Design roughs and range-building **124** /
Fashion design presentation **133** / Showing off – graduate style **136**

6. Historical and Contemporary Fashion Illustration

The beginnings of fashion illustration **140** / Contemporary fashion illustration
showcase **151**

7. The Future: Guidance

Portfolio presentation **208** / The future: making choices **212** / Illustration agent **217** /
Fashion illustrator **218** / Trend forecaster **222** / Commercial fashion illustrator **224**

••• Further reading **228** / Trade publications and magazines **231** / Useful addresses **231** /
Glossary **234** / Index **236** / Picture sources and credits **239** / Acknowledgements **240**

Related study material is available on the Laurence King website at
www.laurenceking.com

LAURENCE KING

Published in 2010 by Laurence King Publishing Ltd
361–373 City Road
London EC1V 1LR
Tel: +44 20 7841 6900
Fax: +44 20 7841 6910
e-mail: enquiries@laurenceking.com
www.laurenceking.com

© text 2010 Bethan Morris
First published in Great Britain in 2006
Second edition published 2010 by Laurence King Publishing Ltd
The moral right of the author has been asserted.

A catalogue record for this book is available
from the British Library

ISBN: 978 1 85669 654 8

Design: Lizzie Ballantyne, Lizzie B Design
Series designer: Jon Allan
Picture research: the author and Peter Kent
Senior editor: Peter Jones
Printed in China

Frontispiece: :puntoos
Front cover: Sara Singh
Back cover: Stina Persson

Fashion illustration titles line the shelves of bookshops, magazines often illustrate features rather than use photographs, and illustration is a popular medium for fashion advertising. The art of fashion illustration is once again in vogue, but will this trend continue? The answer must be yes. In an age of increasing standardization and automation, we yearn for the individuality expressed by the new trend-setting image-makers. Fashion illustrators who experiment skilfully with unusual media and innovative design are warmly welcomed. While fashion illustration continues to develop and offer fresh interpretations, its place in the future commercial world is assured.

Who is this book for?

For the purpose of this book the term "fashion illustration" is broad. It covers a wide range of artwork created by fashion designers and fashion illustrators. Under the umbrella of fashion illustration, this book focuses on the fundamentals of fashion drawing and presentation throughout the design process. As the fashion design student must present fashion ideas to gain employment on graduation, *Fashion Illustrator* explores the skills required to create an effective portfolio. Imaginative research directions are revealed, as well as how to illustrate fashion ideas, how to represent garments technically and how to compile mood boards.

While *Fashion Illustrator* provides a valuable knowledge base for the fashion designer, many successful designers only design clothes. It is common for such designers to employ fashion illustrators to present their collections and promote their labels. The fashion illustration student's portfolio will therefore be geared towards advertising and promotion. A flexible approach is required for working to briefs from a variety of clients, so *Fashion Illustrator* reveals how to experiment effectively with colour, how to use art materials and equipment, and how to select the appropriate artistic style, character and media for a particular client.

Whether you want to be a fashion designer or a fashion illustrator, the most important skill to master is drawing the human figure. *Fashion Illustrator* dedicates a practical chapter to the figure that should be referred to regularly throughout your studies.

Covering the broad area of fashion illustration and presentation, this book will prove invaluable for both fashion design and fashion illustration students. Many books aim to teach the skills required to illustrate fashion, and these manuals are displayed alongside showcase books featuring edited collections of illustrators' promotional fashion artwork. These categories have traditionally been separate, but *Fashion Illustrator* combines a how-to approach with a visual overview of historical and contemporary fashion illustration. By explaining the fundamentals of fashion illustration and presentation, and bringing this rewarding creative process to life with rich detail, *Fashion Illustrator* serves as a valuable resource and teaching aid. It is useful for anyone with an interest in fashion, design and illustration.

What is in the book?

We all know that 'fashion' does not stand still and neither does the illustration and promotional artwork that accompanies it. Fashion illustration needs to keep up with the times and continually reinvent itself. In this second edition of *Fashion Illustrator* I have attempted to incorporate previous omissions and present fresh examples of the fast-moving, ever-changing offerings from the fashion illustration industry of the twenty-first century. Enriched by brand-new case studies, improved example illustrations, extended practical exercises and tips, it covers all aspects of fashion illustration and presentation. The book explores how artists find inspiration in the world around them, how they use this in their work, and it encourages readers to face the challenge of experimenting with varied media, such as collage, different drawing tools, digital enhancement and embroidery. Through an understanding of the figure and experimentation with different illustrative styles, the reader will learn how to present the clothed human form artistically. Examining the work of both past and present-day fashion illustrators gives students the confidence and skills to push the boundaries of their own work. In-depth discussions with leading contemporary fashion illustrators provide insights that inspire students to think beyond graduation to a career in fashion illustration or design.

Chapter One, 'Inspiration', explores the things that inspire the creative mind, revealing how to find rewarding ideas, understand visual expression and produce innovative fashion illustrations, sketchbooks and artwork. The chapter discusses how to find sources of inspiration from which to develop ideas. With this in mind, the reader is encouraged to look at the world with fresh interest. Varied processes for capturing ideas and investigating themes on paper are also explained, helping the budding fashion illustrator tackle the daunting blank page.

Compiling ideas in a sketchbook is also an essential part of both a designer's and an illustrator's development. Updated practical advice is given on completing useful sketchbooks that provide a source of inspiration.

Chapter Two, 'The Figure', focuses on basic drawing skills, providing a solid understanding of anatomy and the physical structure of the human form. Through a series of observational exercises the reader learns to draw the nude and clothed figure from life and photographs, understand correct proportions and draw features of the body accurately. The use of a template and the effective exaggeration of the proportions of a fashion figure are also explained clearly. In this second edition, the diagrams and technical information have been enhanced by providing extra fashion illustrations by professional illustrators. They demonstrate how to draw those challenging figure hotspots with imaginative flair.

A digitally enhanced fashion illustration by Rebecca Antoniou.

Chapter Three, 'Artistic Techniques', gives an overview of how to use art equipment and materials. This guidance has been visually enriched with a series of fashion illustrations from the best fashion illustrators in the business. Illustrator Cecilia Carlstedt also demonstrates how to render a selection of fabrics using the recommended techniques and equipment.

Chapter Four, 'Tutorials', encourages the reader to build fashion illustrations in stages, experimenting with exciting techniques. In this edition the tutorials are all brand-new, featuring personal advice from industry digital illustrators Tom Bagshaw and Marcos Chin. Edwina White explains her commission process for fashion illustrations for *The New York Times Style* pages, and Tina Berning creates illustrations for fashion trend books each season. Louise Gardiner demonstrates how her sewing machine is better than a pencil while Robert Wagt cuts and pastes to create his trademark long-legged women. Finally, Amelie Hegardt transports us into an imaginative world with paintbrushes and ink.

Chapter Five, 'Presentation for Fashion Design', has been improved upon by adding new case studies and fresh examples from the fashion design industry. The chapter reveals how fashion illustration, sketching and considered presentation is significant in a fashion designers's portfolio. It explores the process of producing design roughs to build fashion ranges through the work of womenswear designer Sophie Hulme. The purpose of specification drawings and flats are realised with examples from Bolongaro Trevor. Pages from Iben Høj's portfolio are displayed alongside the 'lookbook' commissioned fashion illustrations of Laura Laine, and graduate Craig Fellows shows how to display the complete package.

Chapter Six, 'Historical and Contemporary Fashion Illustration', describes the social journey of fashion illustration over the last 100 years. The illustrative styles of the twentieth century's most influential illustrators are discussed by decade. Illustrators of today inevitably look to the past for inspiration and this section also features work that demonstrates this synthesis of past styles and modern terchniques. The second part of the chapter showcases work by 28 leading international fashion illustrators from 14 countries. Each illustrator defines his or her work and career by answering a series of interview-style questions. All offer interesting advice and inspiration to students who are thinking of following similar paths.

Chapter Seven, 'The Future: Guidance', takes the reader through the final part of the fashion illustration journey, outlining effective portfolio presentation techniques. There is also instruction on self-presentation, interview techniques, applying for further education and embracing a career in fashion illustration. The role of the illustration agent is clearly described and other industry specialists speak exclusively about their careers in fashion illustration.

In acknowledgement of the wider readership, at the end of the book you will find an extended further reading guide, a list of trade publications and magazines, useful addresses, a glossary, and an index, and in addition the picture credits, which include contact details for the illustrated artists.

1.

This book gives a solid grounding in all aspects of fashion illustration, but it is only a guide to help you on your journey. Sometimes embarking on that journey is the hardest part. Creating something new from scratch is a daunting prospect for any artist. This chapter will help you ensure that your portfolio stands out from the crowd. You will discover how to find inspiration and how to use it.

Discovering sources of inspiration

American painter George Bellows (1882–1925) once stated, "The artist is the person who makes life more interesting or beautiful, more understandable or mysterious, or probably, in the best sense, more wonderful." This is a tall order for the artist. With such expectations you are not alone if you feel daunted by the prospect of creating artwork, and not the only one who finds it hard to know where to begin. To help you to discover a starting point, this chapter reveals how to find inspiration, how to make visual use of the world around you and how to apply your observations in creating innovative fashion illustrations, designs and artwork.

Where exactly do you look for inspiration? As British designer Sir Paul Smith says: "You can find inspiration in everything … and if you can't, you're not looking properly – so look again." This is good advice. Inspiration for creative artwork is everywhere. Begin by wandering around your home, looking at it with fresh eyes. You will be surprised how mundane, everyday objects suddenly have new meaning and potential. The old wallpaper in the sitting room could be a good background for an illustration, or a photograph of your sister may supply the perfect fashion figure silhouette for a template. The illustration on the facing page has a background directly inspired by old-fashioned wallpaper.

When you open your eyes to the world you will discover that it is overflowing with potential to trigger your imagination. Don't be put off if you find that your ideas already exist somewhere else. The truth is that few ideas are entirely new; as Pablo Picasso said: "Everything you can imagine is real." However, when you bring to the idea your own personal response, you provide an original interpretation.

Like all artists, designers and illustrators look for sources of inspiration to develop their work and focus on absorbing new ideas all the time. Read a variety of books and magazines, familiarizing yourself with interior trends, music and lifestyle editorials, as well as fashion. Theatrical costume and set design can also stimulate interesting ideas. Never be without a camera or sketchbook to capture and record inspirational scenes, objects or people.

Experiencing other environments through travel stimulates creative imagination and need not involve the expense of going overseas. If you live in the city, visit the countryside, and vice versa. If you are lucky enough to travel abroad, visit local markets and communities, observe traditional

Taking photographs of, or sketching, people you see in the street gives you a rewarding variety of figures and stances for your illustrations. This girl in a busy Paris street stood out because of her brightly coloured umbrella and coordinating outfit. The image provides an ideal starting point for a fashion illustration.

Left
Vincent Bakkum has created a unique illustration
by focusing on many elements of the composition.
The background is made up of a pencil sketch
inspired by wallpaper. The floating blue bottle
draws in the observer, and the model is wearing a
painted headscarf that flows across the page like
a brushstroke. The artist has used a subtle colour
palette to create a tranquil mood. Few artists can
produce creative ideas without a knowledge base
gained from magazines, books, advertisements
and a wide variety of sources. Keep up to date
with the latest trends and open your mind to new
sources of inspiration.

Beach huts seen on an Australian beach have
added interesting accents of colour to the
dramatic shoreline. This scene could be used
in a fashion illustration, or it could be that the
colours inspire future artwork.

A building's interior structure can be as much
a source of inspiration as that of the exterior.
Interesting lines for fashion design or illustration
can be seen in the timber structure of this
wooden roof.

costumes and everyday clothing, eat new foods and recognize cultural
differences. By embracing the experience, you will come away from your
trip with a wealth of inspiration.

Keep up to date with the news and world events, television and film
releases. Monitor changes and behavioural shifts in big cities around the
world, watching for new trends in cities such as New York, London, Tokyo,
Paris and Copenhagen. For example, how might you apply the trend for
knitting cafés in New York or permanent spray cosmetics (whereby colours
are applied permanently like a tattoo) in Tokyo to your artwork? And never
underestimate the importance of visiting galleries and museums. No matter
how seemingly irrelevant to fashion contemporary art exhibitions might
sometimes seem, it is worth visiting them. Often the exhibition you least
expect to enjoy delivers the most inspiring results.

In museums, too, a wealth of inspiring artefacts and memorabilia awaits
your artistic interpretation. Nostalgia for the past will always captivate us.

In fashion, for example, today's garments date quickly yet bygone eras are always a source of inspiration. Every decade sees a revival of the style of a past decade. It seems that it is second nature for us to draw from the past to illustrate the future.

As an artist, designer or illustrator you are always open to visual stimulation in your normal day-to-day life. Even a trip to the supermarket can awaken new ideas as you look at the variety of vibrant packaging on the shelves. Your journey home might take you past architecture, landscape or gardens whose intriguing shapes and textures trigger your imagination. Your thoughts might be awakened by listening to compelling music, an image in a magazine might inspire a new idea, an absorbing television documentary might activate your creative energy or a favourite poem conjure up engaging imagery. This type of inspiration is all around you waiting to be discovered.

Collecting inspirational items

Artists are invariably avid collectors of what to the uninitiated eye looks like junk. Accumulating anything and everything of interest is a fascinating way to build an ideas-bank for future design or artwork. Keep everything that captures your imagination, as you never know when it might be useful in the future. Arguments about the amount of clutter you possess might occur with those who share your home, but stand your ground! This clutter could one day make you a famous artist – think Tracy Emin's *My Bed.* Art materials, unusual papers, wrapping, packaging and scraps of fabric are worth storing as you may well be able to utilize them in your artwork. In Chapter Three you will find the work of Peter Clark, who uses found papers, such as maps and cigarette packets, to create delightful collaged fashion illustrations.

People collect all sorts of unusual items, either because they get pleasure from looking at them or because they can see creative potential in them. Many illustrators look for interesting stamps, cigarette cards, key rings, handbags, film memorabilia, calendars, buttons and so on in car-boot sales, jumble sales and charity shops. They then put their own original slant on the ideas generated by their collections. The trained eye can spot artistic potential in almost anything. A collection of bangles right, for example, makes a marvellous starting point for a fashion illustration. Look closely at the colours, shapes and details, and see how they have been incorporated into the accompanying fashion illustration.

Books form a particularly useful collection, providing a constant and varied source of inspiration. The further reading guide on pages 228–30 gives a list of fashion and fashion illustration titles worth finding. But remember that books on all sorts of other subjects might spark ideas, too. Look in second-hand bookstores for older, out-of-print titles as well as keeping up to date with new titles, broadening your collection so that it offers an ever-expanding variety of ideas. Collecting books is costly so it is worth becoming familiar with your local library. Just browsing through the shelves in

A trained eye can spot artistic potential in almost anything. Look closely at the colours, shapes and details of these rows of brightly coloured bangles, and see how they inspire the background for the fashion illustration by Gilly Lovegrove above. The striped clothing also reflects the brightly coloured rows.

a peaceful environment can be a stimulating process. If you take a sketchbook along, you could even practise making some observational figure drawings while you are choosing which book to borrow.

Invest in other forms of printed media, too, such as magazines, journals and postcards. As magazines are printed more regularly than books their content is usually "of the moment". Such up-to-date images can inform and inspire your artwork. Postcards from galleries can also be an economical way of taking home a little piece of inspiration, particularly if you can't afford an exhibition catalogue. Many artists have boxes of postcards saved from a lifetime of visiting exhibitions that they use repeatedly as inspirational references for fashion illustration.

Maintaining a lively interest in the world is vital for the fashion illustrator, who must combine keen observational skills with creative interpretation.

Researching themes

There is no doubt that one of the most daunting aspects of creativity for the artist is being faced with a blank page. The prospect of plucking new ideas out of thin air and arriving at an original artistic solution can be unnerving. This is why it is important to develop a knowledge base from which creative ideas can grow.

Above left
This fashion illustration by Gilly Lovegrove has been created in a monotone palette to reflect the black-and-white photograph of a Giorgio Armani dress. The floral design of the fabric is instrumental to the artwork.

Above right
Visit as many exhibitions as possible because you never know which one might provide valuable inspiration. If the exhibition catalogue is too costly for you, buy postcards of your favourite images. This postcard was bought at the Royal Academy of Arts, in London, during the exhibition *Giorgio Armani: A Retrospective*.

Albert Einstein said that "imagination is more important than knowledge". However, before most artists can begin to produce artwork from their imagination they need to establish the knowledge base from which they will work. The simplest starting point for this is to select a theme to investigate and develop. This can be anything that interests you, from an antique Japanese silk fan to graffiti art on train station walls – the range of inspirational resources in the world is endless. With so much to stimulate your imagination, it is easy to become indecisive. The key is to be selective, only choosing themes that truly inspire you. Your chosen theme must continue to hold your attention while you explore its creative elements.

A good starting point in the investigative process is to form a list of words that are associated with the theme. This is known as 'mind-mapping' or 'brainstorming'. A butterfly theme is explored (facing page) by listing the words that spring to mind while concentrating on the image, or idea, of a butterfly. The words create a number of research avenues to follow, the initial subject of a butterfly having a wealth of associations, with almost every word capable of inspiring a new investigation.

The images below show how a theme can also be investigated artistically. Notice how the butterflies have been used to create repeat patterns. The textures of their wings and the symmetrical patterns across them have been represented through painting and drawing. Colour studies have been made of many butterfly varieties. The popularity of the butterfly as decoration in fashion has also been emphasized. This exploration shows how a butterfly theme can be used to inspire fashion designers as well as the fashion illustrators who illustrate their garments.

Four studies investigating the butterfly as a theme show different media, including collage, painting, drawing and cut-outs from magazines, mounted onto hand-made paper. The images demonstrate a visual exploration of the butterfly theme, revealing its diversity as a research direction.

feathers caterpillar symmetry
kites moths colour pattern
birds cocoon summer
fairies
wings alive
flight
aeroplanes natural

repeat pattern fashionable
decoration
delicate
soft jewellery

harmless accessories
transformation:
mystical ugly-beautiful magical
fantasy

Left

This mind-map shows a selection of words linked to a butterfly theme. A pattern of words produced in this way can inspire many ideas for fashion illustrations.

Below

The role of the imagination is as significant as that of knowledge. Once inspiration is found, research material collected and a theme established, the illustrator conceives a wealth of imaginative ideas. This illustration by Jacqueline Nsirim has been created using a mix of traditional drawing techniques for the figure and Photoshop collage to add the butterflies.

Working sketchbook

A sketchbook is a visual notebook or diary. It is a personal response to the world and can assume many different guises, varying from being a portable scrapbook in which to collect interesting pieces of fabric or pictorial references, to a book of observational drawings and ideas. All may, one day, provide that essential spark of inspiration. A sketchbook provides you with the opportunity to practise design, drawing and illustration skills at any time and in any place. You can develop figure studies by sketching the people you see at a local park, or on a train, or even by sitting on a bench in the high street and drawing the shoppers. Sketching scenery, such as interesting architecture, also helps to create ideas for illustration backgrounds.

Most artists keep sketchbooks in which they experiment with ideas and collect insightful imagery. Picasso is said to have produced 178 sketchbooks in his lifetime. He often used his sketchbooks to explore themes and make compositional studies until he found the subject and concept for a larger painting on canvas. Like Picasso, you will have numerous sketchbooks throughout your education and career. Some you will use for researching specific themes while others become constant companions for recording ideas that will provide future inspiration.

Producing useful working sketchbooks is an essential part of an art student's development. Academic design and illustration briefs often request a sketchbook containing appropriate research to be submitted for assessment. Ideally, the sketchbook presents an explorative journey around a chosen subject area.

A working sketchbook should be impulsive, experimental and in constant use, becoming an accumulation of ideas and research from which to draw inspiration for design and illustration. Sadly, this advice is frequently ignored and sketchbooks are produced whose clean pages are decorated with neat cuttings, ordered sketches and unused material from presentation boards. Generally this method of working results in tedious sketchbooks of carefully planned pages, often with Post-it notes acting as a reminder to fill blank pages. By organizing a sketchbook into a precious album in which the artist arranges experimental work at the end of a project, creative spontaneity is often lost. The sketchbook then becomes a useless tool rather than a rich resource for imaginative artwork.

The 'Cold Winter' sketchbook research (opposite) was created by fashion illustrator Cecilia Carlstedt. The page shows various illustrative techniques that became the initial inspiration for a series of commissioned fashion illustrations. Carlstedt uses graphite pencils to draw out ideas for her fashion figures directly onto the sketchbook page. The themes of snow and cold weather are reflected in paper cut-outs and digitally manipulated patterns. The colours that Carlstedt has chosen also guide the viewer to feel the seasonal cold weather. When working as an illustrator for a fashion designer, differentiating between the seasons is vital. A brightly coloured, sunny illustration would not be the best advertisement for a collection of winter coats, for example. This sketchbook page sets the scene for further inspirational illustration or design work and can be referred to time and time again.

The best way to begin creating a useful sketchbook is to gather research material from a variety of sources. This can include any or all of the following:

- observational drawing
- painted visual studies
- colour studies
- photographs
- collage
- relevant imagery, for example from
  magazine cut-outs
- fabric swatches
- found objects
- internet research
- exhibition information
- artist/designer references
- postcards
- historical references (text or visual)
- personal recollections

Research for a 'snow' theme has been collated in Cecilia Carlstedt's sketchbook. She has used a mixture of different media to build up the page, creating paper, cut-out snowflakes, painted and printed snow, and sketches of garments and models in various poses. The artwork has been mounted into her sketchbook for easy reference and keeps a cool, snowy colour palette appropriate to the theme. This collection of research will provide Carlstedt with inspiration for future fashion illustrations.

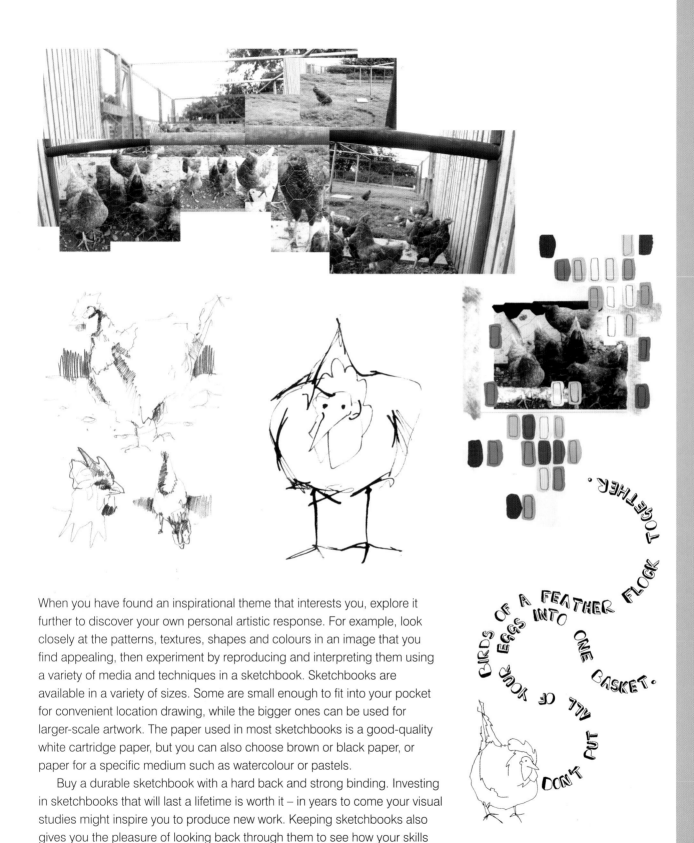

When you have found an inspirational theme that interests you, explore it further to discover your own personal artistic response. For example, look closely at the patterns, textures, shapes and colours in an image that you find appealing, then experiment by reproducing and interpreting them using a variety of media and techniques in a sketchbook. Sketchbooks are available in a variety of sizes. Some are small enough to fit into your pocket for convenient location drawing, while the bigger ones can be used for larger-scale artwork. The paper used in most sketchbooks is a good-quality white cartridge paper, but you can also choose brown or black paper, or paper for a specific medium such as watercolour or pastels.

Buy a durable sketchbook with a hard back and strong binding. Investing in sketchbooks that will last a lifetime is worth it – in years to come your visual studies might inspire you to produce new work. Keeping sketchbooks also gives you the pleasure of looking back through them to see how your skills have progressed.

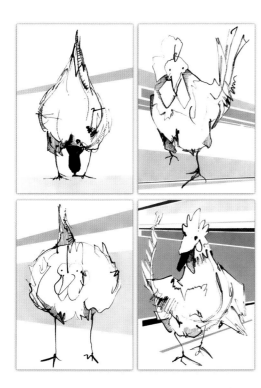

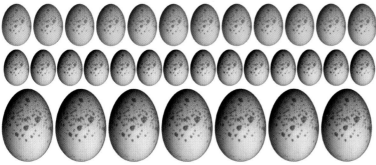

Here, graduate fashion designer Craig Fellows lets us into his working sketchbook to see how some chickens on a farm ended up becoming the inspiration for a beautiful hand-printed womenswear collection. Fellows' sketchbook pages show how he developed a range of prints using his ink sketch of a chicken as a starting point. He added quirky phrases and text that have since become his trademark. Fellows experimented with colour digitally before adding his most successful prints into his sketchbook as a reference point for future design. He also scanned his newly printed fabrics into Adobe Photoshop to create a clever digital presentation board for his portfolio. Again, documenting this style as a point of reference in his sketchbook. Fellows' working books provide a wealth of information that would enthuse anybody who views them. Most importantly, they are a constant source of ideas for his own career as a fashion designer.

Opposite

An unusual starting point for a fashion collection, graduate designer Craig Fellows researches chickens in his sketchbook. He has taken photographs and mounted them to build a new picture. He has drawn the chickens and given them their own unique characters, and added some of his own humour by experimenting with text.

Above

Moving forward in his research Craig records his textile print ideas in his sketchbook. He documents some of his accessories (above right) by adding photographs and print examples to the pages. Craig continually builds records of his ideas in this book which will provide a valuable source of inspiration for his career as a fashion and textile designer.

Following pages

As a designer it is a good idea to record fabric and trim costs and availability. You never know when you may need a similar button or a particular shade of fabric again in the future. Craig Fellows makes notes on everything linked to his collection in his sketchbook. His design sketches are also included alongside the photographs of the finished garments and printed textiles.

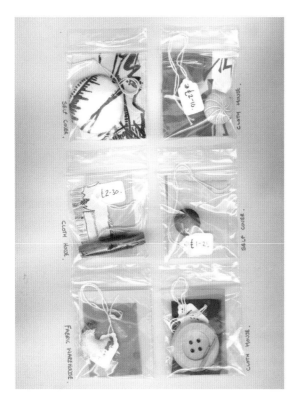

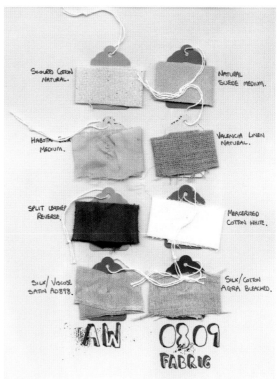

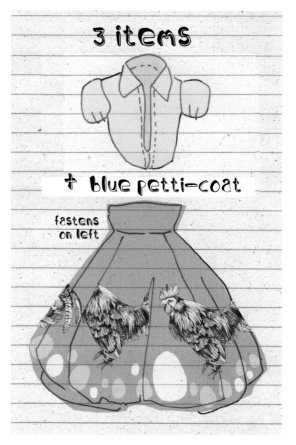

From inspiration to illustration

In 2004 Danish knitwear designer Iben Høj (www.ibenhoej.com) decided she wanted to do something different to promote her fashion collection. What she didn't realise back then was that her simple mail-out folders would become collector items of the future!

Iben Høj's womenswear collections are understated and sophisticated with an emphasis on unique details and refined craftsmanship. She follows her own path, working instinctively and avoids being pulled into the vacuum of isolation by creating her own magical world of beautiful clothing, illustration and art.

When asked about who gets to see the world which Høj and her label inhabit she says, "Aside from showing the current collection on my website and the forthcoming collection at fashion fairs in Copenhagen, New York and Paris, I print a new folder each season and this is used as a direct mail-out. I call it an 'appetizer,' as it is small and only gives a hint of the collection." Høj carefully selects inspirational illustrators and artists from all over the world to promote her label using their own distinctive flair.

There is a very good reason for working in this way. "When I originally decided to print a mail-out folder for the Spring/Summer season 2005 I knew I wanted to do something different. I wanted to show something atmospheric, with the essence of my design at the forefront rather than just the clothes on a model." Høj often found that when working more conventionally with a model on location, the shoot suddenly becomes about the girl, her look and the styling. She asked herself, "How can I show my designs to the public in a more clean form, a simpler way?" The outcome was a striking mail-out containing three photographs of actual designs very simply pictured on a hanger. To complement these, each season she commissioned three illustrations by a new illustrator or artist.

The idea of a collaborative process between designer and illustrator was born and Høj began researching. "I love fashion illustration books and have various publications such as *Fashion Wonderland* and *Romantik* lining my shelves. Once I had found individual illustrators whose work I liked, I viewed further work on their websites and contacted them directly."

With so many illustrators out there it was a difficult decision to pick just one to promote her style. Happily, Høj's first choice in 2005 was fellow Scandinavian Cecilia Carlstedt. "I absolutely love Cecilia's illustrations – she has a lightness, which just suits my work perfectly." (See examples of her work in rendering fabric on pp.75, 82, 84, 86, 88, 90 and p.186 for an interview with her.) For the second collaboration Høj chose Danish artist Cathrine Raben Davidsen. She had admired her work for a long time, believing her creations to possess "great power and an eeriness". Høj was unsure if she would want to work with her, as she is not a fashion illustrator, but a fine artist. Luckily the request was warmly welcomed and the Autumn/Winter 2007 collaboration was a resounding success, resulting in some truly unusual knitwear representation.

Below
An Iben Høj sketch of a garment from her Autumn/ Winter 2007 collection.

Bottom
An Iben Høj sample knit of the detailed knit used in the same garment.

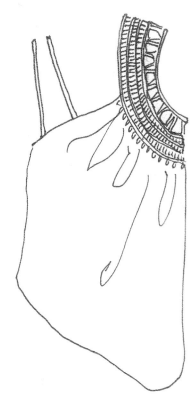

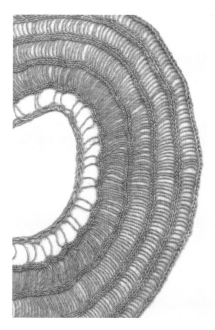

Above
The finished Iben Høj garment of the sketch
opposite photographed for the Autumn/Winter
2007 collection.

Right
The artist Cathrine Raben Davidsen's powerful
representation of the same garment. This
illustration, along with other works by Cathrine
were the basis of Høj's Autumn/Winter 2007
mail-out folders.

"... a collaborative
process
between designer
and illustrator"
– Iben Høj

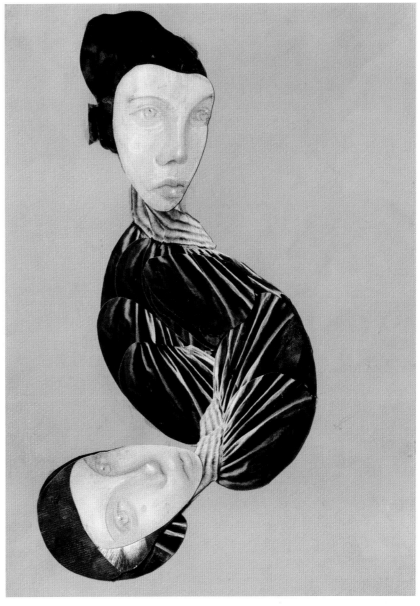

On working with Høj, Raben Davidsen comments, "Iben is a very sensitive
person, and was very open to my world and views, so she gave me total
freedom to enter her world. At the time I was working with a spider theme
(Arachne's Web taken from Ovid's *Metamorphosis*) in my own work. Iben's
knitting reminded me so much of these intricate and very complicated webs."
When asked about her decision to work in a fashion environment Raben
Davidsen says, "Knitting is associated with the female voice, a theme that
I am very interested in. I can really relate to Iben's work on many different
levels, especially as my father was a fashion designer who worked for Yves
Saint Laurent. Fashion has always been part of my life. In my own work I often
use elements from fashion and look towards the big fashion houses for

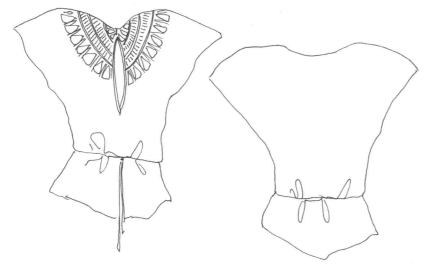

"I give the illustrators
free rein to create
what they like."
– Iben Høj

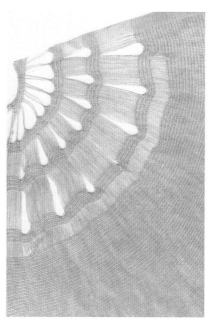

This page
Design sketches, knit sample and finished
garment from Iben Høj's Spring/Summer
2008 collection.

Right
Stina Persson's paper cut-out's, the perfect
technique to illustrate Høj's delicate knitwear
for her Spring/Summer 2008 mail-out folders.

inspiration. At the moment I am working on a series of prints in collaboration
with the Danish fashion designer Stine Goya.

The following season saw Stina Persson take the reins with a mix of
watercolour and paper cut-outs. (Persson's work appears in the showcase
section and on the back cover.) Persson describes how she came to
work with Høj. "In 2007 I had a show at New York gallery hanahou called
'Immacolata and Her Friends' where I had drawn 40 portraits of Italian women
in ink and collaged Mexican *papel picado* (perforated paper) on top. I was
still really into creating portraits this way when Iben contacted me about the
collaboration. The beautifully cut tissue paper of the *papel picado* happened
to be a perfect match to Iben's dream-like knitwear. I also liked the contrast

"The beautifully cut tissue paper of the
papel picado happened to be a perfect match
to Iben's dream-like knitwear." – Stina Persson

from the strong, bold ladies in ink and their delicate paper-thin clothing. This is how I saw Iben's designs and the women wearing them."

Of the German illustrator and artist Tina Berning, Høj states, "I bought her book [*100 Girls on Cheap Paper*] – and fell in love. She has an amazing illustrative style and creates portraits of alluring, strong women. Her style is both old fashioned and yet so modern. It suits my ethos and design perfectly. Working with Tina was like a match made in heaven." Tina Berning also felt they shared the same work ethos and mutual respect for each other's creations. "I immediately fell in love with Iben's knitwear and the idea of creating drawings that could accompany her fragile pieces of wool and art. She provided me with fabric samples and sketches of her new collection and I was allowed to do whatever I wanted. Many clients tend to forget that the more freedom I get for a job, the more I want to give of myself. I have learned to work with strict briefs, but those without any restrictions are always the ones that I liked most, and that I would spend all the time in the world working on. They are also the ones that the clients are most satisfied with."

Berning completed three drawings, interpretation of Høj's designs on old, found paper. She chose china ink and gouache, leaving the paper background itself enough of a space to tell their stories. Everything was created by hand and the original drawings now hang on Høj's walls. (See opposite for examples of Tina's work and p.188 for an interview with her.)

Finnish illustrator Laura Laine was the choice for 2009. Her work can be seen in Chapter Five where Iben Høj's fashion design presentation is examined in greater detail, Høj describes her pencil-and-watercolour women as "fluid, languid and bewitching". Laine's light but striking drawings were a perfect illustrative representation for the Iben Høj label.

With talent like this exhibited by Høj every season, it's no wonder that collectors frequently request back copies of her imaginative mail-out folders. But in a fast-moving, fashion-dominated world where designers are always

Above
A design sketch, a knit sample and a finished garment from Iben Høj's Autumn/Winter 2008 collection.

Opposite
The garment above (along with a few more) are shown here in the Autumn/Winter 2008 mail-out folder illustrated by Tina Berning. The folders always follow the same format, but each illustrator brings them to life in a different way. Tina Berning's strong women exude beauty and personality across Høj's pages. The garments are photographed so that the delicate nature of the knit is highlighted. It is so refreshing to see the garments and their illustrative representations side-by-side in this lookbook format.

working two seasons ahead of themselves, how does the collaboration process actually evolve? "Following the initial introduction I tell the illustrators about myself and my work," says Høj. "I then run through all the facts about the actual job; the timeframe, the number of illustrations required, the inspiration for the collection, etc. I then send a package containing photographs of mock-up styles, design sketches, pictures of knit techniques and a colour card. If they have different modes of working, I let them know which style I prefer. Amazingly, they never see the finished garment before completing the project. The photographs are only taken when the collection is finished and ready for sale. Within this framework I give the illustrators free rein to create what they like." Høj must find this process exhilarating. How magical to pass on these facts and in a few months see these realistic but dream-like representations of her knitwear.

When asked to pick an artist (living or not) to illustrate her collections Høj doesn't hesitate, "I'd probably choose Kiki Smith, because her art is a constant inspiration to me. It would be exciting to see what she could make out of my work! My latest inspirational discovery is the artist Jacqueline Marval (1866–1932). Her work is amazingly beautiful and so strong. Her sense of detail, colour and style would I know be wonderful in one of my folders! I also adore the paper cut-out artist Su Blackwell. She makes enchanting, fairy tale cut-out stories from books – so fragile, poetic and inspiring!

When it comes to commissioning an illustrator or artist, Høj buys the original artwork together with the right to use it. Although she owns the copyright she would never use the work for anything other than the agreed purpose. "After I've compiled the folders and used the illustrations on my fashion week stands, the work is just for my private pleasure on a daily basis!"

Referring to Iben Høj's folders Tina Berning says, "It is always the same design, but the inside reveals a new world with each issue, a new illustrator and a new collection. It is always exciting to receive the new one in the mail. Iben Høj's folders or lookbooks are a wonderful example of how a strong frame opens a huge space for anything, any idea, any style, any technique, any artist, without ever loosing the concept. To illustrate this, I always show them to new students when I teach at art school. It is just such a good example of how consistency is rewarded time and time again!"

Høj says she agrees with Tina Berning's mantra, "A drawing a day keeps the doctor away!". She also reminds illustrators out there to "find your own style – practise, practise, practise – and aim for the stars!"

"…. collectors frequently request back copies of her imaginative mail-out folders."

2.

The Figure

Central to fashion illustration and fashion design is the figure.
An understanding of the accurate proportions of the human body and how
it is constructed is vital for producing convincing fashion illustrations and
garment designs. This chapter provides essential information and advice,
and easy-to-remember tips, that you will find useful throughout your artistic
career. To understand the figure beneath the clothes, practise the exercises
described on the following pages regularly.

Drawing from life

The figure has occurred throughout art history as a central theme for
exploration – drawing the nude figure from life has been practised in art
academies for centuries. Clothing brings further challenge and diversity to
drawing the figure and, from this, the art of fashion illustration has developed.

If you are relatively new to figure drawing, you may feel daunted by the
apparent complexity of the subject. It is a common belief that drawing the
figure is the hardest artistic talent to develop. How many times have you
heard phrases such as "I can't draw faces" or "I can't draw hands"? In fact,
good drawings of figures are not so much the most difficult to achieve as the
easiest to judge. We know the layout and proportions of our bodies so well
that we notice inaccuracies instantly. The result is that, unless a drawing is
remarkably accurate, it is deemed poor and the artist loses confidence.

At its most basic, a drawing is nothing more than a series of marks
made on a surface by one person that another can understand. In fashion
illustration, drawing the figure is more about developing your own style,
and creating individual studies that convey personality and meaning, than
about accuracy. However, this is not an excuse to draw a figure with, say, a
disproportionately large head because you are unable to assess proportions
correctly. An illustrator must understand accurate body proportions before
it is possible to create a unique style.

Through drawing we learn to see. We may think we know the human
figure until asked to describe it accurately. By recording a figure on paper,
we cannot help but understand it better. Our drawings vary because we all
see things differently. Look with fresh eyes to achieve an honest drawing, and
never rely on memory or what experience tells you is correct. Free yourself
from what your mind already "knows" and draw only what your eyes see.

The nude figure

The nude human figure must serve as the basis for all figure study and
fashion illustration. It is impossible to draw the clothed figure without
knowledge of the structure and form of the body underneath. In the
twenty-first century, artists and illustrators no longer tend to study anatomy
as part of their formal training. However, a sound knowledge of how the body
is constructed can only increase your perception. When thinking about the
figure you may use in a fashion illustration, consider the body shapes that lie

beneath the clothes. It is inspirational to look at the work of Michelangelo and Leonardo da Vinci whose observation of anatomy in pen and ink captures the reality and the beauty of the human body.

To broaden your knowledge of anatomy, visit a natural history museum or refer to books to make studies of the skeleton, and the joints and muscles that operate to move the bones. By gaining an understanding of how joints move and which bones fit together, you can create more realistic figure drawings.

A clear understanding of anatomy allowed Pablo Picasso to base a significant amount of his work around the nude human form. The works selected here outline important lessons for the art student. *Two Nude Women* demonstrates Picasso's economic use of line. Both women are lost in thought, and Picasso captures their mood with decisive pen-and-ink strokes. The nudes are drawn on a coloured background, using only a limited palette, enhancing the purity of line and form.

In *Femme nue allongée* Picasso uses mixed media to create blocks of colour and pattern, his experimental approach enriching the artwork.

Left
Pablo Picasso, *Two Nude Women*, 1902–03.
Ink and pencil on card.
With economical line and a limited colour palette, Picasso captures the main lines and forms of two reclining nudes in this uncomplicated image. His technique is bold and decisive.

Left below
Pablo Picasso, *Femme nue allongée*, 1955.
Paper collage and oil on canvas.
Experimenting with mixed media without a fixed idea of the outcome is a way of achieving unpredictable and exciting results, as Picasso demonstrates in this image. He uses haphazard blocks of patterned paper and colour to express his ideas, the finished effect most likely unplanned.

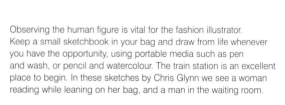

Observing the human figure is vital for the fashion illustrator. Keep a small sketchbook in your bag and draw from life whenever you have the opportunity, using portable media such as pen and wash, or pencil and watercolour. The train station is an excellent place to begin. In these sketches by Chris Glynn we see a woman reading while leaning on her bag, and a man in the waiting room.

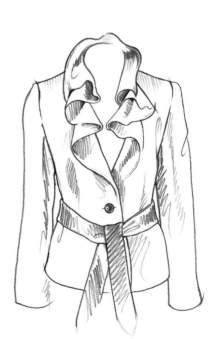

Practise by making quick sketches of clothing detail to increase your understanding of garment construction and the way clothes sit on the body.

It is doubtful that Picasso knew what result he would achieve when he started this piece, once saying: "If you know exactly what you are going to do, what is the point of doing it?"

The clothed figure

An understanding of how fabric drapes around the body is vital for drawing the clothed figure convincingly, as is a knowledge of how seams, gathers, pleats and darts affect the fit of garments on the figure. You do not need to know how to sew to illustrate, but it helps to be aware of the construction of clothing, just as it does to understand the structure of the body. Make detailed studies of sections of clothed figures to build your awareness of the ways in which clothes fit and drape on the body before you begin to illustrate.

An important aspect of drawing the figure is awareness of its scale in relation to its setting. Consider how figures fit into their surroundings, and how much their appearance is dictated by the scene in which they are set. Focusing on scale, composition and clothing, practise drawing figures in various locations: children playing on a beach, customers shopping, teenagers playing football, a couple dining in a café, a person curled up in an armchair or asleep on a sofa, employees in a meeting, friends watching television, passengers on a bus or old ladies chatting on a park bench. This type of sketching increases your ability to create a sense of perspective, and to draw figures to scale in their environments. By sketching on location, you will also gain ideas for backgrounds and settings for your fashion illustrations.

Measuring the figure and using a viewfinder

When drawing the nude or clothed figure from life, the most difficult skill to master is that of correct body proportions. To enhance their skills, many artists use a pencil to measure the figure and a viewfinder to frame a model and give proportionate width to height.

By holding a pencil at arm's length and focusing on your subject you can measure the figure in front of you. Close one eye, then use the pencil point and your thumb as markers to measure each part of the figure in relation to another. You can also hold your pencil at the same angle as the figure's arm, then transfer this angle to your drawing. This method allows you to assess approximately relative angles of parts of the body that would otherwise be difficult to draw correctly.

A viewfinder is a piece of card with a window cut into it of the same proportions as your drawing paper. Hold the viewfinder in front of one eye to frame the figure. A viewfinder helps you to disregard the figure's wider surroundings and draw only what is inside the window. It allows you to try out different framing options for your picture, including more or less of the setting around the figure.

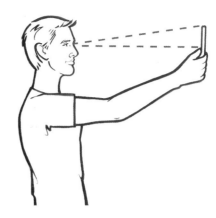

By holding a pencil at arm's length and focusing on your subject, you can measure the figure in front of you. Close one eye, and use the pencil point and your thumb as markers to measure, say, a leg in relation to another part of the body.

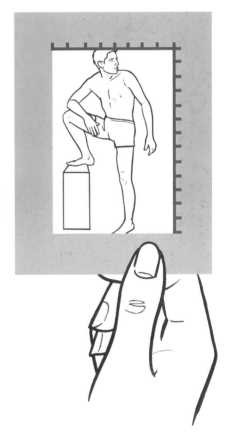

A viewfinder is a simple-to-make device that helps you to select how much of a figure's surroundings you want to include within the confines of your picture. By moving the viewfinder, you can select the view that works best.

Below left
Life drawing on a large scale can be bold and dramatic. Here Marega Palser brings drama and atmosphere to the work by using intense colour, and strong lines, shapes and patterns using charcoal and pencils.

Below centre
Experiment with varied media when drawing from life. While charcoal is a popular choice for many artists because it encourages bold, expressive lines, this study has been created with oil pastels on brown paper. Oil pastels are richly coloured and have a dense, waxy texture that can be exploited to provide additional interest in a figure drawing.

Below right
Here, Marega Palser has used a single page for a series of quick studies. Working with pencil, the artist concentrates on several poses in order to build an understanding of the figure and the way it moves.

Life drawing

The best way to represent figures confidently is to draw from life as often as you can. Many local art centres or art schools offer life-drawing classes. Attending your first life-drawing session can be a frightening prospect. Where will you sit? What materials should you use? Will you feel embarrassed? Where do you start? Many artists advise that in life-drawing classes the best way to proceed is to view the nude figure as a series of lines and shapes and forget that there is a person in front of you. Drawing the nude figure is the ultimate test in observation and understanding, and demands your full concentration, so you will find it easier than anticipated to dismiss other thoughts.

To practise drawing the clothed figure, make the most of opportunities such as family or friends watching television. Most people stay fairly still for about 15 minutes when relaxing. Public transport also offers an excellent opportunity for capturing interesting poses. Always carry a small sketchbook when travelling on a train or bus, or attending an event where there are lots of people to draw.

The sketchbook page opposite shows how Francis Marshall, although famous for couture-show sketches of Balenciaga, Jacques Fath and Dior, has always found time to practise figure drawing.

To improve his talent for capturing catwalk styles, Francis Marshall drew frequently from observation. His sketchbook pages show women walking, detailed pencil drawings of facial features and clothing accessories.

These studies by James Marcus, in charcoal and pencil, demonstrate how drawing from life can help you to gain valuable knowledge of the figure beneath the clothes. Perfect finished artwork is not attempted; instead the artist has focused on understanding particular parts of the body.

Observational drawing and intuitive exercises

Drawing from life is also known as 'objective' or 'observational' drawing, meaning an image that is created to represent what is seen during direct observation. The aim is to show the figure (or object) truthfully, exactly as it appears. Drawing in this way is about believing and trusting your visual judgement as you record what you see. Before embarking on more elaborate studies of the figure, try some simple exercises using intuitive observation. The purpose of these exercises is to train your mind to accept what your eyes – rather than your preconceptions or your mind's interpretations – deem to be true.

The 'don't-look-back' exercise

Focus all your attention on the figure in front of you and draw exactly what you see. Do not examine the drawing once you have started – just look at the figure and recreate its shapes on paper. Try not to use your critical judgement. Concentrate on the contours of the figure and the shapes contained within. This type of drawing is about forgetting what you think you know, and believing in what you see. When you look at a figure, your brain interprets for you what you should see. The result is that you may draw the figure as you *believe* it to be, rather than how it *actually* looks. By checking your drawing constantly, it is tempting to correct what you think are mistakes. Trust your eyes, and you will produce a truthful drawing.

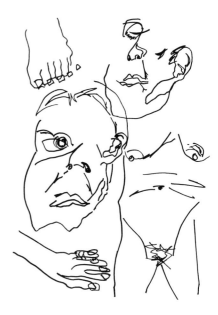

The 'don't-look-back' exercise encourages you to focus your thoughts entirely on the figure you are drawing. The aim is to draw without looking at your page. The result is not supposed to be a perfect artwork, but a valuable lesson in concentration and confident expression.

The continuous-line exercise

Working from observation, make a continuous line drawing of the figure. As you look at your subject, keep your hand moving constantly so that the line remains unbroken. You can complete this exercise using any medium – charcoal, pencil or pen. Avoid the temptation to create accurate details, such as those of the face, with lots of small lines. The purpose of this exercise is to record all information with one single, flowing line. The illustrations opposite (below left and right) have been created using continuous lines. They are extremely free images only refined by a hint of colour added digitally. It is a good idea to experiment with free-hand drawing and the computer to create unique effects.

The outline exercise

A useful skill to acquire when learning to draw the figure from life is to look past the detail to concentrate on the shape as a whole. Simplify what you see, flattening the figure in your mind's eye so that you focus on its outline. Learn to pay close attention to 'negative spaces' – the areas of background enclosed by parts of the figure. If you concentrate on drawing these shapes, the figure should emerge with some accuracy into the foreground of your illustration. Look at the back view of the figure drawn by Matisse (above left). The lines are simply the outline of the shape he sees. Likewise, Ossie Clark shows off his designs with strong outlines. The space around the figure is vital to the outline.

Above left
A master of the outline technique, Matisse captures this figure (1949) with only a few simple lines so that the viewer comprehends it entirely.

Above right
This line drawing, by British designer Ossie Clark, from a sketchbook of *c*.1970, provides just enough detail to appreciate the design of the clothes.

Opposite, below left
The continuous-line exercise involves creating a figure drawing with one, flowing line. Here Rose O'Reilly has scanned the image and blocked in colour digitally to emphasize the hands.

Opposite, below right
Line drawing has been a major influence in this fashion illustration by Louise Brandreth even though there is no obvious outline to the figure. Instead, it is made up from many interconnecting lines. A small amount of colour has been added digitally at the end of the process to finish the illustration.

Putting it all into practice

With all the previous skills obtained and tucked firmly under your belt, you are now ready to begin thinking about illustrating fashion. Fashion adorns the human form so it is usually necessary to include a figure in an illustration. The illustrations by Sara Singh on this page show why observational drawing from life is so important. Singh uses continuous line to capture the models poses as they lounge around the studio. The models faces are depicted but not drawn in great detail. In fact the figures are simply well observed outlines that act as a background for the clothing and accessories. Singh has used ink to capture the flimsy feather boa. It is subtly wrapped around the body hiding the models nakedness. The accessories of Ricci Girl are painted in darker ink than the figure outline to ensure that the observer notices them.

The unclothed body is often a powerful tool in advertising, and is also an inspired background for promoting fashion products. The illustration opposite above by Yuko Shimizu shows a model in a small bikini. Her body has been completely tattooed in place of clothing, however, cosmetic products have been cleverly positioned in the artwork. Shimizu's ink brushstrokes have been enhanced digitally using Adobe Photoshop. This illustration would not have been possible without some knowledge of drawing the human form. Shimizu carefully observes the body in her work. Drawing figures in various poses comes naturally to her, as she does it professionally every day.

Tom Bagshaw's digital fashion illustration opposite below also features an unclothed female. Here Bagshaw uses the figure to showcase the jewellery around her neck. There are no clothes to distract from the necklace, thus ensuring the viewer's eye is drawn immediately to the fashion accessory. Tom Bagshaw shows how he creates a similar fashion illustration in Chapter Four.

Ink sketches by Sara Singh show why observational drawing from life is so important in fashion illustration. The models are drawn with reference to real-life women and their proportions. The figures are well-observed outlines that simply act as a background for accessories and clothing.

Above

Drawing figures in various poses comes naturally to illustrator Yuko Shimizu as she practises professionally every day. This figure, created to advertise skincare products, has been drawn using ink and enhanced in Adobe Photoshop.

Left

Tom Bagshaw has created this fashion illustration digitally. He transforms the model into a magical, almost supernatural being using Adobe Photoshop and other programmes.

Body proportions: theory and practice

The human form

When drawing the fashion figure, it is important to know the standard proportions of the human form, as well as bearing in mind that people vary greatly in shape and size. Clothing the body is a means of self-expression and an opportunity for creativity, so the impression created by a fashion illustration must be based on careful observations. Fashions change from culture to culture, and from decade to decade. For example, a curvaceous figure and short, wavy hair was desirable in the 1950s, while a decade later a thin figure and poker-straight hair was most admired. The fashion illustrator often aims to express the features that society currently perceives as beautiful, and may choose to highlight these features through exaggerated illustration.

The human figure can be divided into 11 basic parts, this assists in seeing the body as a series of shapes.

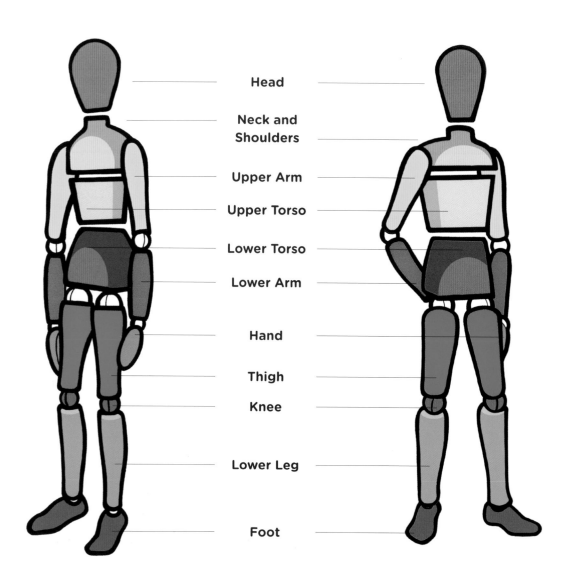

Head

Neck and Shoulders

Upper Arm

Upper Torso

Lower Torso

Lower Arm

Hand

Thigh

Knee

Lower Leg

Foot

So, while body shapes and proportions may vary from person to person and the fashionable ideal may change, the artist must keep in mind the essential components outlined in the following diagrams. The easiest way to begin your study of the human body is to see it as a series of shapes. For simplicity, imagine that it is made up of 11 basic parts (*see* opposite):

These basic parts can be manipulated to create different poses. Practise this by adjusting the parts of a wooden mannequin and drawing it at different angles (below). Your objective is to notice the way the 11 body shapes move in relation to each other. Then, once you understand how all the body parts fit together, focus on remembering their proportionate sizes.

This exercise is an important preparation for fashion illustration, as it will allow you to experiment with poses before you begin to concentrate on the details of the clothing.

Practise drawing poses from a mannequin, observing how the 11 body parts move in relation to each other.

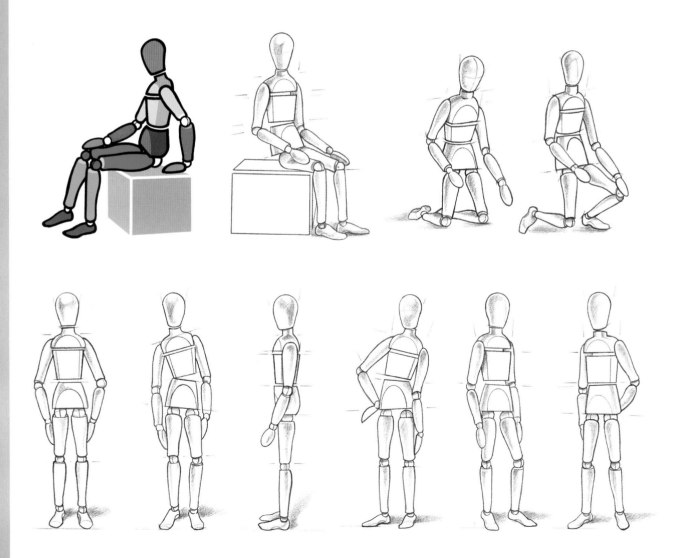

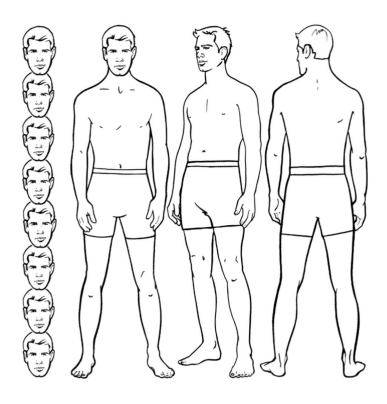

Traditional measuring methods

The Ancient Greeks invented an ingenious method of measuring the height of the human body. They used the length of the head as a unit of measure, then counted the number of times it fitted into the body's total height. During Classical Greek and Renaissance times, the ideal number was eight, which was the standard for perfect proportions. This simple way of measuring is still used today. Try it yourself by using a tape measure to find out how many times your head length fits approximately into your body height, from crown to toe.

Useful body-proportion facts for the fashion illustrator

When drawing the body, a fashion illustrator should remember a few key facts in order to master accurate proportions. For example, in adults, our legs form at least half of our total height. When our arms are relaxed, our fingertips usually reach halfway down our thighs. When standing, our hip tilts down on the leg that is not carrying body weight. When looking at faces, try to remember that the eyes are usually in the centre of the face. The pupil is partly covered by the upper eyelid so don't be tempted to draw a perfect sphere. The position of the eyes can usually be estimated accurately if you remember they are set approximately one eye width apart from the other. The eyes and ears are positioned in line with each other, between the eyebrows and the nose. If you hold your hand up to your face, it is usually the same size, and the sole of your foot (not including toes) is probably the same size as your head.

These diagrams show how the height of the body can be divided into eight equal parts, each equivalent to the height of the head. This fairly accurate system, invented by the ancient Greeks, is still used by artists today. Men's and women's proportions differ greatly, and men are generally taller. Women's shoulders are narrower and slope downwards, whereas men's are broad and fairly straight. Women have proportionally wider hips than men, who have wider necks. The most common exaggerations in fashion illustration are for the female figure to be drawn with longer legs and a smaller waist, and for the male to have broad shoulders and muscular, toned arms.

Exaggeration for fashion

Although it is important to gain a thorough understanding of how the body is constructed, a fashion illustration is not always an accurate representation of reality. Exaggerating some aspect of the figure can add interest and character to the work. Robert Wagt's illustration below pushes exaggeration to its limits with legs that stretch the full width of the page. Fashion designers and illustrators often elongate the figure to give it more elegance and grace. The step-by-step exercise on the following page shows how to exaggerate leg length and fit the tall figure on the page. Use a figure from one of your life drawings for the exercise, or one from a magazine, rather than attempting to draw from imagination.

Below
Robert Wagt uses his signature photomontage technique to create a model with such long legs that they fit the width of the page. Humour is key in Wagt's creations. The image is balanced by the hair flowing widthways in the opposite direction to the legs.

Today contemporary illustrators are not afraid to portray reality and challenge fantasy. Many employ a greater variety of figure shapes and body proportions. Fashion illustration is not only about elegance and beauty, but creating a character that compliments the clothes. Lewis Smith's figures below have very long arms and short legs but their quirky expressions display expressive personalities. These figures are ideal for showing certain fashion garments, such as street, or sportswear, but may be inappropriate for more formal designs such as tailoring.

Bottom
Graduate designer Lewis Smith challenges the fashion world by creating expressive characters that do not necessarily fit a fashion formula. These guys with short bodies and long arms are hand-drawn and then enhanced in Adobe Photoshop.

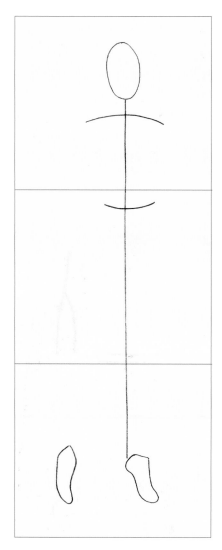

1 Divide the page into three equal sections. Sketch in the waist lightly at the two-thirds line to allow you to elongate the legs of the figure. Then mark the positions of the head, shoulders and feet, and mark a central line down the length of the figure. By drawing simple guidelines, you make sure that the whole figure fits on the page. It is a common mistake to run out of space for the feet. You can erase the guidelines when your drawing is complete.

2 Sketch in outlines for the clothes and any decorative details and decide which colours to use. At this stage the illustrator Carmen García Huerta (www.cghuerta.com) here scans the image into the computer to begin working on her initial sketches digitally.

3 García Heutra completes the fashion illustration using Adobe Photoshop. She adds colour and garment details. The model now has make-up, a hairstyle and the outline of her well-drawn figure can be seen clearly. The guidelines have been left in place to show how this simple exercise, can really help to create a fashion figure that is proportionally convincing, even though her legs have been elongated.

Deciding on a pose

To best promote the garments in a fashion illustration, consider the stance of your figure. The way a person stands expresses much about their mood or emotions. For example, a figure with head tilted and hands behind the back may be thought coy or demure, while a figure with hands on hips and feet apart may be seen as strong or bold. Think carefully about the type of fashion you are promoting. For example, is it your own collection, or are you illustrating for a high-street clothing company or designer with a particular client base? This will help you to decide on the most appropriate pose for your figure.

Left below
Max Gregor draws women in various poses so that he can select the appropriate one when creating a fashion illustration.

Below
Here Max Gregor shows the importance of collecting poses from magazines in order to practise and improve your drawing skills. This pose has been selected from a magazine, hand-drawn and enhanced digitally to create a pose that can be used as a template time and again.

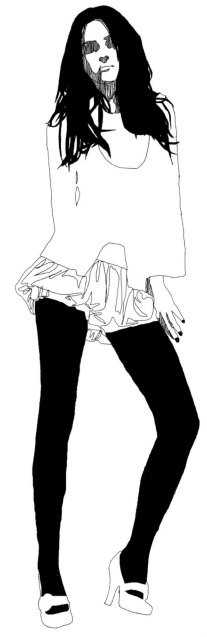

In the illustration above Max Gregor shows models in various poses, but only the outfit he wants the viewer to concentrate on is in focus. The technique of blurring the other poses is clever, as it ensures the viewer sees what the illustrator wants them to see. The same illustration could be used more than once, by blurring different poses each time.

Gregor's other illustration (right) depicts a classic model pose from a magazine. The model has one straight and one bent leg, with head tilted to one side. Build a collection of poses from magazines that you can refer to for your work. Collect images from a range of magazines, including fashion, photography and sports magazines – you may be required to draw action poses for a sportswear range. Look back, too, at your own life drawings and photographs for inspiration.

Gregor's black tights pose could be used as a template to illustrate more than one outfit. The following pages will show you how to create templates to use for fashion design and illustration.

Templates

Tracing from a photograph

Tracing is not always cheating. Sometimes making a simple copy of a figure from a photograph is the most helpful way to start a fashion illustration. You are already working with a two-dimensional image, which is easier than working directly from a three-dimensional figure. Moreover, if you do not have access to a life model at the appropriate time, drawing a figure accurately from memory is not a common skill. Most people need a source of inspiration to begin a drawing. Trace the outline of a figure from a photograph or magazine to give yourself a starting point, then apply your own illustrative style as you develop the artwork.

Place the photograph on a light box, or light tracer, or against a window so that you can see the most important features of the figure clearly. Decide on the main lines that define the figure's shape, then trace them carefully. Use a sharp pencil to avoid lines becoming fuzzy and confusing.

Below
Copying a figure, or figures, from a photograph or magazine can form the foundation of a fashion illustration. Even an ordinary photograph of a couple on a motorbike wearing full leathers can be used as a starting point.

Middle
Trace the main lines of each figure by placing your paper over the photograph on a lightbox.

Bottom
Inspired by the photograph, this is the final fashion illustration. Although life drawing is necessary to understand the human body, it is still valid to use a two-dimensional image as the basis for your figure.

How to use a template

If you select photographs from a magazine that give a clear indication of body shapes and proportions, your tracings can be used as the basis for a fashion-figure template. A figure template is a tool used by fashion designers to help them speed up the design process. It is placed under semi-transparent layout paper upon which the designer draws the garments, moving the template along the page to repeat the process. The template is used as a guide only. When the clothes are sketched in, the template is removed and the artwork completed. Depending too heavily on templates can inhibit a fashion designer's creativity, a common mistake being to design only clothes that fit the templates. Likewise, the illustrator must bear in mind that the template is a useful tool but not a means of creating a unique piece of artwork. The constant use of a template to initiate an illustration tends to lead to stilted results.

Copying a template from a fashion-illustration book as your starting point for an artwork is not recommended. Often, those who view your work will recognize the pose. It is far better to create your own figure using the techniques suggested below.

Creating a template

Select one of your own figure drawings or a suitable magazine photograph, place layout paper over it and trace the image. Now simplify the drawing to create a clear outline, ensuring the proportions of different parts of the body are correct in relation to one another. Suggest the face and hairstyle but do not draw every hair and eyelash. Unless you are adding accessories, the hands and feet also need only be implied.

You may adapt the pose to your own requirements. A simple front and back view of a front-facing figure will enable you to design quickly and precisely, but vary your templates so your work does not become predictable. The easiest method is to develop your first template, repositioning the legs and arms to create a variety of poses. Think about the stance of the templates, too. The way a figure is standing can often reflect the mood of a collection. Study models in magazines and try to recreate similar poses and gestures in your templates. Drawing a line down the centre of the template, front and back, creates a marker against which design details, such as button plackets, pockets and seams, can be positioned correctly. If a template is too large, it can be scaled down by hand or by using a photocopier or scanner. When you have a selection of templates, you could reduce their size to repeat a series of poses across a page.

When creating your templates, consider the market for your illustrations or designs. For example, an expensive eveningwear collection will not look right if templates developed from street figures are used as a starting point. Collect a number of templates with varied looks and character.

Templates are used as an aid to freehand design, but they can also be adapted for the computer. Scan a template and use it as a foundation for your artwork, adding to it with a program that allows you to make decisions on colour and pattern.

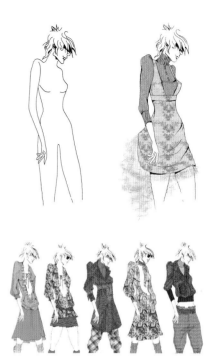

Top left
This female-figure template can be used traditionally on paper, or scanned for use on the computer.

Top right
The template has been scanned and clothing added using the computer. Fabric was scanned then copied onto the garments.

Above
A full collection line-up by Lindsey Collison, which uses the same template and illustration process for each figure.

Overleaf
Templates are created by reducing the body to a clear, simple outline. They enable the designer to work faster, using the template as a guide. To show garments from front, back and sides, the designer creates a range of templates. Templates for design are usually realistic and body proportions are not exaggerated.

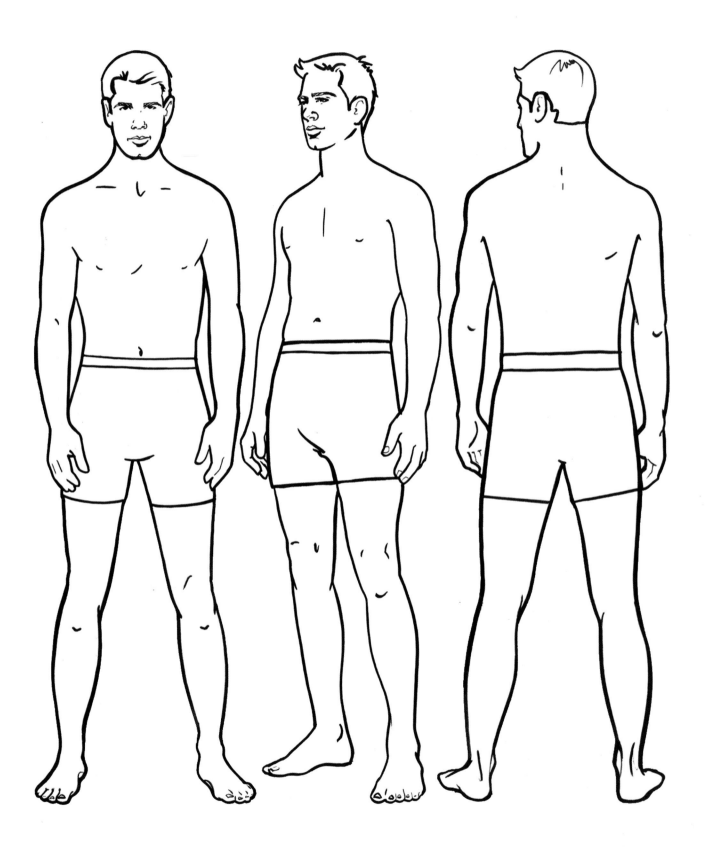

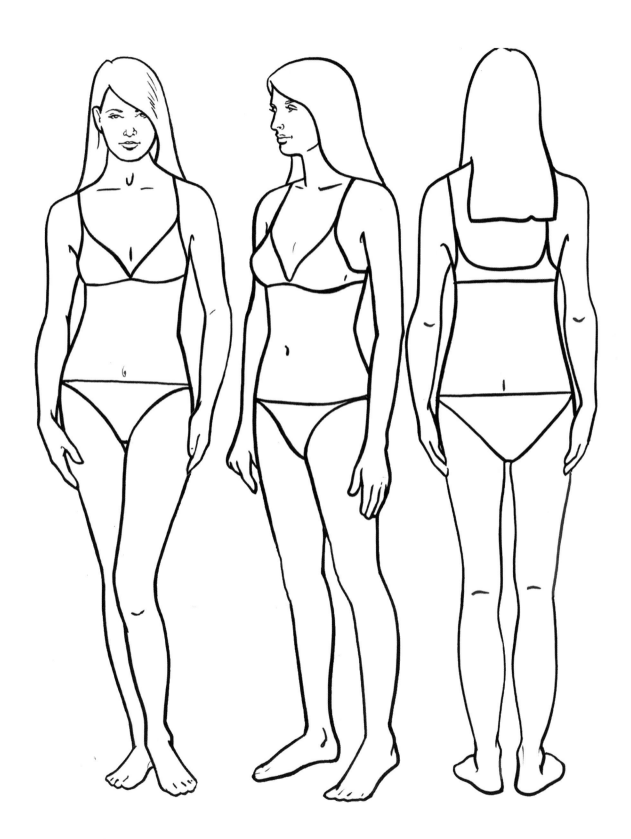

Hot spots

Face

Do you leave out the face in an illustration because you are scared of ruining the image by drawing it in? Do you tuck hands into pockets so that you need not illustrate them? Perhaps you draw the figure off the page to avoid tackling the feet? It is true that one small line in the wrong place can spoil an otherwise perfect fashion illustration, but the best illustrators avoid the temptation to hide these difficult features. By practising until you can approach these elements with conviction, your illustrations will gain in diversity and sophistication.

Indicating these hot spots authentically can be a daunting prospect for the novice, but it need not be. It is increasingly acceptable to suggest features imaginatively, rather than always to represent them correctly. On the following pages are tips on combining an accurate rendering with an imaginative approach to create an illustration that you are happy with.

Montana Forbes uses a strong line to depict the facial features. One eye just peeps out from a heavy fringe and her simple use of colour is well thought out.

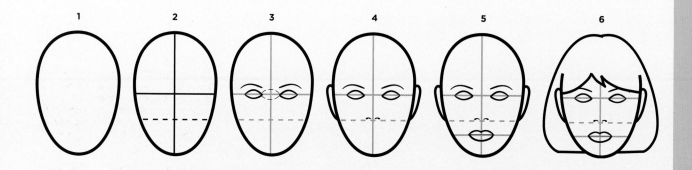

Advice for drawing the head and face

- A ball, egg or square shape can be used to construct the head
- The head divides into three masses: the cranium, the facial bones and the jaw
- Draw in guidelines to define the position of the eyes, nose and mouth
- The guidelines can be positioned to represent the planes of the face looking in different directions
- A male figure has thicker eyebrows, a larger mouth and squarer jaw line than the female
- The face provides a focal point for an illustration, but must harmonize with the rest of the body rather than standing out from it
- When drawing profiles, symmetry does not need to be considered
- A badly drawn face can ruin an otherwise good illustration

1 First, outline the head. This will probably be close to an oval or egg in shape.

2 Divide the head in half vertically and horizontally. Then divide the bottom half in half again in a horizontal direction. These guidelines can be erased later.

3 Map out the eyes on the top horizontal line. Leave a space of one eye width in between the eyes. Draw in the eyebrows.

4 The base of the nose should fit on the next horizontal line. Draw in the ears; their size is usually the distance between the eyebrow and the bottom of the nose.

5 Divide the bottom half of the face again and use the lowest horizontal line as a guide for the mouth. The top lip usually sits above the line and the bottom lip below.

6 Finally, draw in the hair. In fashion illustration it is usually best to attempt to draw the overall shape the hair creates, rather than each individual hair.

Above left

Ed Carosia uses paint and digital enhancement to show the bold facial features of this man. The strong glasses are the main focus of the illustration, but it is the limited colour palette and the decision to use the background colour the same as the skin that set the illustration apart.

Above right

It is hard not to imagine the skull when thinking about drawing the head and face. Here Tom Bagshaw has created an accurate but decorative human skull.

Left

Vincent Bakkum is skilled at painting the facial hot spots. Here he shows how he captures beauty with a paintbrush. The head, neck and shoulders are drawn accurately paying close attention to skin tones and hair colour.

Features

Advice for drawing features

- Suggest the features and, if in doubt, don't draw them in
- Features are usually smaller than you expect. For example, a hand can cover the face easily
- Ears and eyes are in line with each other between the eyebrows and the nose
- Eyes are at the halfway point of the head length – it is a common mistake to draw them higher up
- Most commonly in the centre of the face, eyes are set one eye-width apart
- The iris of the eye is always partly covered by the upper eyelid, creating a shadow on the eyeball
- Eyelashes on both lids become progressively thicker toward the outer corners of the eyes, although the bottom lashes are shorter
- The upper lip often appears in shade as it curves in towards the teeth
- The bottom lip is usually fuller than the top one
- Lips stretch horizontally around the curving face, so do not draw them in a straight line
- Rather than draw each individual tooth, suggest teeth by drawing a shadow between them
- The nose starts at the forehead and has an indentation where the bone ends and the cartilage begins
- Made up of planes that form the sides, top and the base, the nose has a ball at the bottom and wings on either side where the nostrils flare

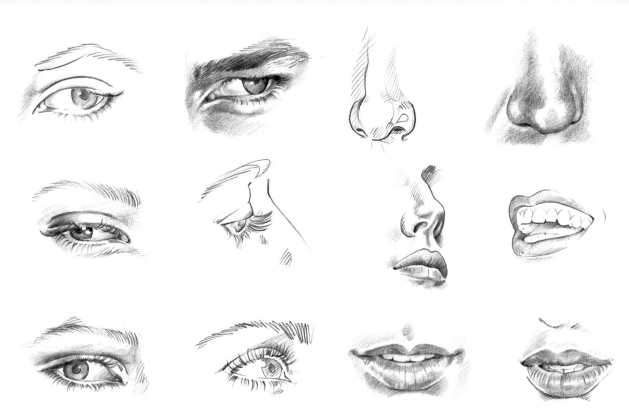

Above left
Sara Singh shows how simple it can be to depict lips using watercolour and a brush. She leaves the white of the page to depict light and to give the lips form

Above right
Singh shows how she can apply the same technique and style to anything, painting facial eyes, lips and eyebrows. She often illustrates a nose by painting a nostril with a single line.

Left
Black ink can be mixed with water to give different tones to an illustration. Here Singh has also added bird and horse prints to the image.

2.

Hair

Advice for drawing hair

- Lines for the hair should flow away from the scalp and continue in the directions set by the chosen style
- Try not to make the hair too uniform or like a hat
- Rather than attempting to draw every individual hair, outline large tufts
- The female hairline is usually higher than the male, emphasizing the roundness of the forehead
- A female's hair is drawn with longer, more flowing lines than the shorter strokes of a male's hair
- Hair should vary in tone, having highlights and definition, rather than be treated as a single mass
- Hair can be styled in all sorts of ways: tied back, neat, wild, trendy, bobbed, wavy, long, curly, fringed, short, spiky, cropped, straight, plaited, and so on

Opposite top left
Watercolour paint is often the chosen medium of Stina Persson. She uses many colours to create the hairstyles of these women, leaving the white of the page as the skin tone.

Oppostite top right
Cecilia Carlstedt has drawn this short crop by hand and collaged the rest of the illustration digitally.

Opposite bottom left
Max Gregor uses the computer to create this wacky purple illustration. The girl's hair has many tones and is a mix of curls and straight lengths.

Opposite bottom right
These girls have been drawn by Edwina White using watercolour pencils. Their cute hairstyles frame their faces.

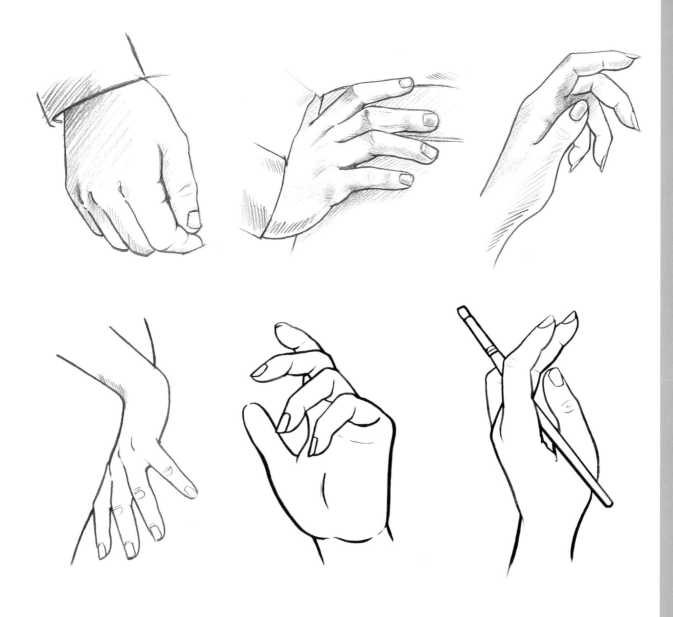

Hands

Advice for drawing hands

- The surface of the hands reveals the skeleton beneath
- It is a common mistake to draw the hands too small
- The hand should cover the face when outstretched – its length is about equal to the face from hairline to the base of the chin
- The palm is concave, the back of the hand convex
- Simplify the drawing of hands in a fashion illustration – you do not need to indicate every knuckle and fingernail

Sara Singh illustrates hands by leaving out the detail. She uses single lines to show shape and form but does not draw in every knuckle, or crease.

Feet and shoes

Advice for drawing feet and shoes

- The body's weight rests mainly on the heel and the outside edge of the foot
- Not including the toes, the sole of the foot is equal to the length of the head
- The big toe is approximately one quarter of the whole foot
- Shoes and boots must be in proportion to the rest of the body – a figure with tiny feet looks as though it might fall over
- When drawing footwear with a heel, ensure that the heel and sole are on the same plane or surface
- The fashion foot is usually drawn long and slender – the higher the heel, the longer the foot appears
- The higher the shoe, the greater the angle in the arch of the foot

Opposite top left and right
These illustrations show how :puntoos can capture shoes at any angle. They work digitally, linking the shoes to the background with colour and pattern to create a fascinating composition.

Opposite bottom left
Stina Persson's unique style of watery paint drips off the page in this illustration of beautiful shoes.

Opposite bottom right
Yuko Shimizu's illustration of bare feet shows clearly their creases and toenails.

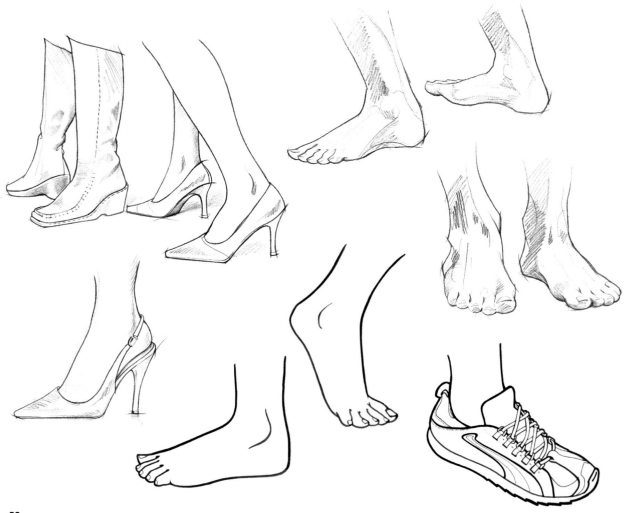

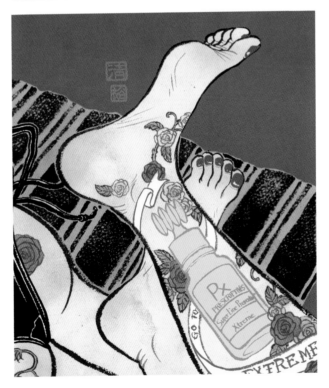

The silhouette

Ever heard the phrase 'less is more'? Well, sometimes when illustrating fashion the details of the figure are definitely worth less! The example below shows an illustration by :puntoos that uses the body in silhouette. This means that the outline of the figure has been drawn and filled in with a dark colour on a light background. The technique is often employed by illustrators to fully emphasize the clothes to the viewer. Here :puntoos manage to successfully add a creative edge to the fashion illustration by adding tabs to the clothes, mimicking the dress-up dolls played with by children. The element of humour displayed here is a valuable tool when illustrating in an advertising world – making the viewer smile is far better than making them cry!

Here :puntoos create a 'dress your own doll' style illustration. The figure is shown in silhouette and the fashion items hold all the detail, leading the viewer to notice them first.

3.

Artistic Techniques

Once you have started finding inspiration, researching themes, using a sketchbook, and practising figure drawing, you will be keen to experiment with different art materials. In this chapter you will find out which art materials to use to achieve particular effects, how to convey fabric realistically and how to select a colour palette. Even professional artists can find these aspects of illustration challenging. To provide a useful reference source, the chapter divides into sections that you can dip in and out of easily to find the information you need.

Art materials and equipment

The range of materials and equipment available to illustrators and artists today is vast and can be a little overwhelming at times. Searching for appropriate materials in an art suppliers can feel like being surrounded by irresistible confectionery in a sweetshop. To the creative eye, everything looks tempting and the correct choice of medium is difficult to make.

Finding a medium that suits your own particular method of working and your style is the best way to proceed. You should feel comfortable enough with it to produce work confidently. Consider your personality when selecting your artistic tools. If you are a careful, meticulous perfectionist you may be most at ease with precise art materials such as a pencil or pen. If you have a more energetic, fast-and-furious approach to illustration, you may enjoy the freedom of oil pastels, charcoal or paints. Experimenting frequently with new materials will encourage you to be more innovative in your work. Brand-new pots of ink, sharp, colourful pencils and acrylic tubes just waiting to be squeezed may look inviting but, to a beginner, they also hold an element of anxiety. The next section covers how to use art materials and equipment in fashion illustration, so that you can make your selection with confidence.

The *sewing machine* is an important piece of equipment for many fashion illustrators. If possible, yours should offer a number of embroidery stitches. Many now have computer-software programs that link the sewing machine to your computer, allowing you to stitch a design created on screen.

A *photocopier* can save you time by enlarging and reducing images or by providing you with repeated copies for collage. Having inexpensive, throwaway copies of artwork to manipulate and experiment with can help you find new techniques and styles, without having to worry about perfection.

To cut out mount boards and papers, the *steel ruler* is useful as both a measuring and a cutting tool. It is preferable to a wooden or plastic ruler, as it is more difficult to slice into steel and create unwanted irregularities along the cut edge. A *cutting mat* provides a safe, steady surface for cutting with a sharp *scalpel* or *knife*. The most useful blades are those with an angled top over a straight cutting edge.

A *light box* is a handy tool for the illustrator. It is simply a screen lit from below that allows you to see through paper placed over photographs and magazine cuttings, so that you can trace figures or other elements. As light boxes are fairly expensive, you might prefer to use a window for the same

Opposite
A selection of art materials and tools that can be used to illustrate fashion.

purpose. However, if you can afford a light box, you will own it forever.
They are also useful for looking at details in photographs or transparencies.

Spray adhesive is an essential for the illustrator. It should be applied evenly
to one surface in a well-ventilated room. Be careful to protect areas you want
to remain free from glue, as spray adhesive can be messy. It does, however,
provide the most professional results when producing presentation boards,
collages and illustrations.

Masking tape is essential for fixing paper to a drawing board, and it peels
easily off the board and your artwork when you have finished.

The aforementioned tools and equipment are essential for traditional
fashion illustration. However, many illustrators work with machines rather than
by hand to create contemporary effects, and working digitally is increasingly
popular for fashion illustrators. For this you will need a computer (desktop
or laptop) and possibly a scanner and digital camera. There are many
creative software programs to help you draw, manipulate images and alter
photographs, the best known being Adobe Photoshop and Adobe Illustrator.
You will find tutorials on how to use these programs in Chapter Four.

Paper

Paper is the first element to consider when beginning a fashion illustration. There are many types to choose from, available in various colours and thicknesses. All can be used as a surface on which to work or as a material from which to create a collage.

Cartridge paper is one of the most basic, commonly used papers, and is suitable for drawing and dry artwork. It is not generally recommended for painting or heavily rendered work, as it is made of wood pulp, so that moisture causes it to buckle.

Layout paper is a fine, semi-opaque paper that allows you to see an image faintly beneath it. Suitable for roughs, marker drawings and colour tests, it is often bleed-resistant so that colours do not run. The translucency of layout paper enables you to trace over it to produce one rough from another.

Unlike smooth cartridge paper, *pastel paper* has a grain running through it. Soft art materials such as pastel and charcoal pick up the grain, and the artist can exploit this effect in the illustration.

Watercolour papers are supplied in many weights and textures. With its ability to absorb liquid, watercolour paper can be used with many wet media, such as ink, paints or watersoluble crayons.

Tissue paper, card, coloured backing papers, wrapping paper, wallpaper, sweet wrappers and *other packaging* can all be used in fashion illustrations. Use your imagination as to how to incorporate them into your work.

While paper is the background for many fashion illustrations, it can also be used as the media to create them. Collage and paper sculpture are the chosen techniques of the illustrators shown on these pages.

Opposite
Peter Clark uses old paper because of the way that it can be manipulated and because he prefers the colour and texture. "In my pieces I try to use mark-making in an innovative and humorous way to create a collection of clothing that exudes character and wit."

Below
Jeff Nishinaka is a paper sculptor of the highest quality. In these images he has created the background for a fashionably dressed doll and a bedroom setting for luxury accessories.

"As a paper sculptor, it can take me two weeks to cut, layer and glue my creations."
– Jeff Nishinaka

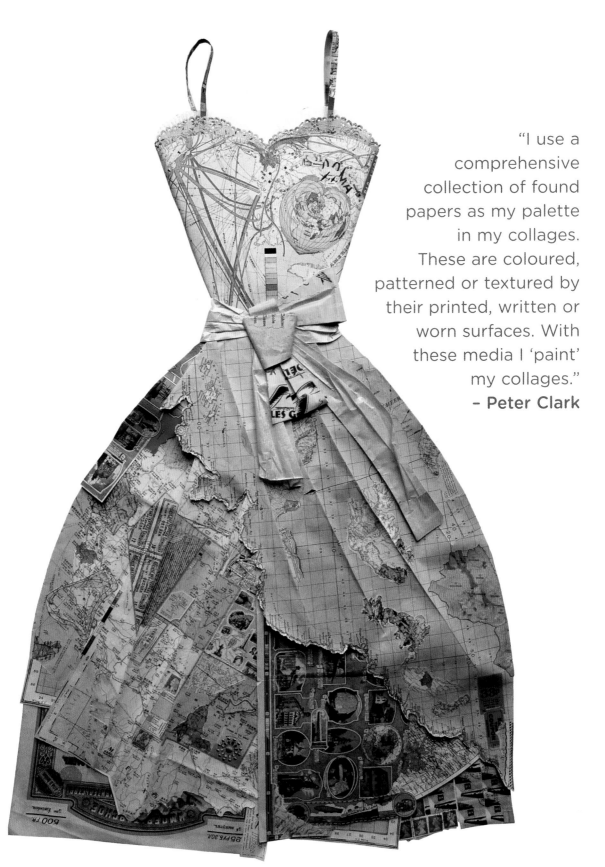

"I use a comprehensive collection of found papers as my palette in my collages. These are coloured, patterned or textured by their printed, written or worn surfaces. With these media I 'paint' my collages."
— Peter Clark

Drawing

Pencils

There are many types of drawing media and mark-making materials. However, every artist – even painters, sculptors and printmakers – benefits from being skilled at drawing with a pencil. The pencil is a convenient and expressive means of evolving a composition and of recording visual information quickly for translation into another medium later on. Most works of art begin with a pencil drawing.

Lead pencils are available either in the form of traditional wood-cased pencils or in a mechanical pop-up style. The advantage of a mechanical pencil is that it is always sharp. You can also select a variety of lead thicknesses for this type of pencil ranging from 0.3 to 0.9. Pencil leads are graphite and they are made in several grades ranging from hard (H) to soft (B – the "B" stands for black).

Soft pencils are ideal for rapid sketches and expressive line-and-tone drawings. They work especially well on textured paper, but take care when using them, because they smudge easily. Hard pencils best suit artists with a confident, clean and accurate style of drawing. *Graphite sticks* are made of compressed and bonded graphite. They glide across the page to produce the boldest and most expressive drawings. You can change the marks they make by using the point, side or the flattened edge of the stick. The water-soluble versions produce beautiful, silvery grey washes. Graphite sticks are especially popular for life drawing and clothed-figure drawing because they allow a fluid technique.

Coloured pencils are made from a mixture of pigment, clay and filler bound together and soaked in wax before being encased in wood. Use them like a graphite pencil to shade areas, only in colour. You can also blend shades together carefully with a paper stump (a tightly rolled, tipped paper), eraser or your fingers. As with all pencil drawing, tonal areas can be built up with hatching (short parallel lines drawn closely together) or crosshatching (a fine mesh of criss-crossing lines that builds depth of shade).

Water-soluble art materials

Water-soluble pencils offer the advantages of coloured pencils, but they have a water-soluble ingredient in the lead. This means that you can apply the colour dry, but create a subtle watercolour effect by loosening the pigment with brushstrokes of water. The advantage of both water-soluble pencils and crayons is that they are easy to carry with you, allowing you to sketch figures quickly on the street or catwalk. You can develop a picture further with paint when you return to your home or studio, if you so wish.

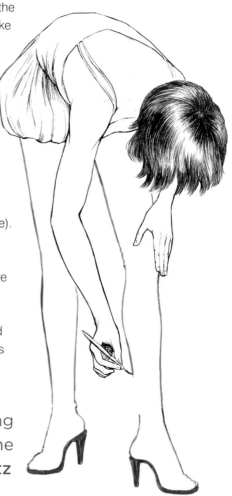

"I came up with this while thinking how everybody would love to 'redesign' some part of themselves if they could." – **Silja Goetz**

Pens

There are all sorts of *markers*, including a variety of felt- and fibre-tip pens. High-quality markers can be costly but give good, non-blotchy results. They are usually supplied in packs of toning colours or sold singly. The best types have a variety of nibs – wide, medium and fine. Wider nibs are useful for blocking in areas of colour evenly. Skin-tone markers are invaluable for fashion illustration, giving a realistic flesh colour. However, while using markers is a quick, convenient way of adding colour, it takes a confident illustrator to apply them with conviction.

Ballpoints, although not always considered an art material, are worth experimenting with. Working in a single colour with a line quality that does not alter can produce interesting results. A ballpoint is often easily at hand and doodling in a relaxed atmosphere provides a perfect creative environment.

Fineliner pens are wonderful for emphasizing fine details, such as intricate embroidery or knitted textures, in fashion illustrations. A non-permanent type can also be watered down to create a flowing line.

"I experiment with techniques, mix them up and see what's happening."
– Tina Berning

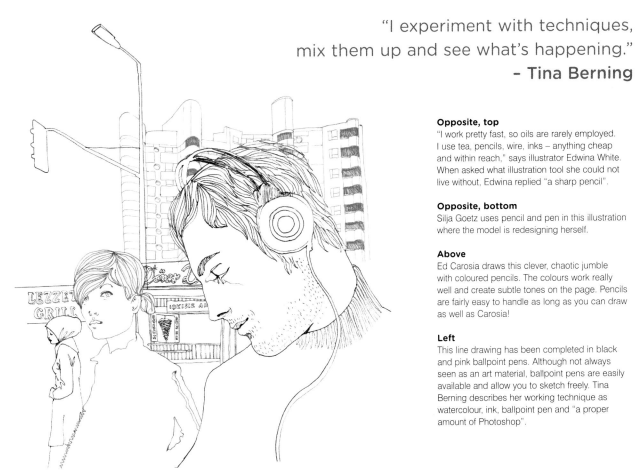

Opposite, top
"I work pretty fast, so oils are rarely employed. I use tea, pencils, wire, inks – anything cheap and within reach," says illustrator Edwina White. When asked what illustration tool she could not live without, Edwina replied "a sharp pencil".

Opposite, bottom
Silja Goetz uses pencil and pen in this illustration where the model is redesigning herself.

Above
Ed Carosia draws this clever, chaotic jumble with coloured pencils. The colours work really well and create subtle tones on the page. Pencils are fairly easy to handle as long as you can draw as well as Carosia!

Left
This line drawing has been completed in black and pink ballpoint pens. Although not always seen as an art material, ballpoint pens are easily available and allow you to sketch freely. Tina Berning describes her working technique as watercolour, ink, ballpoint pen and "a proper amount of Photoshop".

Ink and watercolour

Black waterproof Indian ink is the first choice of most illustrators as washes can be applied over a shiny line drawing. A monochrome illustration is then created using a dip pen, brush or bamboo stick. By varying your drawing tool, you can achieve a range of wonderful effects.

Non-waterproof ink sinks into the paper and dries with a matt finish. Diluting it produces a wide range of lighter tones. You can experiment with non-waterproof inks by dropping them onto paper soaked in water. The ink disperses in the water, creating beautiful patterns and textures on the paper surface. Painted lines will be fuzzy rather than sharp as the ink spreads.

Watercolour paint is sold in tubes or pans. Tubes are available in many sizes and are recommended because you can mix stronger colours in larger quantities. Pans are small slabs of solid paint that fit into easy-to-carry boxes, the box lid usually acting as a palette for mixing colours.

"I do many drawings of the same subject until I get it right. Each drawing takes only minutes. It's the scanning and post-production that takes time." **– Sara Singh**

A watercolour illustration by Sara Singh. The jewellery has been added using Photoshop. Sara's illustration technique combines traditional and digital techniques.

"My technique is very raw and simple, and really, my tools are just some random brushes and my fingers. Sometimes it takes weeks, a day or even seconds to complete a fashion illustration."
– Amelie Hegardt

Above
Cecilia Carlstedt sketches with a graphite pencil and then uses inks and watercolour to add atmosphere and style to her fashion illustrations. She is a master at mixing media, scale and technique to create a versatile approach to her work.

Left
Amelie Hegardt uses pastel, ink water and graphite on paper. She says that it can take her weeks, a day, or just seconds to complete a fashion illustration.

Watercolour is the perfect medium for adding subtle colour to pencil fashion illustrations. It is also excellent for applying washes to pen-and-ink drawings and for adding coloured details to sketches. You can exploit its natural properties by allowing a thin wash to run and drip over your fashion figure, adding a sense of movement to the illustration.

"A painting according to the old school, done with the hasty speed of nowadays. Not because I'm in a hurry, but because that's the way I like to work." **- Vincent Bakkum**

Vincent Bakkum describes his illustration 'Delphine' as "a drawing in paint". It is created with acrylic on canvas and at 150 x 150 cm (59 x 59 in) it is quite big, so that he can really brush into it. "I work like a house painter almost! Strong strokes so that I can feel myself an artist," he says.

Left
"In Photoshop I added the yellow background that was created with acrylics and a spatula on cardboard as well as adding the lady's make-up and the purple blouse under the coat." You can see how Tina Berning works with paint in her fashion illustration tutorial in Chapter Four.

Below
For the illustration below Tina Berning drew the woman in Adobe Photoshop with the paintbrush, her embroidered top was painted, dot by dot, using a Wacom pad. Initially the girl had dark, drawn hair, painted in Photoshop, but the artist deleted this and let the painted brushstrokes complete her hairstyle instead. The background is hand-painted purple with acrylics on paper.

"To create a more hand-made element I added a painted structure over the whole drawing, you can see this in her skin."
– Tina Berning

Paint

Many illustrators favour a particular paint, but it is sometimes difficult to decide which type will most suit the style of your work. Qualities of the different paints available are described below to help you make a selection.

Acrylics are incredibly versatile as they can be applied straight from the tube, or diluted, using a brush or knife – the latter creating a dense texture. Producing strong colours, acrylics dry with a tough, plastic waterproof skin. Try painting fashion figures onto fabric in acrylics. Once dry, use a sewing machine to add decorative stitching.

Oils are historically the professional painter's medium. The buttery consistency of the paint arises from a high concentration of pigment mixed with the finest-quality oil. Although rarely used in fashion illustration today, oil paint is not as difficult to handle as you may think. The advantage of oil paint is that you can model it on the canvas, moulding the textures you want in your fashion illustration and even creating a three-dimensional effect by applying the paint with a knife.

Gouache is a type of watercolour that has been mixed with white to make it opaque. It is excellent for laying flat, solid colour as it dries without streaks, and is popular for illustration because its strong, matt colours are suited to reproduction. To use the paint creatively, apply the colours boldly in undiluted form. Imagine your illustrations as poster art, making them powerful and eye-catching.

Spray paint gives unexpected results, and is therefore the medium to have fun with. You can buy fairly cheap cans of spray paint for artistic use in a wide range of colours. It is excellent for stencilling and adding finishing touches to your fashion illustrations.

"My greatest achievement is to translate the application of materials and techniques traditionally related with 'women at home' into a fashion language." **– Paula Sanz Caballero**

Embroidery and fabric

Hand embroidery threads offer a vast choice of colour. Stranded cotton is the most popular type, and the strands can be separated to give you the thickness you want. Silk, wool, linen, synthetic and metallic threads are also available, giving you a variety of options ranging from smooth, shiny stitches to textural, matt ones.

Machine embroidery threads are presented on reels and also vary in colour, thickness and finish. Usually made of rayon or cotton, they come in a wide range of single colours or variegated shades, matt, shiny and metallic.

To embroider, use the needle as a drawing tool on the fabric. There is a great variety of different embroidery stitches you can use to create patterns on the fabric, demonstrating creative flair in your fashion illustration. In Chapter Four you can see how embroidery illustrator Louise Gardiner creates a fashionable shopping character using free machine embroidery techniques.

Above
Paula Sanz Caballero uses hand-stitching and fabric collage to create her art.

Opposite
"With a Bernina sewing machine, I either draw freely onto canvas or I paint with acrylic onto the stitched drawings and then embroider again, mixing intricate, coloured-thread patterns into the shapes and spaces with the drawing"
– Louise Gardiner.

"I collect ideas in sketchbooks and do figurative drawing as often as possible." **– Louise Gardiner** (opposite)

"The flat, black silhouette makes the 'real' fabric scarf stand out more dramatically. I like illustrations that are simple and effective in this way."
– Silja Goetz

Mixed media collage

'Collage' was originally a French word, derived from the word *coller*, meaning 'to paste'. In fashion illustration collage is primarily an illustration or design created by adhering flat elements such as paper, wallpaper, printed text, newspaper, or photographs with three-dimensional elements or 'found' materials. It is a technique or mixing art with imagination. Most collage artists don't really rule any objects out. They use thread, yarn, buttons, fabrics, wood, feathers, and wire – in truth, any bits and bobs that may inspire them.

However, it is the advances in digital technology that has enabled the new technique of mixed-media collage. This is where collage and assemblage art is scanned and manipulated digitally on the computer. Today, illustrators use various computer programs such as Adobe Photoshop to paste objects into their illustrations and flatten their artwork. This way they create a single sheet illustration that can be printed. Many students use this technique to document their research and compile their portfolio pages.

"The hand-drawn girl and the leaves rendered in pencil were scanned as the base of the illustration. Then I placed the jewellery from supplied photographs on top using Adobe Photoshop." – **Cecilia Carlstedt**

"In this composition [above] we decided to play with the bikini fabric and the background, creating a communication between them."
– :puntoos

Digital illustration

Digital illustration is the use of digital tools to produce images under the direct manipulation of the artist, usually through a pointing device such as a tablet or a mouse linked to a computer. When looking to purchase a computer consider both PC and Mac, desktop and laptop. The most important elements are the quantity of RAM and a generous hard-drive space. Image files tend to take up more space than text files, so you may need to invest in an external hard drive. This gives you extra storage space, and also acts as a back-up, protecting you against computer breakdown or accidental deletion.

A scanner is also useful equipment to have in your studio. You can get high-quality scans done professionally at reputable reprographic stores.

Many illustrators use a graphics tablet for digital painting. Buy a superior, large-surface input device that will be extremely precise, making the freehand drawing experience more accurate and enjoyable.

Most people own a mobile phone with an in-built camera, so there is no excuse for not capturing on-the-spot inspirational images. A good-quality digital camera is an investment for your fashion illustration work.

There are two main types of tools used for digital illustration: bitmapped and vector. With bitmapped tools, the content is stored digitally in fixed rows, columns, and layers, containing information about each pixel's hue,

Above left
In Vince Fraser's front cover illustration for *Trendsetter* magazine the original model photographs were retouched in Adobe Photoshop while the background was created in 3D Studio Max, using abstract shapes. All the vector special effects were drawn in Adobe Illustrator and exported into Photoshop for the final post-production compostion.

Above
Working with vector illustration is the easiest way for :puntoos to take in the client's feedback, applying changes on composition, colours, etc. They usually scan a photograph into Adobe Illustrator, lock the layer, and start drawing with lines in other layers. For ease with vector drawing, they use a small Wacom tablet, and a 24" iMac. After completing the outlines, they put colour into them, group them by elements (bikini, background, etc.) and then play around with different compositions.

luminance, and sometimes filter settings. With vector-based tools, the content is stored digitally as resolution-independent mathematical formulae describing lines, shapes, and colour gradients.

There is a variety of image manipulation software available on the market. Some of the most popular are: Adobe Photoshop, Paint Shop Pro, Corel Paint Shop Pro, Corel Painter, Adobe Illustrator, CorelDRAW and Macromedia Freehand.

Most digital fashion illustrators work with a mixture of programs, to correct, retouch, manipulate, compose and paint. Take a look at the tutorials by Marcos Chin and Tom Bagshaw in Chapter Four to see how they create their work using Adobe Photoshop and Illustrator. There are also many online tutorials and journals that can help with trouble-shooting. The further reading list on pp.228–30 recommends a selection of current books and websites.

Below
Paris-based fashion magazine *Jalouse* provided illustrator Kate Gibb with a series of digital photographs to turn into silk-screened illustrations. After transferring the photographs onto screen she worked on them by hand using brushes and inks. She felt this allowed the image to come alive and appear less flat, which is often a problem with silkscreen technique.

"Although I had artistic license on the look of the pieces, it was important to remain truthful to the garments depicted, their colour, feel and most important the inherent printed qualities of the cloth." **– Kate Gibb**

Colour

In our daily lives we are surrounded by colour and make choices about it regularly in the way we dress, decorate our homes, even when we buy a car. Having an eye for which colours work well together is essential for the fashion designer or illustrator, whether you are choosing a scheme for a portfolio project, planning a colour-themed collection or selecting colours for a dramatic fashion illustration.

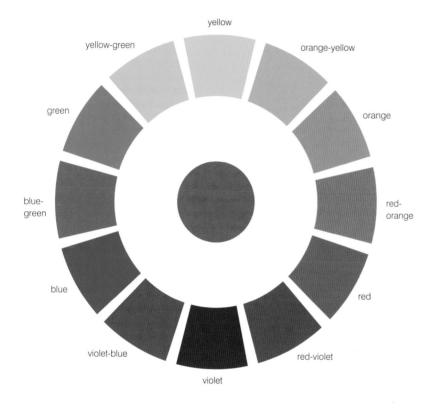

yellow

yellow-green

orange-yellow

green

orange

blue-green

red-orange

blue

red

violet-blue

red-violet

violet

The colour wheel

Understanding the basic principles of colour theory, and knowing how to apply colours, will help boost your confidence as a fashion illustrator. The simplest way to learn about the theory is to study the colour wheel. When the sun shines on a rainy day, a rainbow often forms. The basic colours in a rainbow are red, orange, yellow, green, blue, indigo and violet. The colour wheel is a simplified version of this spectrum (excluding indigo) and arranges six colours into a circle. The wheel is then made up of colours that fit into the following categories: primary, secondary, tertiary, warm, cool and complementary.

Primary colours

red

yellow

blue

Secondary colours

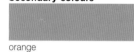
orange

green

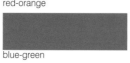
violet

Tertiary colours

orange-yellow

red-orange

red-violet

violet-blue

blue-green

yellow-green

Primary colours

Primary colours are ones that cannot be made by mixing other colours. The three primary colours are red, yellow and blue. They are equidistant on the colour wheel.

Secondary colours

The secondary colours are orange, green and violet. They are produced by mixing two primary colours. When mixed, red and yellow make orange, blue and yellow make green, and red and blue make violet. The secondary colours are also equidistant on the colour wheel, in between the primary colours.

Tertiary colours

Mixing a primary colour with its adjacent secondary colour on the wheel produces a tertiary colour. For example, mixing red with orange creates red-orange and red with violet creates red-violet. Again, these are equidistant on the wheel.

Warm and cool colours

All colours have associations. Warm colours such as reds, oranges and yellows are associated with sunlight and fire. They tend to stand out in an illustration and seem closer than cool colours, which recede into the background. Cool colours include the blues of the sky and water, and the greens of rolling hills and landscape. Bearing in mind how warm and cool colours affect the viewer enables you to enhance the atmosphere of your artwork.

Complementary colours

The opposite colours on the colour wheel are contrasting partners called complementary colours. The partners consist of one primary and one secondary colour. The pairings are red and green, blue and orange, and yellow and violet.

They appear brightest when placed next to each other. When mixed together complementary colours produce a grey, neutral tone. To make a colour darker, add its complementary partner rather than shading with black. For example, if you would like a darker yellow, add a hint of violet.

Using colour-wheel theories

Mixing colours yourself in your chosen medium is the best way to discover how the colour-wheel theories work. Start with three primary colours – red, yellow and blue. When the primaries are mixed together they produce a muddy black. Experiment by mixing the secondary colours, then the tertiary colours. The amount of any one colour added to the mix affects the shade produced. Make notes on how you mix the colours so that you can recreate them in the future.

Three distinct characteristics account for the appearance of colours: hue, value and saturation. Each of these can be manipulated by colour mixing or, more subtly, by altering the context in which a colour appears. *Hue* is the name of a colour – for example, red, green or blue – that identifies it in the colour spectrum. *Value* is the relative quality of lightness or darkness in a colour. This varies on a scale of black to white. *Saturation*, also known as intensity, is the relative purity of hue present in a colour. A highly saturated colour will give a strong sense of hue, and a low saturation will have a weaker presence.

The result of mixing a colour with white is known as a *tint*. Mixing grey with a colour is known as a *tone*. Mixing a colour with black creates a *shade*.

Hue

Value

Saturation

Colour forecasting

Have you ever wondered how the colours for fashion, interiors, cosmetics and even cars seem to complement each other every season? How do fashion designers all decide that, say, green is this summer's colour? Or that our homes will be decorated in brown? The answer is that there are teams of professionals – known as "colour forecasters" – analyzing data to provide colour predictions for up to two years ahead. Chapter Seven contains an interview with Promostyl, a fashion-and-colour-prediction house. The company has a series of agents that travel the world to research upcoming trends. Promostyl then produces seasonal books recording their predictions, which are sold as reference sources to designers and businesses worldwide.

Using colour in fashion illustration

In the fashion industry colour palettes for clothing change from season to season. When designers produce new collections they are aware of the season's predicted colours through attending trade shows and seeking advice from fashion and colour-prediction agencies. However, the illustrator is free to select a personal palette for fashion artwork. Although it is important to describe the garments, using colour confidently is preferable to paying too much attention to the seasonal colour trend. Be bold with colour, keeping in mind the way that children splash colour onto a page and experiment with bold brush strokes and strong shades. Not adding colour for fear of ruining a perfectly drawn figure is self-limiting for an illustrator.

Think about the viewer and what you want the eye to be drawn to in your illustration. Limiting your colour palette, then using an accent colour cleverly is one way of controlling what the viewer notices. By adding a few, carefully placed accessories in the accent colour, you can create a flow across the page from top to bottom, left to right. In this way the accent colour guides the viewer's eyes over the illustration. For example, think of an illustration of a man in a black suit wearing a red belt, red hat and red shoes. The red would draw the viewer's eyes to follow it over the ensemble but without detracting from the predominant black suit.

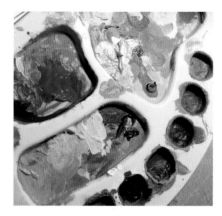

Top and above
The palette (top) shows how paints are mixed together to create the background colours for the embroidered illustration 'Glamour Girls' by Louise Gardiner (above).

Left
Max Gregor uses various shades of blue to create his 'Blue Girl.' Don't be afraid to stick to one colour. Sometimes using a variety of tonal shades works better than mixing many contrasting colours.

The illustrations on this page are also made up from a monotone palette. The interest is added, by clever use of pattern and line by the illustrators. In Shimizu's 'Now Hear Stripe' (above) the fashion figure blends into the black and white environment that she lays in. However, the red shoes and lipstick allow the figure to stand out from a background that is as striped as her clothes. Gregor's 'Meeeee' (above right) has been created digitally with patterns of various shapes and sizes. This build-up of pattern and therefore colour (even though it is only black on a white background) allows the garments to be the main focus of the illustration.

Louise Gardiner creates her intricate embroidered illustrations by drawing and painting the figure onto fabric first. In 'Glamour Girls' and the corresponding paint palette (opposite), you can see how she has a natural flair for balancing the colours in the illustration. See more of how Louise works with colour in her tutorial in Chapter Four.

The subtle palette in Max Gregor's 'Blue Girl' (opposite below) is a striking contrast to some of the other illustrations in this book. Gregor uses various shades of blue to create this play-on-words for his fairly miserable 'Blue Girl'. The expanse of plain blue background draws the viewer to focus on the character. The shadows are also applied with the same tonal qualities as the rest of the illustration style.

For further inspiration, look at how other artists and illustrators use colour in their work, for example the contemporary illustrations in Chapter Six use colour in many imaginative ways. Try similar techniques yourself, adding your own fresh, individual response.

Above left
Yuko Shimizu shows how a monotone palette can be enhanced by introducing a hint of red.

Above
Max Gregor also uses a mono palette but he uses pattern to differentiate between the garments and make them the main focus of the fashion illustration.

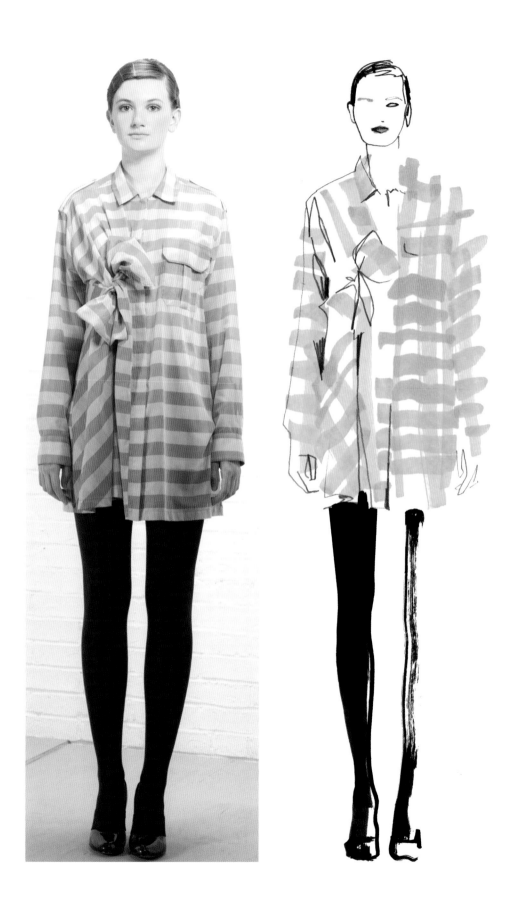

Fabric rendering and pattern reproduction

Depicting the qualities of fabric accurately brings authenticity to a fashion illustration. To achieve a professional standard of fabric representation, develop an understanding of different fabrics and observe the way in which they drape and fall on the body. The best way to gain this knowledge is to sketch clothed figures. Notice the shapes the fabric makes around the body, rarely lying flat but moulding itself around the contours of the figure. Observe the way that looser garments hang while tighter fabrics stretch on the body, and practise drawing the effects. It would be useful to collect a range of fabric samples and practise drawing them, observing the way they fold and fall.

Always keep in mind that, although your fashion illustrations may be highly creative and individual, the intention of the artwork is to convey a garment or outfit. The representation of the fabric from which the clothing is constructed must play a significant role in your artwork.

Stripes and checks

When drawing stripes, keep in mind that they move with the body. Stripes run across, down or around the body, regardless of their width or the direction of the print. A common mistake in fashion illustration is to render stripes using straight, parallel lines. If you look at a horizontal-striped jumper off the body, then the lines of the stripes are indeed straight. However, imagine a person wearing that jumper. The stripes will wrap around the torso and arms so must be drawn with curved lines.

The correct way to draw stripes is to begin at the centre of a garment, then follow the lines of the stripes over the curves of the body, up to the shoulder and down over the hips to the hem. It is a mistake to start from the top or bottom, as the direction of the stripes will become confused with the shift in hip and shoulder positions of the figure. When you plot your stripes from the centre of the garment, ensure they are of equal proportion if that is true of the fabric. Some striped fabrics have uneven stripes that are not symmetrical. Stripes may run in a vertical, horizontal or diagonal direction.

Checks, or plaids, are stripes running in two directions. Like stripes they can be drawn straight or on the bias (diagonally) to form either repeated '+' or 'x' shapes. Again, checks are made up of straight lines that will curve with the body. These lines usually run down the centre front of a garment and are equidistant from each other.

Plan your drawings with faint pencil lines before you begin to render striped and checked fabrics. Accuracy at this stage is vital if the finished artwork is to look professional.

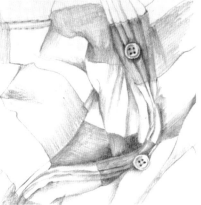

Top
A mix of pencil and paper collaged together in Adobe Photoshop.

Above
A mix of coloured and lead pencil adjusted in Adobe Photoshop.

Opposite
Cecilia Carlstedt illustrates this checked shirt by Sophie Hulme with a flat-headed, thick Priscolor Premier marker pen. The tights are painted with Cretacolor calligraphy ink. The brush Cecilia uses is Beckers 440 synthetic acrylic. Cecilia likes working in marker pen because "… it gives a sketchy look and since every line you draw is permanent you have to make more considerate lines, that creates a certain confident style."

Wool

Woollen fabrics are generally woven in a variety of weights, and include flannel, gabardine, fleece and mohair. They can also be patterned – for example, tweeds, pinstripes and herringbone. Wools are best rendered in a soft medium that will produce one base colour and a darker shadow because, unless it is textured, a drawn woollen surface often appears flat. Markers are excellent for drawing flat fabrics, and you can soften the edges with a non-permanent fineliner, sweeping a wet brush over the outline. Other art materials that work well for rendering wool are pencils, inks, watercolour and gouache. Try applying the base colours with paint and the highlights or shadows in pencil.

Textures and weaves can be rendered with a dry-brush technique, in which a fairly limited amount of almost-dry paint is applied, leaving part of the page white. You could also try scratching directional lines into the surface of wet paint. Tweeds and herringbones can be represented with inks and markers, which convey the fluidity of the pattern. To create the intricacies of the weave, crosshatch with two or more colours.

Below
The illustration by Cecilia Carlstedt of an Iben Høj design is all drawn in pencils (HB and 2H) by building up the rough sketch and filling in the more detailed parts of the knit. On finalisation the illustration was slightly colour adjusted in Photoshop using the Adjust Colour/Balance tool.

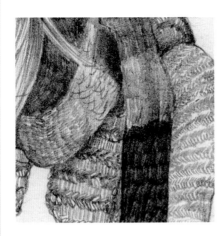

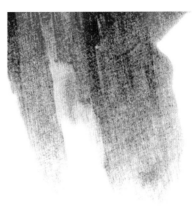

Knit

This fabric has a texture created by its looping and twining threads. Knit differs from woven fabric in its stretch as well as its texture. Knitted garments are either constructed by hand or machine, and produced in various wools and yarns, such as angora, cashmere, mohair, chenille, bouclé and metallic. Gain awareness of knitwear variations, because they demand very different rendering techniques.

   To render knitwear differently from a woven fabric you need to draw in the rib. Rib, or ribbing, is the term used to describe a series of raised rows in knitted fabric. Ribbing is often found around the neck, cuffs and edges of a garment and can be indicated with repetitive line. You will also need to master authentic representation of the stitches used in knit. For example, cable and braiding can be indicated with a combination of curved and straight lines in a rope pattern, while purl and garter can be rendered with a series of loops and ellipses. Knit patterns often include geometric shapes, raised textures and flowers. These are usually known as Fair Isle or Argyle and are best shown by blocking in the patterns before adding texture and colour.

Woven

Denim, a heavy, woven fabric, is often adorned with topstitching, rivets and prominent seams, all of which can be rendered by the illustrator. If you look carefully at a piece of denim, you will see that it is made up of a series of diagonal lines broken up by the weave. Copy this effect using sharp, watersoluble pencils of varying shades of blue. Use darker shades for the diagonal lines and paler ones for the weave. For areas where the denim is worn, dilute the pencil marks with water to create the effect. Denim rivets are often metallic and can be rendered effectively with a metallic pen or paint. Highlight the topstitching in areas where it is prominent, using a simple, broken line. Today, denim is often customized to include embroidery, rips, print and jewelled accessories, all of which the fashion illustrator must draw attention to.

Left
Pencil drawing to capture hand-knitted stitches.

Middle
The woven qualities of denim are rendered in pencil.

Right
Here denim has been depicted with blue paint screenprinted on to rough paper so that the paper mimics the texture of denim.

Sheers

Sheer fabrics are so fine that a single layer is transparent, and you can see skin tone through it. With the exception of lingerie, most garments in sheer fabrics are made up of many layers, or include undergarments.

Sheers can be categorized into two groups: the softer sheers, such as chiffon, voile, georgette and some laces, and the stiffer types, including organza, tulle, net and organdie. To render transparent fabrics, begin by applying skin tones to your fashion illustration. Add the colour of the fabric over the top of the skin with a light touch in either pencil or marker, avoiding

Above

The illustration by Cecilia Carlstedt of a Bolongaro Trevor dress is a collage where transparent tissue papers are layered to create the sheer, multi-layered dress. It has been stuck down with a small amount of spray adhesive. The collage was then scanned into Photoshop to add extra details.

heavy outlines. The skin must be visible under the fabric, so be careful not to choose too dark a colour.

Where sheer fabric touches the body, shading should be darker. Where it floats freely, use lighter tones. This technique also applies if you are rendering many layers of chiffon – the more layers, the denser the shading. For lace or net, the appearance of the fabric as it lies over the skin must, likewise, be rendered sensitively. These mesh-like fabrics can be represented with fine crosshatching that becomes darker where the fabric folds. For lace, you can build up the floral patterns and embroidery by using a fineliner to indicate the details. Your drawing lines for such a delicate fabric should be fluid and without sharp corners. The edges of lace may be scalloped and heavily patterned, but it will be impossible to draw every intricate detail. Simply suggesting the style is perfectly acceptable in fashion illustration.

Organza and organdie have a stiffer consistency than the sheers discussed above. Garments made from these fabrics stand out from the body and create a sense of drama. They can be rendered with the same techniques used for other sheers, but there is a difference in the way that they fall and catch the light. When sketching them, try overlapping blocks of colour to show where one fold of fabric lies on top of another. The deeper shading conveys the double thickness of the fabric.

Embellished and embroidered fabrics

Not all fabrics are the same through their length; some vary in texture. Hand-made fabrics are often embroidered or otherwise embellished, and you will need to change your rendering style accordingly. Embellished fabrics are often manipulated through stitching. For example some are raised with padding or wadding, then decorated with hand- or machine-stitched patterns. To capture such techniques on paper, the fabric must look raised from its background. Embellishments will appear closer to the viewer if worked in light colours on a darker background. Embroidery thread also catches the light, so again this should be rendered with highlights. It is impossible to record every detail, but draw in elements every now and again to indicate the presence of decorative stitching.

Top
Transparent petals made in Illustrator overlaying each other in gradient shades of red.

Middle
Pencil sketch scanned into Photoshop with tones of yellow overlaid to create a deeper pattern.

Bottom
Vector pattern made in Illustrator to create a lace effect.

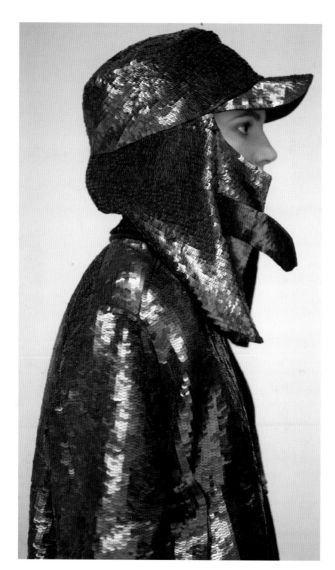

Above

This completely sequinned hooded jacket by
Sophie Hulme is painted with different shades
of black Luma Brilliant concentrated watercolour
by Cecilia Carlstedt. The colours were built up
in layers, lighter shades first and darker on top.
Carlstedt then inverted the colours in Photoshop,
so that the dark patches became light, to give
the shimmering feeling of glistening sequins.

Shiny fabrics

To illustrate shiny fabrics, observe where the light source falls on the garment. Clever rendering will create the illusion of reflected light. To add a highlight to the garment, draw on a white shimmer line or leave the white of the page to shine through.

Shiny fabrics divide into three categories. First, there are the light-reflective types, including firm fabrics such as taffeta, satin and leather, and softer velvet and velour. Secondly, there are the decorative fabrics with a sheen, which are usually beaded, and sequinned lamés. The third category includes heavily patterned reptile skins and brocades.

Shiny fabrics are usually rendered in three shades. The darkest shade is for the folds and shadows, a medium shade is for the general garment colour and the lightest for the highlights. The lightest shade, usually white, often surrounds the dark shadows, and touches of it should be added to the edges of the garment. Add highlights where the body juts out from the fabric, at the chest, arms or legs, for example. Choose any art material for these three shades, but focus on imitating shine.

Softer sheens such as that on velvet should be approached in the same way, only without areas of solid colour or solid outlines. Instead, create feathery edges. A soft, dry medium such as pastel is ideal for creating a velvety smooth surface to your fashion illustration. Treat the shimmer of lamé, sequins and beads as a pattern, stippling with a hard brush using fairly dry paint and creating sharp white highlights. Alternatively, tap all over the drawing with a medium-nibbed marker. To give your illustration extra sparkle, use metallic pens.

Feathers and fur

Both natural and imitation feathers and fur are difficult to render realistically. It is a common error to overwork these parts of an illustration by sketching in too many lines. The best method is to use watercolour paper, dampening the page then adding ink or paint in light touches. This creates fuzzy, soft lines that represent the delicacy of feathers and fur well. For white feathers or fur, paint a dark background then use bleach to add fine lines.

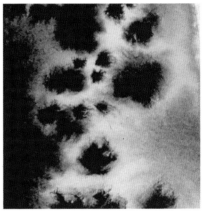

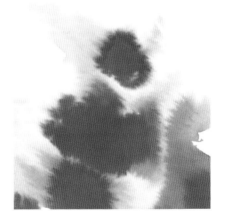

Top
Pencil drawing, scanned and inverted in Photoshop to create long fur.

Middle
Ink on wet paper blurs to give the effect of short-haired animal fur.

Bottom
Pink watercolour on wet paper spreads out feather-like to mimic a boa.

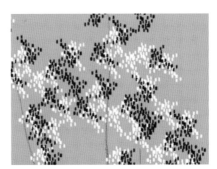

Opposite
This illustration by Cecilia Carlstedt of the dress shown left is made up of various mixed media. The base is watercolour and the golden pattern is drawn with the real fabric layered on top using the Lasso tool in Photoshop. The Fill tool has been used to colour the fabric appropriately. This gives an interesting mix of the flowing fabric in watercolor and the more graphic, computer-generated print.

Above left
Garment by Bolongaro Trevor.

Top
A small repeated pattern created in Illustrator.

Middle
A repeated pattern created using Photoshop with different colours overlaying each other.

Bottom
Collage of coloured paper created in Photoshop.

Pattern and print

Fashion fabrics can be printed with almost any design or motif, including floral, abstract, animal and polka dot. A design that is duplicated or copied is called a repeat pattern. In addition to the repeat, you need to bear in mind scale. For example, a life-size floral fabric must be reduced to fit into the proportions of a drawn figure. The simplest way to calculate this is to hold the fabric up to the centre of your body and count the repeat in the directions of the side seam and along the waist. To achieve the scale, fit the same count into your drawn figure.

When you reduce a fussy print, remove some of the detail as it can look overworked on a smaller scale. Render some of the pattern and disguise areas with soft shadows, using a limited colour palette.

Drape

Examining the way clothing drapes, hangs, falls and clings to the body is of the utmost importance when illustrating. The previous pages have looked at how various fabrics can be illustrated in order for them to be realistically represented. However, an illustrator must also be aware that the body is a moving three-dimensional being, and fabrics will take on different forms depending on the body size and shape and the part of the body it is next to. Sometimes a fabric will fall in loose folds, rest limply or cling tightly to the body. Fabric sometimes bunches up, is tied or gathered together. The direction the fabric is being often pulled by gravity while at other times it can be stretched tightly across an arm or torso.

It is necessary to look closely at how clothing fits the body as patterned fabrics will change directions, areas of light and dark shade will be visible and hem lengths will alter accordingly. The illustrated example of check fabric right clearly shows the drape in the clothing. The lines move in different directions and it is possible to see how the garment hangs and folds. Remember to use shading to give the illustration more form. Generally, you should shade along a fold line or any places that you think a shadow would be cast. Don't forget no two folds are ever the same when it comes to fashion. Take a further look at the fashion illustrations by Laura Laine for Iben Høj (p.135). Laine has a remarkable skill at capturing the drape and folds in fabric.

Fabric reference exercise

To make the most of the information discussed in this section, experiment by rendering fabrics yourself to create a set of reference illustrations. Divide a sheet of plain paper into a grid of blank squares. Place a viewfinder with a square view over various fabric samples. Try to create the same effects that you can see through the viewfinder in your squares. Experiment with a range of media until you find the best way to represent each of the fabrics. Make notes next to your accurate renderings to remind you how to create similar effects again. Building up a library of authentic rendering techniques is certain to be a useful aid when creating fashion illustrations in the future.

This vector illustration created in Adobe Illustrator by Cecilia Carlstedt, shows how fabrics drape and fall. A checked fabric is a good example to demonstrate how directions change as the fabric falls and how light and shade hit different areas of the fabric create depth of colour.

4.

Mixed Media: Tina Berning

Tina Berning originally studied graphic design with a specific focus on illustration in Nuremburg, Germany. Besides her commissioned illustrations she continuously elaborates fine art projects such as her book *100 Girls on Cheap Paper*. This originated as an ambitious project where she completed 100 illustrations in as many days. In a collaboration with Michelangelo Di Battista for *Vogue Italia* models were photographed with Berning's illustrations held over parts of their faces. This work is interesting, as the mix of media is also a mix of creative people (photographer and illustrator).

When new digital techniques are being used by artists on a daily basis, it is natural to mix media when illustrating the fast-moving world of fashion. In this tutorial Tina mixes the traditional painting techniques of ink and acrylic with Adobe Photoshop to demonstrate how she works through the process of illustrating for *Fashion Trends* books each season.

www.tinaberning.de
www.cwc-i.com
agent@cwc-i.com

You can see more of Tina Berning's work on pp.27, 67, 71 and 188–89.

1. The job is the cover for *Fashion Trends Summer 2009*. This is a fashion report magazine aimed at people in the fashion business, like designers, fashion companies and retailers. It shows and analyzes the latest trends. I do the title and five inner pages four seasons a year. The title can be folded out, so I have to make sure it works cropped, but also as a spread.

The client sent me a choice of fashion items and I chose a Dior Summer 2009 dress to show on the cover, because the pattern works nicely in a drawing. The image above shows an earlier title that I did.

2. For the rough I use the Path tool to cut the dress out of the Dior photo that I got from the client. Then I select the path and position the girl in the layer. The shape cut out of the photo does not really fit my girl, so I flip it and use the Transform (control T) option to fit it to the right position.

4.

3. Doing the first sketch in Photoshop helps me check if my illustration fits the strict layout guidelines. I get a template from the client and apply it as a separate layer in Photoshop. Then I check if, for example, the eye falls within the left-hand page, when the right side is folded.

4. Using the rough layout as a guide, I do a fine drawing with ink. Ink is not light resistant, so the image will fade when hung on the wall, but the washes are beautiful. I always use a Venetian glass quill. If you ever get hold of one, buy it: the ink flows very evenly and long and it makes a nice line. Then I take a large watercolour brush, and wash the lines with a lot of water and ink. Ink – in contrast to China ink, is water-soluble, so, when I touch them with the brush, the lines wash too, which merges the two steps nicely, lines and washes.

5. In Photoshop I add a little make-up to my drawing. Everything I do in Photoshop is done in layers, so if I don't like the lipstick colour, I can always change it. The colours are applied with the Brush function. Using a Wacom pad, I can control the pressure and thickness of the brushes.

6. From my archive of backgrounds that I have collected over the years, I chose this apricot-coloured one. It is done with acrylics on cardboard, the different layers smoothed with a spatula. The contrasts are not too great with the face, and the texture is very subtle. I open the background in Photoshop and drag the drawing of the girl in as a separate layer. The drawing layer is put on Multiply. To exclude the dress from the background colour, I use the Path tool to define the selection of the dress, invert the selection and turn the selection to a mask. Using a mask instead of erasing the background where I don't need it enables me to make changes later. If, for example, I decide the background looks better upside down, I can flip it, and the mask will not be affected.

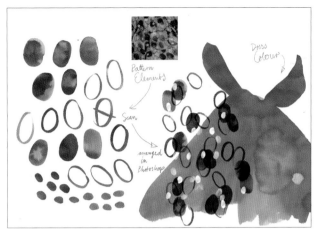

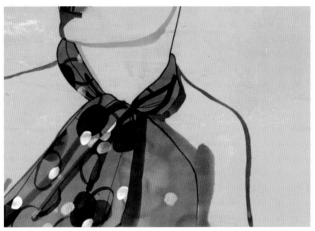

7. The pattern and the colour of the dress are drawn separately. I draw the pattern elements and arrange them in Photoshop according to the fabric in the photo. I make each dot and circle a separate layer, then I Duplicate, Flip, Transform and set the transparency to Multiply, and push them around, until they look like part of the fabric. The white spots are actually inverted dark spots (below in the scan), with the Photoshop layer on 'Screen'. This Photoshop file probably has about 30 layers, so it is better to do this as a separate file, and drag the result into the main file as only one layer later. That way you avoid ending up with 300 layers in a file, where you can't find anything anymore.

8. The arranged pattern element is integrated into the dress in separate sections, defining the different layers and pleats of the cloth. Instead of just adding an overall pattern, which would look flat, I select sections of the dress within the drawing with the Path tool and apply a mask to the pattern layer with the selection. I duplicate the pattern layer, make a new mask of another section of the dress and move the pattern within this new mask to a different position. In the example here I made five layers of pattern for the fabric.

10. Finally check if the illustration works nicely with the layout, especially when it is cropped as a cover. The colours of the typography will be done by the graphic designer later, so this is just a mock-up. I received the typography mock-up from the client as a PDF. You can open every PDF in Photoshop, so you have the precise dimension, and then drag the PDF as a separate layer to your file (multiply).

9. A shadow is added, and a sprayed element. With a very watery ink I paint a shadow on a separate piece of paper, scan it, and drag it as a separate 'multiplying' layer in Photoshop. Of course the shadow has to fit the shadows in the face. When you're doing an illustration like this in several steps, you sometimes forget this. In this case the light is coming from the right side, so the shadow has to be on the left of the face.

To make the illustration look less bold, I start playing around with the elements in Photoshop, which can be wonderful and surprising. The drawing itself is done, now the 'decoration' begins – the experimenting with different elements of the design. I found that some elements from the dress pattern, swirling around the girls head, look like a beautiful hairdo, and it makes the forehead, which is a little too blank, look much nicer.

Allow yourself to play around and try out things you might not have planned initially.

fashion trends

casual

HEADI: SUMMER 2009

MODE

Hier steht der text,
Hier steht der text,
Hier steht der text,

MODE

Hier steht der text,
Hier steht der text,
Hier steht der text,

ISSN 0940-7278   # 01.2008
GERMANY 135.00 €, FRANCE 135.00 €,
ITALY 135.00 €, UK 90.00 £.

TM

fashion trends   PUBLISHED BY BRANCHE & BUSINESS
FACHVERLAG GMBH, DÜSSELDORF

Illustrator: Marcos Chin

Marcos Chin graduated from the Ontario College of Art and Design, in Toronto, Canada. Since then, his work has appeared on book covers, advertisements, fashion catalogues, magazines, and CD covers. Perhaps the most recognizable work in his portfolio are the illustrations he created for Lavalife's international advertising campaign, which appeared on subways, billboards, print and online.

In this tutorial Chin explains how he use's Adobe Illustrator to create a fashion illustration used for *Complex* magazine. Illustrator has become the standard application when clients want slick illustration design. Artists, illustrators and graphic designers use it to create vector-based graphics that can be easily rescaled without loss of quality. The software is often used to transform hand-drawn sketches into lively, detailed digital images.

Chin explains how he spent days drawing thumbnail sketches of figures and environments before he deconstructs them and begins to bring the layers to life. It is a very organized way of working which may not suit illustrators who prefer to work in a more craft-like manner.

marcos@marcoschin.com
www.marcoschin.com

You can see more of Marcos Chin's work on pp.142, 151, 162–63.

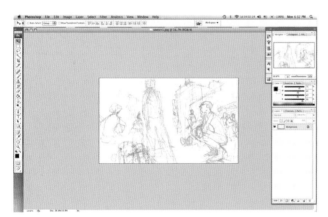

1. The starting point for an illustration is a sketch. I spend hours, even a couple of days, working out ideas for an illustration. For me, the idea is paramount in any image. I love beautiful pictures, images that engage me visually but also those that have some sort of concept of narrative. In the above example, the assignment was for *Complex Magazine's* 'Hooked Up' section, which featured different fashion items. Instead of placing them on a blank background, I choose to embed the clothing and accessories within an environment; doing so inspires the picture's narrative. This stage of 'brainstorming' exists as quick gesture drawings, usually no more than a few inches large, thumbnail size.

2. Once I have come up with an idea that works, I begin to tighten the drawing in order to establish a stronger sense of the characters, environment and composition. I like to use markers or pens during this stage because of their fluidity and the fact that I can't erase any parts of my drawing. Before I produce a more tightened sketch, it is important to be 'free' and not to hyper-focus on any one part of the drawing. Paying attention to the overall shapes and curves of the elements on my page affects the entire composition, and prevents parts of it being overworked or looking too stiff.

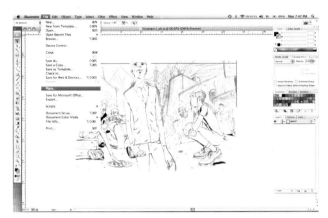

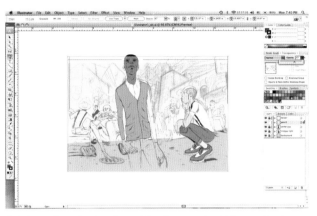

3. If I have some time I like to further tighten my drawing and then ink it with a brush. Often I don't get to do so because I work on very tight deadlines, but in this example I have. I scan the tight drawing into Adobe Photoshop and save it as a 300dpi, jpeg, greyscale (colour). Afterwards I 'Place' it into Adobe Illustrator, so that I can use it as a template to trace over using vectors. The area that you work on in Adobe Ilustrator is called the Art Board.

4. I always deconstruct my image into a foreground, middleground and background by adding additional layers. However, if the image is more complicated as above, then I label the layers according to what will be drawn in each one (see figure 4). Notice that the 'pencil layer' is the top layer in the layer window. On your art board, the 'pencil payer' will be the foreground layer. Moving from top to bottom on the layer window corresponds to moving from foreground to background on your art board. The layer opacity is set at 67 per cent. This is not a required number, but I used it for the purpose of illustrating this step. Essentially I reduce the opacity of my pencil layer in order to see what I am drawing underneath it. I also 'Lock' the pencil layer so that it will not move by clicking on the 'Lock' icon that appears on each layer.

5. I use the pen tool to trace over my drawing. The tool has a kind of connect-the-dot system. As I move over the line of my drawing, I place down a point until it forms a shape. Here the shape that is being formed is the character's arm. Notice the colour swatch fill and outline. You can change the colours of each one by moving the CMYK colour sliders (C=Cyan, M= Magenta, Y=Yellow, K=Black).

6. I usually simplify my images by blocking in the overall shapes of the elements of my picture. Here they are the figures centre, left and right. This technique is similar to how painters create an under-painting in order to establish an overall colour palette, after which they build up their painting by adding more layers or details at a later stage. I have also added more layers and named them according to the elements in my illustration, (i.e. 'yellow box' and 'motorcycle'). Whenever I am not working on a layer I like to 'Lock' it so that I won't accidentally move or delete parts on that layer.

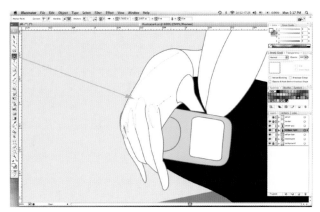

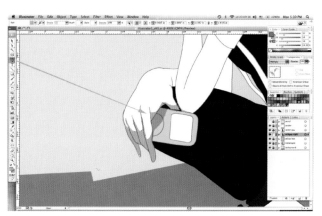

7. Once I have blocked in overall shapes I begin to hide parts of the drawing. When I build figures I reduce them into simple parts. In the hand of the person right, I have drawn four fingers and connected them to a shape that looks like his palm. I have hidden some of the lines where his fingers connect with his palm to make the picture look more believable. The outline colour is 'empty' and the colour fill matches the colour of the character's palm and fingers.

8. I add shadows to parts of my drawing. Often I will select a darker variation of the colour on which I will add the shadow, and then select Multiply from the Transparency window. I draw the shadow the same way as I draw the rest of the figures, like shapes of colour.

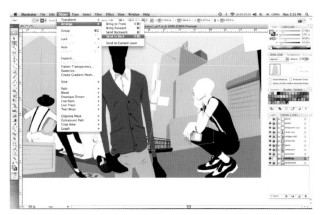

9. I continue to draw the rest of the image, the middleground and background components such as the buildings, and place them on a separate layer. To send drawn objects to the back I pull down the Object window from the Menu bar, and select Arrange and then Send To Back. Conversely if I want to bring objects to the foreground, I will select Bring to Front. This only works to move objects from foreground to background within the same layer.

10. To draw the decorative background elements, again I use the Pen tool and Stroke menu option which is located under Window in the menu bar. Once selected, the Stroke window will appear on the right of your Art Board. Here you can adjust the weight of your line, as well as the characteristics of the (cap) end of it.

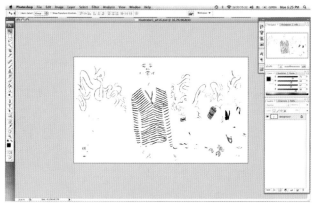

11. This is an example of the finished vector drawing. As you can see, parts of the drawing are still missing, but they will be completed in Adobe Photoshop. In order to open the illustration in Photoshop, you can save it as an Illustrator EPS file.

12. A sample of some of the inked details that will be laid on top of the vector file. It was scanned into Photoshop as a 300dpi file, RGB colour.

13. Some of the inked lines from the previous step were layered on top of the vector drawing (in Adobe Illustrator). Select Multiply in the Layers box.

14. Here the remaining inked lines are added on top of the image from the previous steps, adjusting the characteristics of each layer in the Layers box, i.e. Normal, Multiply, etc. After this I 'Flatten' the image by selecting the icon on the top right of the Layers box.

15. The final image saved as a 300 dpi tiff or jpeg file, CMYK or RGB colour, in Adobe Photoshop.

Embroidery: Louise Gardiner

Louise Gardiner graduated from Goldsmiths College, London with a textiles degree and completed an MA in illustration at Manchester Metropolitan University. She creates figurative and floral one-off pieces of artwork using rhythmic drawing, intense and intricate free-machine stitches, paints, appliqué and inks. She has exhibited worldwide, won numerous awards, completed large-scale public commissions and contributed to books and other publications. She also has her own greetings cards range.

Here, Gardiner creates a quirky back view of a character. Stitching by hand or sewing machine is a lengthy process that could be expensive for a client. However, a designer or fashion label that wanted to show off a creative, unique collection would benefit from this lively, one-off approach. The recent trend for 'hand-made' has made embroidered illustration or text a popular way for graduates and designers to liven up their portfolio pages.

www.lougardiner.co.uk
loulougardiner@hotmail.com

You can see more of
Louise Gardiner's work
on pp.72, 80 and 194–95.

1. Choose the drawing that you wish to embroider.

2. Trace this sketch and place the tracing paper onto a piece of fabric. A heavier weight fabric is best (e.g. thick cotton or denim) unless you want to use a hoop. Here I have chosen a heavy weight calico to avoid being restricted by a hoop.

3. To use your sewing machine and create free embroidery you need a 'free machine embroidery foot' or 'darning foot'. The dog's teeth feed should be down so that you can slide the fabric around without any tension, drawing with the needle as if with a fixed pen. Once your machine is sorted and you have the right foot, follow the lines of your drawing, transferring your design with stitch through the tracing paper onto the fabric. Here, I have used black thread but you can choose any colour. When finished, remove the tracing paper.

4. (opposite) Go back to your sketch and spend some time contemplating colour. How do you want the design to look – is it specific to a collection in the making? What is your theme? Decide, collect and mix the colours you want to use. Here I have chosen mixed fabric paints and collected the threads I wish to use.

COLOUR PALETTE

1) sassy lady - pink/red/gold
green, white, yellow

2) Slightly Clashing Colours for punchy
appeal.

3) gold + glittery threads for luxury.

PAINTS — MIXES.

Range of Base Colours
Mixed Acrylic - combining colours
THREAD to keep palette tight.

5. Return to the stitched piece and paint the design with your chosen base colours. Here I have used a tidy and neat brush, creating a solid graphic style. You could work more loosely with more spontaneous mark-making or work with inkier washes if you wish for a more subtle finish.

6. Here you can see the free machine embroidery foot as I work a fishnet pattern into the legs of the figure.

7. Once you are satisfied with your base colours, and the paint has dried, start to use the gorgeous coloured threads that you have chosen. By stitching different colours of thread over the paint base layer, you will be creating a more three-dimensional look and colours will take on different hues. Here I have added a few black details and started to embroider red thread into the design. If you have the choice, use a multitude of stitches on your machine. If not, straight stitch and zigzag are fine, if mixed with a little imagination.

8. Continue to stitch different coloured threads into the different areas of the design. Carefully guide the needle and develop your own patterns or textures within the clothes. The piece will get richer and richer with each stitch used.

9. Usually towards the end of a piece I will spend some time adding more intricate details which add that extra something special. You could use sparkly or metallic threads if you want to add an extra air of glamour. Some more delicate sparkly threads can keep snapping and drive you mad, but remember you can always wind your metallic thread into the bobbin and work upside down! That's the beauty of embroidery – your designs are two-sided and the back (shown here) is often as beautiful

10. This will take a bit of practice but once you have given your embroidery a good iron, you can stretch it to make it neat and flat, if that's the look you want. Do this by pinning the fabric into the edges of the mount board. Start in the middle of each side and gently pull the fabric as you pin away from the centre.

11. (opposite) Here, I decided to add a couple of splatters of fabric paint to liven the figure up, add movement and tie the design into the background. *Voilà*, a beautiful, sassy lady stitched to the nines!

Photomontage: Robert Wagt

Dutch-born illustrator Robert Wagt graduated from the Minerva Academy of Art in the Netherlands, specializing in photography and fashion illustration. He has done numerous publicity campaigns in both the US and France where clients include Waterman, Ford, Coca-Cola, and Gillette. Wagt is a regular contributor to international magazines and has also illustrated for fashion designers Jean Paul Gaultier and Pierre Cardin.

Robert Wagt's work is interesting because he uses photo reference and realism, but is not bound by them, instead he distorts the body shape to create humour and effect. In this tutorial Wagt shows how he glues bits of magazines and photographs to create a trademark witty and whimsical photomontage. He also uses Adobe Photoshop to give his hand-made work a clean, digital edge.

www.lindgrensmith.com
pat@lindgrensmith.com

You can see more of Robert Wagt's work on pp.43, 178–79.

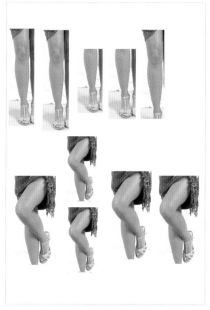

1. I usually have a central character in most of my illustrations. Here I have completed a detailed drawing that will be the same size as the final illustration. The size of the initial sketch is important because I will be using collage to add parts from photographs and magazines by hand throughout the illustration process, therefore they need to match in scale.

2. The next stage is to decide on the composition of the illustration. I take inspiration from magazines, news articles and generally any little quirky things I see on the street. Humour and a sense of fun are key elements to my work, so most of my figures are usually enjoying themselves. For this illustration the central character is being dressed and adorned.

3. In my studio I take photographs of a female model standing in a similar pose to the illustration's central character. I take many photographs in order to build a large collection that forms the basis of the photomontage. Parts of the photographs will be cut and pasted into the illustration.

4. Next I divide the figure into sections and work out which photos I will use in the montage. I place the figure outline onto a light box and then draw the correct sections accurately onto the photographs. I then cut out the relevant sections and glue them onto the paper illustration.

5. This process is then repeated with images collected from magazines. For example, if I do not have the correct skirt fabric photographed I will search for a print in a magazine and cut and paste this onto the illustration instead. At this stage, all of these processes are completed by hand, not digitally as some might expect.

6. When the photomontage figure has been completed to my satisfaction, I scan it, and open the file in Adobe Photoshop.

7. I am unsure about the clothing the model is wearing in this illustration. At this stage I scan another garment and try it on for size using Adobe Photoshop.

8. I then make detailed drawings of the secondary background figures in the illustration, and scan them.

9. The background figures are filled with a green colour using Photoshop, and arranged around the photomontage illustration. The final image is cleaned up by smoothing out the cuttings and removing the pencil marks, before a tonal background is added to complete the illustration (*see* over).

Drawing: Edwina White

Raised in Australia, Edwina White studied visual communications at the University of Technology, Sydney. Her fine art career has been enhanced by her illustrations appearing in international publications, including *ID*, *Print* and *Vogue*.

This tutorial shows how White's sparse drawings on found papers are enhanced with a painterly touch in an article commissioned by Barbara Richer of *The New York Times* Style pages. White tells the story of how the job unfolded, from initial sketches to a full-page spread in the daily newspaper – and how her phone has not stopped ringing since!

You can see more of Edwina White's work on pp.54, 66, 198–99.

www.edwinawhite.com
fiftytwopickup@gmail.com

1. I got a phone call from my agent. I was on holiday in Miami and she asked if I could do the cover for *The New York Times* section while I was there. Of course I said yes.

Usually I receive comprehensive copy, but for newspapers, writers are down to the wire, the story can change a lot between the pitch and the final piece for publication. So.. from the art director, Barbara Richer: "This is the lead story and for beginning sketches why don't you think in a square-ish shape, then I'll quickly as I can work it into a layout and you can modify width or height as necessary. This piece can certainly be simpler than the last one you did, even if it's an event 'at a hotel suite' or something."

And the story description from the editor:

"This is a story about luxury shame. A lot of people regard it as unseemly in these dire economic times, when so many people are hurting financially, to be seen leaving Neiman Marcus, say, carrying refrigerator-size shopping bags. But there is a kind of woman who can't curb her appetite for luxury even in a recession. So some of them have taken to shopping in private – at shopping events arranged in hotel suites, at friends' apartments and online, where they can spend freely yet keep their purchases anonymous (or known only to their fellow travellers). They want to shop without being judged."

I started thinking and sketching immediately.

2. Then further correspondence from Barbara Richer: "I was just talking to my head styles editor and he is talking about someone coming out of somewhere and heading off papparazzi – 'no photos please!' And I was thinking quite the opposite – a string of collar-up, trench-coated, big-sunglassed chicks slinking into somewhere to shop. And, since we don't have a strip ad on the bottom of the page and because this is our 'resourcefulness' package I was thinking maybe we could have people snaking up from the bottom of the page to somewhere, and that would divide the stories. Or maybe slinking in somewhere and then out with packages."

3. I sent the two edited pages of sketches with this explanation in an e-mail:

"What I have attached is a series of characters that you can plot around your page, with various frenzied shoppers. I have situated most with bags and large swing tags. I am envisaging the large swing tags and shoe boxes and bags can be dotted throughout, like stage props. Most of the women are wearing dark glasses or they are propped on their heads.

The first character is a fellow… only because of the other article on the list of ten staple garments for men. Have a good look. I want you to play around with them and then I can put more stage elements in.

I will attach luxury brand logos on the bags and swing tags and to credit cards too.

How's Chanel, Louis Vuitton, Louboutin, Gucci, maybe a DVF, Balenciaga, Lanvin? That's for your people to choose. I do hope I'm on the right track, a flexible one at this point of course."

4. After an editorial meeting particular sketches were selected and arranged in a dummy page layout by the art director

After co-ordinating the characters, I had to dress them, in the very latest, as the fashion press are up to the minute, especially in newspapers. So further research was required at this stage. A Google search for the latest in luxury bags, dresses, coats and sunglasses. From brands such as Chanel. Louis Vuitton, Hermès, Prada, Alexander McQueen. With a quick look at *Vogue* magazine advertisements as well.

5. The pencilled artwork is transfererd to paper, old paper that carries a yellowish tone, a warm background ideal for skin colour. And then I coloured in the figures with fabrics and logos, according to the research material, with pencil, and ink wash. The first I sent to Barbara with this note attached "…shaded lady is wearing zero, an Hermès scarf and bags by Burberry, YSL and Chanel".

When that was approved, I knew I was on the right track, so I painted and scanned and sent another, "This one is wearing McQueen, carrying Hermès, with Dior and Vuitton shopping bags".

And gradually… "This one wearing Marni-ish thing and carrying Marc Jacobs and Gucci shopping bags"

I send them step by step because the editing process at *The New York Times* is very acute. Accuracy is key, as the fashion press is very observant and particular.

"This one with Hermès and Prada shopping bags, platinum card and Prada lace leggings."

6. All images were placed and all approved, except for the photographer who I had to reposition.

I then edited the background paper, so that the figures were silhouetted. That was just a stage in Photoshop, utilising a tool that selected and deleted all the area outside of my lines.

Barbara placed them on the page, with final text at the ready, to be printed for the following day's paper. My phone rang from 9am onwards. It was a huge success!

And I was on holiday, remember?

Photoshop: Tom Bagshaw

Tom Bagshaw is a UK-based illustrator who, despite a stint at graphic design college, is pretty much self-taught. His webfolio is proof that practice makes perfect, showcasing his work and home to a truly inspirational blog. If you are struggling with digital illustration technique or composition, Bagshaw's informative yet creative blog probably has the answer.

This extended tutorial shows his digital painting talents and process, using mostly Adobe Photoshop. He explains in detailed stages how to create a hi-res fashion illustration. His visual style combines the look of traditional painting, the feel of fashion photography and elements of graphic design.

www.mostlywanted.com
tom@mostlywanted.com

You can see more of
Tom Bagshaw's work
on pp.39, 51, 158–59.

1. To start I create a new document in Photoshop at print resolution A4 with 3mm bleed all around. I fill the background layer with 50 per cent grey, it helps keep a constant mid-tone for later. Next come my guides, I split the document into thirds for pretty much everything I do. I don't always stick to these guidelines but it can be a good way to help compose your image. My initial sketch was created in ArtRage. You can generate your sketch however you like, digitally or analogue, just bring it into the document on a separate layer and turn the blending mode to Multiply so that any white areas dont show, just your pencil or pen lines.

2. I want to have a textured background to this piece so I open up ArtRage again and paint with thick oils on a rough, textured plaster and canvas layer, layers of paint built up showing plenty of texture and colour. When I am happy, I export the file to Photoshop and bring it in on a layer below the sketch. This stage could quite easily be done in Photoshop using scanned or sourced textures, or simply brushed onto another layer, it's really just personal preference.

3. The background is a little too even, so to create a more pleasing backdrop a hue saturation adjustment layer is used to knock back some of the blue. I add a gradient of white to transparent, set to a softlight blending mode. The opacity is dropped down to allow some of the underlying texture to show through. Finally another layer is added and the Gradient tool used to add a circular burst of light behind the model. Again I set this to softlight and reduce opacity until I get the effect I desire.

4. For the model's skin I switch to Painter and use the oil brushes to paint her head and part of her hair. You could use Photoshop but I prefer the way Painter handles painting blended tones – especially skin – so I use it for that specific task. Once I'm happy I can just switch back to Photoshop as Painter also handles psd files without any problems. Once back in Photoshop I use a custom brush to finish off the hair and add a few touch-ups to the skin with some light air-brushing.

5. This is a short step as it is really just adding some touch-ups. Shadows are added below the strands of hair that fall over the model's cheeks. I add some spatter effects to her eye-shadow, spatter and paint drips added to layers below the hair help tie the hair into the shoulder and around the neckline. These are custom brushes that can be created yourself from scanned images or there are resource sites online that can furnish you with brushes to suit.

6. Using the Pen tool I create vector paths for the arm and legs. Then I open the path's palette and save the work path. I select a hard-edged, round brush and reduce the size to that of a pen line. I set colours to default by hitting 'D', create a new layer, then switch to the Arrow tool (A). Then I select my paths and right click. In the Content menu I click on 'Stroke Path'. This brings up a dialogue box allowing me to choose to stroke the paths with various tools. Using the brush option will stroke the path with the last-used brush and the foreground colour, which is why you need to set your brush up before this step. You can check the box to simulate brush pressure but in this instance I leave it unchecked to create a smooth, constant line.

7. To create the pattern for the dress I'm going to use some stock images of flowers and design a rough poster/screenprint effect. It takes some time but can produce some good effects. I prefer it to some of the filters that could be employed to a similar effect. The bigger your images are, the better. It is far easier to work large and scale down than try and scale up small images to fit a larger size. I use another A4 300dpi document so that I can work on the pattern at the same resolution as my final artwork.

8. Once again, I select the Pen tool and start to draw a path around the flower. This can take a little time but eventually I have a vector outline around the flowerhead. I select the path and right click, there is an option to 'Create Vector Mask'. This has the effect of using the path to remove extraneous imagery in a non-destructive way, it also gives a good, clean edge to the image.

9. With the layer still active, I create a 'Threshold Adjustment Layer' above it. This converts the image below to simple black and white. Moving the slider left or right will remove or show more of the shadows, and highlight information in the image. A little trial and error will show you what's happening, so aim for a mid-range and click OK.

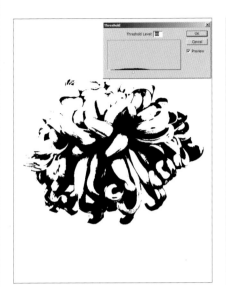

10. To create the desired effect I need to add a few of these threshold layers, each with slightly differing levels. We are in effect replicating basic screenprinting technique in Photoshop. Once you are done with one threshold layer, turn off its visibilty and repeat the process with another adjustment layer at a differing level.

11. Once all the threshold layers are done, a selection is made from the results. Turn the visibilty of a threshold layer on with the underlying masked flower. Click on the Channels palette to view the channel information. You will see four channels, RGB and then the split channels that make up that information. Hold down 'Ctrl' and click the thumbnail image in the blue channel once. This makes a selection from that channel.

12. Back on the layers palette, click on the 'Create a New Fill or Adjustment Layer' icon again and select 'Solid Colour'. As you have a selection active this allows you to create an editable colour layer that uses the selection area only. Add the new base layer to the bottom of your colour fill layers and adjust its tone so that the above layers will show properly.

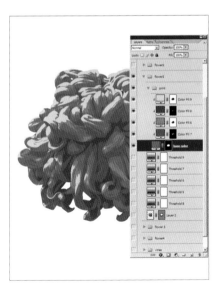

13. With the base layer still selected, place the cursor between it and the layer above, hold down the Alt key – note the cursor changes – this denotes that you are about to make a clipping mask. Click and the layer moves to link it to the layer below, add the others in the same way. You may need to play with inverting the layer masks or alter the order of the layers, but you should end up with something similar to the above.

14. Once all the chosen flowers are done, I have each flower in its own folder. When selected, this means that I can move and scale the group as needed. I move the flowers around to make a pleasing composition and then turn off the visibility of everything but the flowers (not forgetting to turn off the background white layer too.) I hit Ctrl + A to select everything on the canvas, I then hold Ctrl + Shift + C to copy everything visible to the clipboard.

15. Back on the artwork document I create a new layer folder under the hair and skin and add in a new layer. From here I can now hit Ctrl + V to paste the flowers in and free transform the pattern to best suit the compostion. Then using the Polygonal Lasso tool (L), draw out the shape of the dress and with the pattern layer still active hit the mask icon on the layers palette to hide the unwanted areas.

16. The pattern is too bright, so with the flower layer selected I create a new hue/saturation adjustment layer. I hold down Alt and click on the dividing line between the flower layer and the adjustment layer above. This creates a clipping mask so that the new hue/saturation adjustment layer will only affect the layer below. I double click the thumbnail of the adjustment layer to bring up the settings and bring the saturation down to a more acceptable level.

17. To create some subtle folds on the dress, I hide the flower layer (this also turns off the clipping mask) and create a new layer above the now-hidden adjustment layer. Usng the sketch as reference and with a brush with a couple of pixels softness I brush in some folds. I've used a bright green so it's easier to see but the colour isn't important, just the shape. Once you're happy, lock the transparent pixels by hitting the '/' key.

18. Now the layer's transparent pixels are locked off I can paint the folds with a purple selected from the dress. I set the layer to 'Screen' and adjust the opacity to about 90 per cent. To erase the brush strokes outside the edge of the dress I add a layer mask using the same shape as the pattern layer. I Ctrl + click on the mask thumbnail of the pattern layer to select the dress shape and with the folds layer still active hit the 'Add Vector Mask' icon at the bottom of the Layers palette.

19. In order to add some shape to the edge of the sleeve, I create a new layer and, using a spatter brush, lightly paint some spray roughly around that area using a brown sampled from the hair. I lower the opacity and set the blend mode to Multiply, then once again, add a mask the same shape as the dress. This also has the effect of darkening the top part of the flower print and the opacity helps to match the same tones as the hair at the top end of the print.

20. Moving on to the arm and legs we can employ similar techniques as on the dress. Taking the arm as the example, I use a new layer and textured brush to paint in some tone and colour then, using the saved work path from the line work, I create a selection of the arm and add a layer mask, resetting the blending mode and opacity as needed. To paint some additional brush strokes into the mask to remove or lighten some of the arm, make sure the mask thumbnail is active and use black to paint where you want to knock the arm out.

Finishing touches
Small details such as the sun and abstract shapes are added. The flowers were copied from those created for the dress and treated to blend in. A mask is added to the hair and airbrushed lightly. Finally, select all, copy everything visible and paste it back on the top layer, apply some gaussian noise and then fade the effect slightly. Save the final layered file, then 'Save As' a hi-res jpg or flattened tif file format ready for delivery.

Ink: Amelie Hegardt

Amelie Hegardt studied fine art at the Stockholm School of Art and Design, and continued at Central Saint Martins London. Her tightly rendered, doodle-like, overloaded Indian ink and watercolour images have been commissioned by the likes of Mac Cosmetics, Godiva chocolates, Bloomingdales, Umberto Giannini and *Vogue Italia*.

In this tutorial Amelie explains the process of capturing the spontaneity of ink splashes and the fluidity of bleeding, watery ink to create a beautifully controlled fashion illustration. She completes this provocative artwork by adding a background in Photoshop.

www.trafficnyc.com
www.darlingmanagement.com
ameliehegardt@gmail.com

You can see more of
Amelie Hegardt's work
on pp.69, 190–91.

1. Going through fashion magazines is great for inspiration. Sketch several different postures and work out what you want to say with your mannequin. I've always been interested in body language and how the models move and communicate with the camera. Even though I am very seldom aware of it myself, the pose often reflects my mood that particular day. With this illustration I found a girl that was protecting her self in a seductive way, a little bit of a female warrior with mystical powers, yet fragile and perhaps slightly suspicious. With her shoulders raised towards her neck she might resemble the way a cat responds to something she dislikes but won't fear.

2. I use graphite on paper to make up a sketch for what I want to do. To give some depth to this particular drawing I also use pastel on her shoulders. Mixing pastel with bleeding ink is my trademark. When I started I mainly used pastel, not for any particular reason, but it has been with me ever since I started to illustrate. I like the contrast between the smudginess and the bleeding ink. There are many types of paper that can be used with water-based colours. At art school I learnt how to put the paper in water and glue it onto a board, but I like it when the paper is 'bulking up' and shows the reaction to the water. Normally this disappears when I scan the illustration. It's just visible on the actual original which I get to keep for myself.

3. To create a background I add ink with a brush. It's very random which brushes I use. Normally I just take the nearest brush to me, one that is not already wet with colour. Sometimes I use one of the brushes that I bought in Beijing, the ones they use for writing, or just a traditional brush. It's very random and depends on how messy my desk is. Usually it's just a chaotic mess where I work, so I don't really plan the process.

After that I refine details such as shoes and hands with very thin brushes. Have a look at the latest fashion shows and use accessories you like or think would suit your character.

I was inspired by the Dolce & Gabbana fashion show, Fall 2009, I saw these very girlie shoes and added gloves and a clutch bag to them. There is no definite plan for the process, it mainly just happens. I think you just have to listen to your own feelings.

5. Now I paint her dress with ink and water. I always try to find some sort of movement in the drawing. I make sure the ink and water don't dry up so that I can move the colour around rather than actually colour it. It's like cooking a soup, it's really random. I make mistakes and then I have to throw it away and redo the illustration.

4. I use a very thin brush to refine the details of facial features. When the eyes and eyebrows are completed, the next step is to add blusher with the pastel. I just draw it the way I like the face to be covered, normally it is a pink or red colour. No brush is used. This is usually the moment when I know whether I have found the right girl and if I will continue or move on to a new theme.

6. I refine accessories and decide what colours would be suitable for the character. I use watercolour, spectrum red, applied with a rather thin brush. And black ink for creating her gloves. This too is done with a very thin brush. You have to keep your hand very steady. It's really just that. I wanted the shoes and clutch bag to go with her blushing face. I like this strong, feminine colour contrasting with the dark cloud of ink around her body. When I have no restrictions, I prefer to just use black and red.

7. I scan the illustration and then use Levels in Photoshop to get rid of uneven marks. I never send out originals. Clients buy the rights for a digital file. When you scan an illustration, there will always be uneven marks, in my case, because of a paper that is bulking up a bit. Be sure to add some contrast. If you use darker colours, they might be a bit lame in contrast to, for example, black graphics. It all depends what expression you are looking for, and where the illustration will be used. Use hue/saturation if you want to change

any colour. In this illustration I added a little more background in Photoshop. I drag the final illustration to the chosen background as a layer. When I have finished, I flatten the image.

5.

Throughout your education and career as a fashion designer, you will need to present your design ideas, technical drawings, mood boards and promotional fashion illustrations in an effective way. This chapter looks at how to use your initial inspiration and sketchbook ideas to create original designs and build ranges. It will show you how to present your ideas to a professional standard without limiting your creative flair, and how to gear your presentation style to suit a particular client or market.

These pages focus on how professional and graduate fashion designers present their ideas to the industry and the buying public. The fashion labels of Sophie Hulme, Bolongaro Trevor, Iben Høj and Craig Fellows are discussed in the case study boxes.

Mood boards and portfolio presentation

Creating a mood board is an excellent way to organize your research and ideas at the beginning of a project. It captures the style and theme for a set of designs by displaying images, fabrics and colours that are to be influential in the creative process. An effective mood board will make a clear, cohesive statement to the viewer, who gains an understanding of your design direction. A mood board is also sometimes known as a story, or concept, board.

First, lay out all your research material and decide which image, or images, best define the mood or theme for your design ideas. These images can be photocopies from a sketchbook, magazine cuttings or photographs. If you use more than one image there should be a common link between the colours, patterns or themes. The images all need to tell a similar story.

Pay attention to prevailing colours as you select images. Colour choices must be coherent throughout the project, so think about them as you compile your mood board. When you have selected your colour palette, decide how to display it creatively. Means include cutting out paint-swatch cards, wrapping threads around card or painting your own samples. Limit the amount of colours you display otherwise the board will become confusing.

Fabric samples should complement the images in colour and theme. Think about how to display these samples, too. Untidy, jagged and frayed edges will spoil your mood board. Frame your fabrics, stretching them over card, or neatly sewing the edges. Treat any textile sampling, such as embroidery or fabric manipulation, in the same way. If you want to apply text to your mood board, avoid doing so by hand. Unless handwriting is particularly beautiful, it can make a mood board look amateurish. Use a computer to print text, or use Letratone. The next step is to plan the layout of the mood board for maximum impact. Make some rough sketches to see how best to arrange your items, and decide on the colour of the mount board and backing papers you will use. Decisions made in the mood-board process can be applied later when illustrating, a fact that demonstrates the importance of planning ahead.

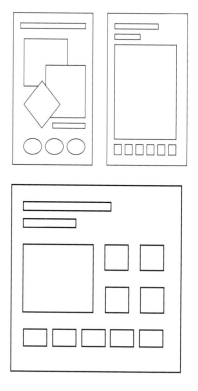

Above
Example diagrams of possible layouts for mood boards. Plan your ideas before fastening elements in place and use the shapes in these diagrams to represent the things you will place on your mood board. For example, the boxes represent the colour palettes and the larger rectangles the defining images that illustrate your mood or theme. A checklist of items to use would include: mount board, defining image(s), backing papers, foam board, spray adhesive, cutting equipment, colour samples, fabric swatches and text (to include title and season).

Opposite
Sophia Bentley Tonge a graduate of Nottingham Trent University describes this moodboard and design development board that she created for a Fashion Awareness Direct project.
"The brief was quite specific, listing areas that we should research, and asked that we design two space hostess uniforms, looking at travel, commercial aviation, the 60's airhostess and the aircraft. My slant on the project was inspired by flight safety cards. I titled my project 'Crash Landing' and researched emergency equipment needed to survive a crash landing into the sea. I did quick drawings using a pen or biro to express my initial idea. Later I created this mood board, scanning in pages from my doodle book. The design development board includes sketches of an airhostess that later became the silhouette template for my fashion designs."

Design roughs and range-building

Fashion designers produce a series of connected ideas that are later realized in their clothing range. While garments work as part of individual outfits, they share linking elements such as colour, fabric, shape and styling so that, when viewed together, they create a cohesive collection. When a collection is shown on the catwalk it is easy to wonder how fashion designers produce so many new garments. How do their ideas get from paper to the bright lights of the fashion show, and how many designs do they complete to present a full range? Also, how do they create the story of their collection? The simple answer to all these questions is "careful planning".

The first stages of planning should include a thorough breakdown of the design brief. Gain an understanding of who you are designing for, identifying your target market and customer profile. Ask questions such as who will be wearing the clothes you design – how old are they, and are they male or

Case study: Sophie Hulme

Sophie Hulme graduated from Kingston University, UK in 2007 with Student of the Year and Best Collection awards. After much interest in her graduate collection, she set up her own label a month later. Having grown up in North London she now works from a studio in the same area.

Her concept is an armouring of womenswear: created by integrating traditional military clothing and detailing into luxury garments. The result is a luxury look, not military or utility as such, but with a hard edge. Menswear influences and hard detailing give feminine pieces a certain toughness. Many pieces from the collections have also been sold as menswear.

The unique approach and style of the brand has quickly gained interest. The *Daily Telegraph* has named her as one of London's brightest talents. The 'Sophie Hulme' collection is stocked in stores worldwide including Selfridges (London), Bettina (Greece), Space Mue (South Korea), Plum Concept (Beirut), Kniq (Hong Kong) and Midwest (Japan).

Contact information:
www.sophiehulme.com
info@sophiehulme.com

PR contact:
katie@cubecompany.com
sarah@cubecompany.com

Opposite
Designers jot down their ideas in different ways. Some draw onto the body while others sketch the garments straight onto the page. These examples show fashion designer Sophie Hulme doing the latter. She uses a sharp pencil and a layout pad to bring her ideas to life. Sophie makes notes about construction details, trims, garment shapes as she goes along. This way, when she looks back at her designs she has an accurate log of her thought process for the collection. Detailed design roughs also help to build up a coherent range.

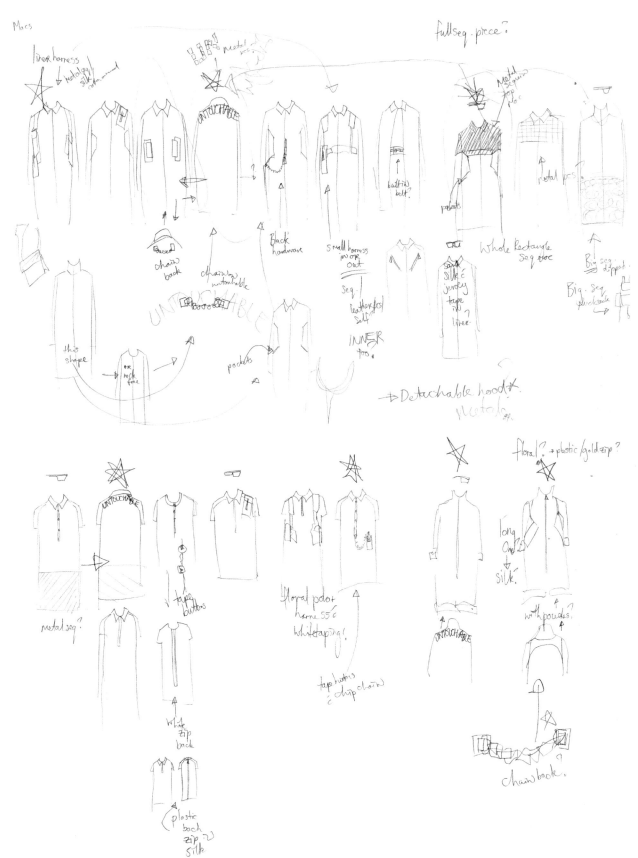

female? Pinpoint the budgets and price points you are aiming for. Is it a couture clothing range or a collection for a high-street store? Are you producing a casual range or occasionwear? What season is the collection destined for? It is only when you are clear on all these points that you can begin to design.

Remember the lessons from previous chapters when planning your fashion range. From discovery of sources of inspiration, and the exploration of ideas in your sketchbooks, will often spring the theme for your collection. This foundation work provides a starting point for experimental fashion sketches, known in the industry as 'design roughs'. When representing your thought processes on paper, forget about perfection and let your ideas flow freely. Have the confidence at this stage to draw rough sketches without worrying about mistakes and bad designs, although do keep in mind correct body proportions. In this way, you are most likely to commit unique ideas to paper.

Some designers draw ideas onto the figure using a template (see pp.48–49) while others prefer to design flat, drawing garments directly onto the page. Find the method that best suits your personal design style, again always using correct body proportions.

A design rough does not have to be well executed or a perfect piece of art. Faces and figure details are not important when designing at this stage. Do not worry about creating beautifully finished sheets – the purpose of design roughs is to assist you on your design journey. As your skills continue to improve, your presentation style will develop.

When producing design roughs, decide which fabrics and trims your garments will be made from. Source fabrics by visiting shops and contacting factories that supply via mail order. For specific fabrics, look on the internet. Always ask to see a sample and check that you like the way the fabric handles before buying. Attach small pieces of your chosen fabrics to your designs as you draw, to enable you to see which fabrics and designs complement each other. When designing, avoid portraying flat, lifeless fabric. Instead, see it as three-dimensional, considering how it will drape and hang on the body. Take into account any embellishments you might add. For example, if you intend to embroider or manipulate the fabrics, add experimental samples to your design roughs.

To develop your designs, use a layout pad. This is a pad of thin paper that allows you to trace ideas easily. Place a template underneath a page and design over the top, adapting the original design but keeping the related template outlines. This method of working not only saves you time, but allows you to see the range developing. Repeating this process of designing over a template encourages a cohesive collection of designs.

At the rough-design stage, start making decisions about colour. Designers often use a limited palette when building a range so that colours harmonize and outfits can be co-ordinated. As you produce design roughs your ideas will flow like these, and your designs should be linked by colour and shape. Importance should be placed on the clothes themselves, rather

These images show how Sophie Hulme's intitial design rough evolves into a sketch on a fashion figure. She has drawn the grey, dazzle sequin vest onto a figure to position the seams in the correct place, etc. Sophie can also ensure the sequinned pattern falls in the right place, drawing it proportionally onto the figure. The photograph shows the finished Autumn/Winter 09 garment ready to hit the shops.

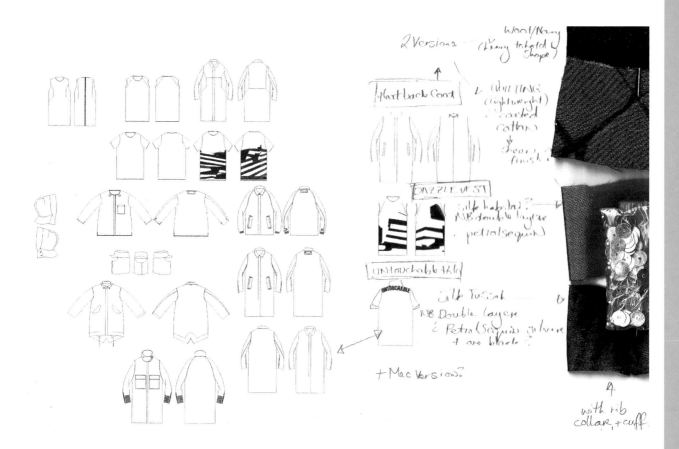

than on the figure. At this stage you should not aim to produce a polished fashion illustration, rather an image that focuses all attention on your designs. The next step is to build your designs into a range. As you select outfits, you will notice common design themes running through your choices. Repetition is an important tool in creating a cohesive collection. For example, incorporate frills into a series of garments, changing one feature with each new design. Repeat this process of design experimentation until you have a store of fashion designs from which you can build your range.

The easiest way to make a selection for your range is to lay out all your design roughs and choose the outfits that look good in their own right, but which also sit well with others when mixed and matched. You may need to include a selection of balanced separates such as skirts, tops, trousers, dresses and outerwear. A complete, interchangeable wardrobe, in which garments work in harmony with each other, is often the ideal.

When you have built your range, draw it onto one page so that it can be easily viewed as a complete collection. Depending on the size of your range, you may need to reduce your designs on a photocopier or scanner to fit them onto a single page. Think creatively about how to present your collection at this stage because it is the first time you are telling its story.

Above

This page from Sophie Hulme's layout pad shows her design thought-process. Alongside the sketches of garments from her Autumn/Winter 09 collection she has attached swatches of the potential fabrics she will use. The sequins are to be stitched as blocks of pattern or lettering on the garments.

"UNTOUCHABLE POLO

"UNTOUCHABLE" FOUND ACROSS
THE BACK OF AN ARSENAL
FOOTBALL SHIRT FROM
THEIR 49 UNBEATEN
       GAMES

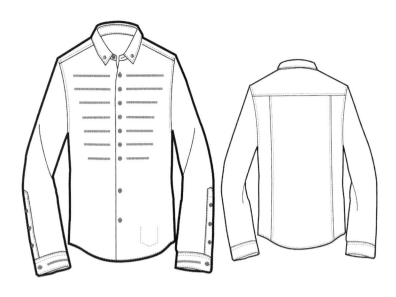

Flats, specification drawings and production sheets

A variety of terms are used to describe the drawing of a detailed garment specification. Flats, working (or technical) drawings, specs (or schematics) all describe the diagrammatic styles of representing an item of clothing. They are two-dimensional drawings of garment construction, showing front, back and side views with technical descriptions. They also show design details such as topstitching, trims and pockets. This style of drawing is most often used to accompany a fashion illustration, giving the viewer more information about how the garment is made to back up its visual description. Without roughs, it would be difficult to imagine the shapes that make up the outfit. Some designers actually work out their design roughs in this way if they find it easier to design ranges flat, rather than on a figure, in order to consider technical aspects as they work.

Drawings for flats should be clean, sharp and precise. This style of accurate drawing is difficult for those who like to draw freely using sketchy lines. Practise drawing clothes from your wardrobe and, to enhance your understanding of your own designs, from your design roughs, too. You will learn about the construction of garment details by drawing them. In particular, practise drawing more complicated details such as trouser seats, collar revers, pleats, pockets and unusual sleeves.

The simplest way to produce a flat is to sketch a garment in pencil, then draw over the top in black ink. For this purpose, buy a set of fineliners made up of three different nib thicknesses. Use the heaviest to outline the garment, the medium line for the garment structure and the finest to emphasize the details. In industry and the commercial world, the details indicated in the flat are also shown in a more precise version known as a spec (specification), or schematic, drawing. For this, a garment's correct specifications are mapped

Top left
An accurate specification of a Bolongaro Trevor shirt drawn to scale has been worked using fineliners of varying thickness. It is important to show both front and back views to enable correct construction.

Above
The shirt made up for Bolongaro Trevor's Autumn/Winter 09 collection.

Case study: Bolongaro Trevor

Bolongaro Trevor is the complete menswear/womenswear collection designed by Kait Bolongaro and Stuart Trevor. The range is stocked in over 100 stores worldwide including Selfridges London, Atrium New York, Fred Segal Los Angeles, and independent stores throughout the UK.

Trevor and Bolongaro were the driving force behind London label All Saints, which eventually evolved into a landmark fashion brand in the 1990s and remains a high street leader today. On selling All Saints and following a short career break to "fall in love with fashion again" Bolongaro Trevor was born, launching its first collection in 2007.

Bolongaro holds the main focus for the women's brand, where silk chiffon dresses, semi-structured tailoring and draped silhouettes combine to create an elegant yet directional aesthetic. The menswear features Trevor's trademark jerseys, skinny denims, detailed, slim-fit shirts and shrunken tailoring. T-shirts are the strongest part of the range having sold out in Selfidges in just three weeks.

Contact information:
www.bolongarotrevor.com

The designers at Bolongaro Trevor have created a working collection space in their studio. By sticking all the design flats into this space, it is possible to see how the whole collection fits together.

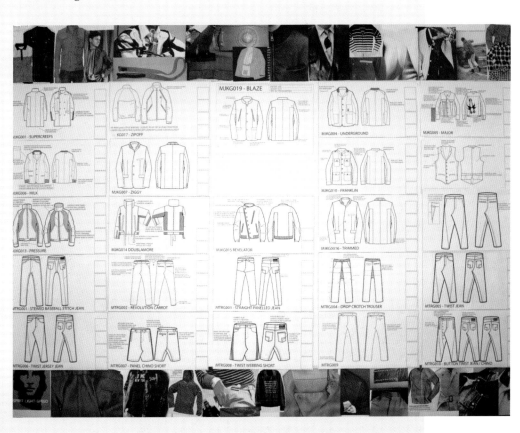

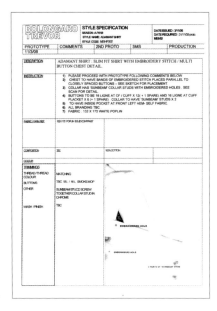

out to the last millimetre. Accurate measurements are added to the drawing, along with details about lining, trims, threads, fusing and fastenings. A sample specification sheet used in factories (such as those shown above and right) will even have meticulous details about darts, pleats, pocket placement, pattern matching, hems, buttonholes and pressing. Compiling this information on a sheet, with a detailed spec, means a sample machinist is able to make a garment simply from the information provided. Creating the design from an illustration would be almost impossible, with the machinist having to make crucial decisions about the garment construction that could differ from the designer's ideas. Specs provide a safety net for all and eliminate the possibility of error. They are also vital in the costing process. From a spec, it is possible to work out all the materials required to make a garment and cost its production accordingly. Much of this information is compiled using a computer system often known as CAD/CAM (computer-aided design/computer-aided manufacture). CAD/CAM systems speed up many of the manual-design procedures and operate specialist-manufacturing machinery efficiently. Specific training is required to be a CAD/CAM operator, but with every detail of the garment logged, it should be simple enough for the garment to be produced anywhere in the world.

Above

An example of an industry-style specification sheet produced using CAD/CAM software and based on the original scaled drawing on the previous page. The more complex parts of the garment are clearly explained.

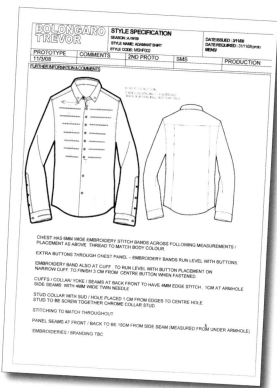

Fashion design presentation

When you work in the industry as a fashion designer you have to make presentations to representatives from many types of companies. Whether it is to buyers from new stores where you hope to sell your label, or displaying your latest collection to existing stockists, the way that you present your work is key.

Fashion designers work in two ways, they either compile a portfolio for each collection or they mail out lookbooks. The knitwear designer Iben Høj does both. She creates a portfolio that is available for buyers to view at fashion weeks, and trade shows. Her delicate sketches shown here are brought to life on the following pages where the completed garments are shown next to the bewitching commissioned illustrations of Laura Laine.

A lookbook is a small book or folder that captures the essence of the collection. It mostly contains photographs of the garments pictured simply on a model with a numbered reference system. Stockists or press can then select the garments they want with ease. Some designer lookbooks are extremely creative works of art. They are highly coveted designer diaries documenting collections season after season. Iben Høj describes her collectable mail-out folders in Chapter One.

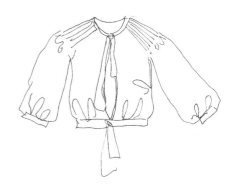

Design roughs by Iben Høj sketched with a fine pencil. Shown here are the shapes of the garments placed alongside each other to see if they fit together as a collection.

Case study: Iben Høj

Iben Høj is a small company founded by Danish knitwear designer Iben
Høj in 2002. Høj studied Fashion Knitwear at the University of Brighton,
UK. Since graduating in 1997 she has freelanced for a knitwear agent,
selling her work to design labels such as Marc Jacobs, Donna Karan and
Marni. Between 1998 and 2001 Høj was the knitwear designer of Danish
fashion brand Bruuns Bazaar. Høj launched her first collection in
Spring/Summer 2003.

The Iben Høj signature style is highly unique and technically complicated
knitwear. Materials are sourced from exclusive Italian spinners focusing
on new developments, rich fibres and luxurious draping.

Styles vary from the finest delicate top or dress to more classic pieces
– all with unique detailing and beautiful finish.

Over the years Iben Høj's knitwear has been bought eagerly by a devoted
fan base and is available worldwide in exclusive and innovative stores.

Contact information:
www.ibenhoej.com
info@ibenhoej.com

The enchanting illustrations of Laura Laine commissioned by Høj for her Spring/Summer 09 lookbook/mail-out folder. Laura was given sketches, colour swatches and knit samples of Iben's latest work, and 'free rein' to create illustrations that would capture the mood of the Iben Høj collection.

Showing off – graduate style

As a fashion design student you are expected, on completion of a project brief, to present not only a fashion illustration but all the design work leading up to it in a portfolio. If you have planned carefully, then the same colour palette, characters, media and so on will have been used to work through the project, building a cohesive theme for the final artwork.

Chapter One featured some inspirational sketchbook pages from Craig Fellows' 2008 graduate collection 'A Hen That Struts Like a Rooster Is Often Invited to Dinner…' The images here and overleaf show how Fellows completes the whole design process of his collection in a series of extra portfolio projects. His attention to portfolio detail gained him press recognition and his garments were a huge success on the runway. As a graduate it is extremely important to get excellent promotional features in your portfolio. Fellows has a distinctive artistic style that even carries over into his professional website and promotional literature.

See Chapter Seven for more advice on creating a cutting-edge designer portfolio and some valuable information about the increasing popularity of digital portfolios.

Graduate Craig Fellows shows a collection line-up from his portfolio in a clean, uncomplicated style. His text and layout complement the rest of his portfolio, allowing a buyer to gain a clear vision of his collection.

5.

Case study: Craig Fellows

After gaining a first-class honours degree in Printed Textiles for Fashion from University of Northampton, UK in 2008 Craig Fellows has been the one to watch in the fashion press. *Vogue* says that since Fellows launched his graduate collection of rooster-inspired prints onto the runway "the farmyard has never been so chic". His quirky poultry-inspired scarf designs saw him gain runners-up prize in the coverted Society of Dyers and Colourists Award. Established in 1884, the Society of Dyers and Colourists is active in the development and understanding of colour and how it is applied in the fashion industry.

Fellows' use of traditional silk-screen techniques combined with digital printing allows him to explore his passion for drawing and mark-making. At the time of publication he is completing a Masters in Textiles at the Royal College of Art, London.

Contact information:
www.craigfellows.co.uk
info@craigfellows.co.uk

Below
Craig also includes a series of 'extras' in his portfolio to show that he not only has a creative mind, but also one for business. A set of packaging is displayed featuring his trademark prints and text. Swing-tickets for his garments have also been designed. A future employee will always be impressed by a graduate who is prepared to go that extra mile.

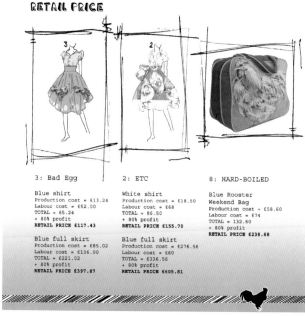

RETAIL PRICE

3: Bad Egg

Blue shirt
Production cost = £13.24
Labour cost = £52.00
TOTAL = 65.24
+ 80% profit
RETAIL PRICE £117.43

Blue full skirt
Production cost = £85.02
Labour cost = £136.00
TOTAL = 221.02
+ 80% profit
RETAIL PRICE £397.87

2: ETC

White shirt
Production cost = £18.50
Labour cost = £68
TOTAL = 86.50
+ 80% profit
RETAIL PRICE £155.70

Blue full skirt
Production cost = £276.56
Labour cost = £60
TOTAL = £336.56
+ 80% profit
RETAIL PRICE £605.81

8: HARD-BOILED

Blue Rooster
Weekend Bag
Production cost = £58.60
Labour cost = £74
TOTAL = 132.60
+ 80% profit
RETAIL PRICE £238.68

This portfolio page outlines the ability to calculate realistic designer costings. Yet again, Craig shows off his flair for business.

6.

The story of fashion illustration is one of change. Through the last century alone, distinct changes in illustrative styles, and the popularity of the illustrated figure, have taken place. Different drawing styles have emerged, encouraged by the development of new media. Fashions have evolved constantly and the representation of the fashion figure has altered dramatically. This chapter will examine why these changes occurred and, more significantly, how styles from the past still influence illustrators' work today.

The beginnings of fashion illustration

Throughout the centuries, artists have been inspired by costume and fabric. Fashion illustrators have depicted the latest fashions, publicizing not only the garments but their creators. As early as the mid-seventeenth century, the detailed and descriptive etchings by Wenceslaus Hollar represented the beginnings of fashion illustration.

By the eighteenth century, fashion ideas began to circulate via newspapers and magazines in Europe, Russia and North America. The first engraved fashion plates were published in *The Lady's Magazine* in 1759 and, by the nineteenth century, technical improvements in print meant fashion, and the outward expression of wealth it conveyed, was never out of the press. At the turn of the twentieth century, fashion illustrators were strongly influenced by art movements such as Art Nouveau, Art Deco and Surrealism. These were instrumental in determining new styles of illustration. During the same period, artists such as Matisse, Degas, Dalí and Toulouse-Lautrec demonstrated a keen interest in what their subjects wore. Their work also had a vast impact on the way that fashions were illustrated.

Charles Dana Gibson illustrated for magazines such as *Time, Life* and *Harper's Bazaar*, but it was the creation of the "Gibson Girl" that made him most famous. This character was tall and slender, and said to be based on his thoroughly modern wife. She was realized on stage, endorsed products for manufacturers and even inspired songs. Women everywhere tried to emulate the "Gibson Girl" by copying her clothes, hairstyles and mannerisms. This truly shows the influential power of fashion illustration at the time.

Pre-1900s

Before the turn of the twentieth century, Alphonse Mucha and Charles Dana Gibson had both begun to make their names for painting beautiful women, and would go on to become famous illustrators of fashion in the new century. Their drawings had a profound effect on the fashions of the time.

Alphonse Mucha created posters in the style of Art Nouveau with swirling, floating and twisting lines, and detailed patterns. Mucha's women were languid, with flowing hair and dramatic elegance, and many society women tried to imitate the beauties he portrayed in their styling and dress. In the same way, others emulated the clothes, hairstyles and mannerisms of the tall, slender "Gibson Girl" created by Charles Dana Gibson. Gibson first worked with paper cut-outs and silhouettes before becoming famous for his pen-and-ink drawings. He illustrated for magazines such as *Time, Life* and *Harper's Bazaar*.

The early 1900s

The first 30 years or so of the twentieth century were the golden years for fashion illustration. These were the decades before the photographer and camera took over the task of showing fashion to the world. In the early 1900s, illustrators such as Leon Bakst and Paul Iribe captured the true spirit of the new fashion trends and portrayed them in an individual manner, conveying the mood and hopes of the time.

The elaborate Ballets Russes and its costume designer, Leon Bakst, introduced brightly coloured oriental fashions to the world, challenging the subtle shades of Art Nouveau. The vivid colours of his drawings influenced fashion for years to come. Through Bakst, an enthusiasm for Orientalism was introduced to fashion, influencing the couturier Paul Poiret to produce his innovative designs. These feature in the colourful fashion illustrations of Georges Lepape, many of which were line drawings, highlighted with watercolour through finely cut stencils. This technique, known as *pochoir*, originated in Japan. Stencilling is a simple form of printing that is still a popular means of adding colour to an illustration today.

Pochoir images from the book *Les Choses de Paul Poiret* by Georges Lepape. This technique of simple stencilling originated in Japan.

The Teens

Contemporaries of the illustrators discussed above, Georges Barbier and Pierre Brissaud were French illustrators working for an early fashion magazine called *La Gazette du Bon Ton*, eventually acquired by Condé Nast. Many of the illustrators later went on to work for the company's prestigious fashion magazine, *Vogue*. Georges Barbier was the chief illustrator. His style owes much to oriental ballet, theatre and the sinuous lines of Art Nouveau. He also greatly admired the work of Aubrey Beardsley, whose influence can be seen in Barbier's strong outlines and bold figures.

The illustrative styles of the decade from 1900 to 1910 were landmarks in the development of twentieth-century illustration. Many illustrations now showed fashions in busy social scenes, a trend followed by some of today's fashion illustrators, including Marcos Chin. Art Deco design also began to feature heavily in illustration, and Cubist geometry influenced the work of illustrators such as Charles Martin. Similar Cubist shapes were revisited in the 1980s by fashion illustrators such as Mats Gustafson and Lorenzo Mattotti.

The First World War had a significant impact on fashion illustration. Printed journals and magazines declined as a vehicle for fashion illlustration, but the film industry grew dramatically. During this decade many fashion and costume designers for stage and film hit the headlines, the most famous being a Russian-born painter known as Erté. Perhaps best known for his elaborate costumes at the Folies Bergères in Paris, Erté also designed many lavish costumes for American movies. His life's ambition to become a fashion illustrator was fulfilled when he signed up with *Harper's Bazaar*, where he continued to contribute fashion drawings for the next 20 years.

Today's illustrators are also fond of showing their fashion figures in a busy environment. Marcos Chin's illustration shows a well-dressed woman at a music gig sipping a glass of wine, surrounded by other revellers.

The Twenties

The First World War was a period of great social upheaval, which had a dramatic influence on culture and the arts. The emancipation of women resulted in a new female image that rejected unnecessary flounces of fabric and impractical, ornate frills. Two of the most influential women in the fashion world at this time were Coco Chanel and Madame Vionnet. Chanel's simple styles, teamed with compulsory costume jewellery, and Vionnet's bias-cut dresses defined a new era. Both designers opened shops in this decade and went on to clothe women for many more.

Until the twenties, the illustrated fashion figure had been drawn with fairly realistic proportions. However, as artwork and fashions became simplified, angular and linear in the twenties, so too did the fashion silhouette. Illustrations now featured longer and leaner figures. Exaggerated fashion figures appeared in the works of Eduardo Garcia Benito, Guillermo Bolin, George Plank, Douglas Pollard, Helen Dryden and John Held Jr. In his many memorable covers for *Vogue* in the twenties, Benito captured the essence of the strong, emancipated women that epitomized the decade. His figures were elongated and somewhat abstract in style, appearing in graphic designs enhanced by subtle colour contrasts.

The "flapper" became an iconic figure of the "roaring twenties". The cartoons of John Held Jr during the "jazz age" adorned the covers of *The New Yorker* and *Life* magazine. His style, featuring funny dancing cartoon characters with bright backgrounds and humorous scenes, is still mimicked today, and contemporary illustrators such as Stephen Campbell use character and humour in their fashion illustrations too.

Below left
The cartoons of John Held Jr became iconic in the "roaring twenties" and adorned the covers of society magazines.

Below right
Modern illustrators such as Stephen Campbell use personality and character to show off fashionable clothes. Campbell's preferred tool in creating his popular cartoons is the computer.

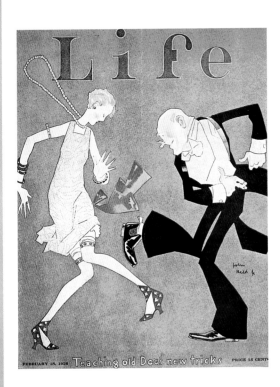

The thirties

The beginning of the thirties saw fashion magazines truly utilize fashion illustration, in both editorial and advertising formats. The fashion silhouette returned to a more realistic feminine form, and drawing lines were softer, textural and curved. A new romanticism was reflected in the illustrations of Carl Erikson, Marcel Vertes, Francis Marshall, Ruth Grafstrom, René Bouët-Willaumez and Cecil Beaton.

Carl Erikson, known as Eric, emerged in the thirties as a remarkable draughtsman who would become an influential fashion illustrator for the next three decades. Eric represented every detail of garments with the lightest of brushstrokes. An advocate of observing the human figure and capturing the beauty of real life, Eric drew only from life, never memory.

Vertes worked for *Harper's Bazaar* and *Vanity Fair*, his illustrations characterized by an economical use of line and colour. He also illustrated the advertising campaign for Schiaparelli perfumes. Today freelance fashion illustrators still work for advertising companies: the image (below) is an advertisement for the UK high-street retailer, Topshop, by David Downton. Cecil Beaton contributed amusing fashion sketches and cover designs to *Vogue* throughout the thirties but became most famous for Oscar-winning costume designs for stage and screen, and his photographs of Hollywood actresses. Towards the end of the thirties, the fashion photographer began to overtake the illustrator as the camera replaced the paintbrush as the favoured means of advertising fashions.

Above
Eric, cover of British *Vogue*, 2 September 1936. Schiaparelli's flaming red velvet hat and caracul (lamb's wool) scarf streaked with blue-green owe their wit and inspiration to the Surrealists with whom she was closely involved. Eric's association with *Vogue* lasted for many years, on both sides of the Atlantic.

Left
Fashion illustrators still contribute to advertising today. This image shows an illustrative advertising campaign for Topshop, by David Downton. Promotional postcards featuring his work were available in the store for customers to take away as a keepsake.

The forties

During the Second World War, many European fashion illustrators went to the United States, where there were more work opportunities, and some never returned. The early part of the decade saw illustration styles continuing in the same romantic vein they had embraced in the thirties. Dominating forties fashion illustration, along with Christian Bérard and Tom Keogh, were three illustrators who coincidentally shared the name René. René Bouët-Willaumez worked for *Vogue* in the thirties but continued throughout the forties, using an Expressionist style influenced by Eric. René Bouché began illustrating exclusively in black and white, though in his later illustrations he developed a strong sense of colour. His decisive and accurate drawing style was derived from strict observation, and his images often appeared spread across double-page *Vogue* editorials.

René Gruau is perhaps best known for creating the advertisements for Christian Dior's 'New Look', establishing a professional relationship with the Dior design house that lasted more than 50 years. He painted in a bold style, influenced by Picasso and Matisse, using black brushstrokes to outline the form, minimal detail but a generous amount of movement and shape. Gruau's style gives the illusion of speed and hastiness. However, he admitted that he completed at least 30 preparatory sketches before creating an illustration. A lesson to us all.

Above left
René Bouët-Willaumez was influenced by Eric, but refined his own style through adventurous use of colour, swift, sharp hatching and vigorous shading. His illustrations had a dramatic sense of style and commanded space on the pages of *Vogue* for many years.

Above right
René Bouché had a firm and accurate drawing style that derived from strict observation. He used pen and ink or crayon, and cleverly merged the character of the garments with that of the wearer, as in this example from 1945. Bouché had a strong sense of colour and he passed on his knowledge to fashion illustration students at the Parson's School of Design in New York, where he taught during the forties.

The fifties

Following the war, the fifties were a time of development and increased affluence. Technological advances introduced plastic, Velcro and Lycra, creating for illustrators the challenge of representing new synthetic fabrics. The glamorous life depicted in the movies and on television showed up-to-date images of beauty and the use of illustration began to decline. However, many illustrators from previous decades continued to work in the fifties, while new artists such as Kiraz and Dagmar arrived on the scene.

A self-trained artist, Kiraz, who emerged in the fifties, still illustrates fashion today. From Cairo, he moved to Paris where he drew sexy, sophisticated Parisians as cartoon-style characters. His method of illustrating personality as well as fashion has influenced many contemporary illustrators such as Jason Brooks, who draws gorgeous comic-book girls with character. Dagmar had a simple, clear-cut and direct approach to representing fashion. She worked at *Vogue* for 20 years, her modest graphic approach distinguishing her from some of her predecessors.

The sixties

In the 'swinging sixties', youth culture was predominant, and being young, carefree and abandoned was the fashionable ideal. The emergence of the teenager in the late fifties meant that fashion acquired a younger, modern look. Illustration poses altered from demure to witty and dynamic. However, the fashion illustrator had become less important than the photographer for magazines, so much so that photographers and models became celebrities in their own right.

Just one illustrator shone like the stars of illustration from previous decades – Antonio Lopez. His versatility meant that he went on to illustrate for the next three decades, but it was in the hedonistic sixties that he truly made his mark. Through his illustrations he portrayed the rebellious attitude of the young generation and reflected fashion as it took centre stage in this colourful, visual decade. His wide imagination led him to experiment in every possible style using a wealth of media and techniques. Each season he tried a new illustrative technique, discarding styles as they became popular and were taken up by others. He was, and still is, a great influence on fashion illustrators.

The seventies

In the seventies, photography still dominated fashion editorials and advertising. Antonio Lopez continued to work, however, and was joined by a variety of new illustrators influenced by Pop Art and Psychedelia. In the early part of the decade, illustrations featured dramatic colours and bold patterns. New ideas were developed by illustrators such as Lorenzo Mattotti, Mats Gustafson and Tony Viramontes, whose striking images began to make their mark in the fashion world.

Top
Kiraz is a self-trained artist who emerged in the fifties. The sexy, sophisticated *Les Parisiennes* cartoon characters from his books became his trademark, as seen in this cover of 1953, and he still illustrates fashion today.

Above
Jason Brooks works digitally, yet draws from historical influences such as Kiraz to capture his infamous comic-book girls. This is a computer-generated flier for the London nightclub Pushca.

Opposite
In the hedonistic sixties, Antonio Lopez's fashion illustrations showed the rebellious attitudes of the younger generation. His huge imagination meant that he drew in every style possible, using a wealth of media and techniques. In this 1964 artwork we see how the background and furniture play just as an important part as the figure.

An illustration in watercolour by Tony Viramontes for an advertising campaign for Valentino couture.

By the latter part of the seventies a highly finished realism emerged in illustration. This is evident in the work of David Remfrey, whose pen-and-ink drawings coloured with a faint watercolour wash show realistically rendered women. The artist's straightforward technique captures the sexy, bold women of the era. Remfrey most recently illustrated the successful Stella McCartney advertising campaign with nostalgic, seventies-inspired drawings.

The eighties

The eighties saw the emergence of a style so distinctive it seemed impossible that fashion illustration would not return with a vengeance. The large shoulders and harsh angles of the fashionably dressed were crying out to be drawn by the great illustrators of the decade. Make-up was expressive, and poses were theatrical – a perfect excuse for fashion illustration to creep back into magazines.

6.

Antonio Lopez once again answered his calling to epitomize the men and women of the time. He did so alongside illustrators such as Zoltan, Gladys Perint Palmer and Fernando Botero who were all producing innovative and experimental work.

Zoltan was one of the first illustrators to produce a series of fashion images ranging from three-dimensional photo-drawing montages to collage with found objects. He used fabrics, flowers, gemstones and inorganic or organic materials to recreate fashion in the same way that illustrators had previously become more liberal in their choice of artistic materials. Palmer illustrated for magazines and various advertising campaigns for Vivienne Westwood, Oscar de la Renta, Missoni and Estée Lauder. A well-known artist in the eighties, when asked to capture the French fashion collections Fernando Botero did not alter his artistic style. The result was a series of fashion illustrations featuring large, rounded, voluptuous women. He confronted the view that "fat" can never be "beautiful" by illustrating high fashion with delightful results.

Zoltan became famous for his three-dimensional photo-drawing montages and collages of found objects. He represented fashion with a creative choice of artistic materials.

The nineties

By the end of the twentieth century fashion illustration was no longer considered the poor relation of photography but instead a credible rival to it. Illustrators such as Jason Brooks, François Berthold, Graham Rounthwaite, Jean-Philippe Delhomme and Mats Gustafson spearheaded illustration's comeback.

Berthold created a series of fashion illustrations that challenged previous styles. He presented cropped illustrations so that the head, shoulders, calves and feet were missing. The viewer's full attention was thus given to the garments illustrated.

Computer-generated images and digital technology in the nineties signified boom-time for illustration. There were illustrators who created small subcultures with intense fashionable followings: Brooks produced his computer-generated fliers for the nightclub Pushca, and Rounthwaite created a set of New York street kids generated on a Mac. His ads for Levi's were projected onto huge billboards on the side of buildings – a true sign that illustration was back in town. Moreover, illustrations of the emerging, couture-clad supermodels by the likes of David Downton were splashed across every newspaper and magazine.

Above left
The digital age could not be more clearly outlined than by the work of Jason Brooks. His Pushca fliers became collectables, and his illustrative style is instantly recognizable even when you only see legs and feet!

Above
Graham Rounthwaite's street kids show how, by the late nineties, fashion illustration began to depict real people rather than focusing solely on the perfection of fashion models.

'Hackysack with Comme Des Garçons'
A digital fashion illustration created by Marcos
Chin featuring clothing inspired by Comme
Des Garçons.

Contemporary fashion illustration showcase

The turn of this century has brought about a new world that reflects on the old. Traumatic terrorist events and natural disasters have encouraged society to crave the comfort and safety of the past. There is an increasing desire to look back to old-fashioned values and explore bygone days.

Advances in technology will always improve and develop the artistic performance of fashion illustrators, but the return to safe traditional methods has brought about a new way to work. Today's illustrators use established hand-crafted techniques such as drawing, embroidery or collage and mix them with their digital counterparts to create a modern medium.

The next section provides an in-depth look at a selection of contemporary fashion illustrators from the twenty-first century. It focuses on their varied use of media and examines the way they clothe the body in art. Through a series of questions and answers, the illustrators explain what inspires them, how they create their work, and what it means to them to be a fashion illustrator.

Vincent Bakkum

www.saintjustine.com / vincent@saintjustine.com /
www.pekkafinland.fi / pekka@pekkafinland.fi

Describe your fashion illustration style.

A painting according to the old school, done with the hasty speed of nowadays. Not because of a hurry, but because that's the way I like it. A drawing in paint maybe?

Which media and techniques do you use?

Acrylic on canvas.

Which fabrics are hardest to illustrate?

I find all fabrics hard to illustrate. Please give me skin, lots of skin, and shadows!

What fashion illustration tool could you not live without?

Pictures, paints and brushes.

What artistic training have you undertaken?

I have been 'stealing' and 'robbing' until I developed this particular style of my own.

What was your first illustration job after leaving college?

My first illustration jobs were book covers and children's book illustrations.

Do you have an agent? If yes, how does this benefit you?

I have a couple of agents. Through agents clients find out you exist. Clients also believe they choose from the 'créme de la créme' by using agents, which in some senses is true.

How do clients find out that you and your work exist? How do you promote yourself?

Through agents, published illustrating jobs, my website, exhibitions and by word of mouth.

How does your website benefit your career?

It helps to give people an impression of what I do. It's essential, especially for my mother to see what I have been up to.

Is being a fashion illustrator a good job?

Excuse the cliché but it is a terrific job if you're passionate.

What do you like most about being a fashion illustrator?

Most I enjoy the trust I have been given by the client. It's extremely pleasant to be able to realize someone's dream with your own.

Do you work in any other areas of illustration, art and design?

I exhibit in the occasional one-man show. I enjoy painting murals.

What is your greatest achievement?

My greatest achievement is not a job for a magazine or a fashion designer, but I'm extremely proud of certain paintings I did. 'Altina' for example is one of them.

What is your one tip for a new fashion illustrator?

'Rob and steal' until you get tired of it; then you have found yourself. If you don't get tired, change your profession.

Stina Persson

www.stinapersson.com / www.cwc-i.com / agent@cwc-i.com

Describe your fashion illustration style.

Lush watercolours. Edgy ink drawings. Beautiful women. Taken together, this gives my illustrations a kind of 'fashion feel'. In reality, I rarely do work for fashion clients. Instead, my work tends to end up with any and all clients who want that fashion feeling, like airline companies to pharmaceutical clients. I think this is quite common as fashion illustration is gaining in interest. More people want it, even if they don't create clothes.

Which media and techniques do you use?

Watercolour, ink, paper, gouache and Photoshop.

How long does it take you to complete an illustration?

I want my work to look spontaneous and maintain a sketchy quality. I do a lot of drawings quickly, maybe 20 until I get it right. So the actual time for an illustration maybe isn't so long, but to get there takes a while. Then there's the scanning and computer work which can take forever. That's why it's worth getting it right on paper. Making five extra drawings to get the original right is much faster, and better, than trying to digitally fix something bad afterwards.

Which fabrics are hardest to illustrate?

I find fabrics with tiny, floral patterns really tricky to render in fluid watercolours when maintaining a loose and fresh feel.

What fashion illustration tool could you not live without?

Ink I think. Which is funny as I mostly use watercolour. But if I had to choose only one technique, I think I would choose ink. Regular, black India ink. And a stick.

If you could illustrate for any fashion client in the world, who would it be and why?

I'd love to work for *Vogue Italia*. If it came to prints for fabric, I would love to work with Prada, Eley Kishimoto or Marimekko.

Do you have an agent? If yes, how does this benefit you?

I have and it's the wisest and best career move I have made. I get to focus on the work rather than payments, agreements, invoices and contracts. My agents have also become good friends and colleagues, something that is very precious as a freelancer.

How do clients find out that you and your work exist? How do you promote yourself?

I do try to keep my website updated, and my agent does promotional mailings. And work seems to generate work.

How does your website benefit your career?

I think it is a great complement to the portfolio. Often even more important as the website creates that important 'first impression'.

What do you like most about being a fashion illustrator?

I like the freedom and the variety. And that I get to be creative for a living. And I get to use my brain solving problems daily.

Do you work in any other areas of illustration, art and design?

I work in most illustration fields from museums to perfumes. I would love to make children's books as I have three sons under the age of six.

What is your one tip for a new fashion illustrator?

Try to constantly get better, and try to stay away from the computer as much as possible. It's the biggest time thief.

Paula Sanz Caballero

www.paulasanzcaballero.com / nairobiflat@paulasanzcaballero.com

Describe your fashion illustration style.
I think it is quite narrative and based specifically on irony.

Which media and techniques do you use?
Hand-stitched embroidery and collage mainly

How long does it take you to complete an illustration?
A hand-stitched one could take from two weeks to two months. A collage may last a week.

What fashion illustration tool could you not live without?
A pencil and fabrics.

If you could illustrate for any fashion client in the world, who would it be and why?
There are so many… Jil Sander, Chanel, *Vogue Italia*…

As a child, what did you want to be when you grew up?
I always knew I was an artist and never dreamed of being anything else.

What artistic training have you undertaken?
I studied Fine Arts in Spain, plus a masters degree in graphic design, also in Spain.

How do clients find out that you and your work exist? How do you promote yourself?
The main promotion is the published work itself. Then, of course, a website where they can contact me. Books, interviews, etc.

How does your website benefit your career?
As much as I hate the risk of people getting my images in blogs, I assume it's a necessary tool to be in the commercial art market.

Is being a fashion illustrator a good job?
It is a vocation job, in my opinion, so I love it.

What do you like most about being a fashion illustrator?
To work in what I really enjoy.

What do you like least about being a fashion illustrator?
Dealing with clients who try to change the illustrations for absurd reasons, both during the process and after the work is finished, in Photoshop. The lack of respect for our profession from some clients, the lack of confidence in our criteria, taste and ability to interpret what they need.

Do you work in any other areas of illustration, art and design?
Yes, I work as an artist, showing my work in art galleries.

What is your greatest achievement?
Perhaps to rethink the application of materials and techniques traditionally related with 'women at home' into a fashion language.

What is your one tip for a new fashion illustrator?
To learn more about human anatomy, drawing and human expression, and not to focus so much on fashion.

Tom Bagshaw

www.mostlywanted.com / tom@mostlywanted.com / www.centralillustration.com

Describe your fashion illustration style.

Figurative, painterly, digital.

Which media and techniques do you use?

I predominantly use Photoshop, Painter, ArtRage and Illustrator but also use some 3D software if I need it in the work. Sometimes analogue tools make their way in but this is becoming quite rare for me now.

How long does it take you to complete an illustration?

My portfolio is based around a few different styles, each taking a slightly different approach, so the timescale can vary quite a bit. Some can be turned around in a day, others can take a couple of weeks to complete.

Which fabrics are hardest to illustrate?

Each fabric I try throws up challenges – I love them all. Lace can be a pain to get looking right but usually ends up being quite rewarding when you see the finished result. It's just the time it can take to do that can drive you mad!

What fashion illustration tool could you not live without?

Photoshop without a doubt, it's the core of all my working process.

What artistic training have you undertaken?

I am self-taught with pretty much everything but I do have some graphic design college under the hood.

What was your first illustration job after leaving college?

An album cover. It sounds totally cliché but was a pretty big deal at the time.

Do you have an agent? If yes, how does this benefit you?

I do indeed, CIA. They are great and are able to attract clients that might otherwise never come across my work.

How do clients find out that you and your work exist? How do you promote yourself?

My agent and my website are the main tools for my promotion but blogs, mail-outs and other marketing is handy for additional marketing.

How does your website benefit your career?

I tend to get a lot of my work via my online portfolio. I can't stress how important a webfolio is these days, even if you sign up with illustration sites that give you a portfolio space, a dedicated webfolio is a must.

What is your greatest achievement?

Apart from my daughter? – seeing my work in print on the news-stands is a fantastic feeling.

What is your one tip for a new fashion illustrator?

Learn to adapt when the need arises but don't let your portfolio get all over the place. It's a tricky thing to juggle but clients and especially agents like to be able to pigeonhole you, even if only a little bit, which can help when a client is searching for a 'look'. Conversely if your style doesn't change with the times, you can end up losing out on work.

Masaki Ryo

www.masakiryo.com / www.cwc-i.com / agent@cwc-i.com

Describe your fashion illustration style.

I strive for a style that is not so complex in its organization, but very expressive and daring without sacrificing a delicate feel.
I incorporate these elements into my paintings of feminine, attractive women and fashion accessories.

Which media and techniques do you use?

I use a painting knife with acrylic paints, and then process the image with Photoshop.

How long does it take you to complete an illustration?

On average, it takes about one week for the rough sketch and one week to finalize the artwork after that, so a total of two weeks. The duration varies according to the project.

What fashion illustration tool could you not live without?

For me, that would be my painting knife. It's an extension of who I am as an artist.

If you could illustrate for any fashion client in the world, who would it be and why?

That's a tough question. I guess I'd have to say Dolce & Gabanna, because their designs are always interesting.

As a child, what did you want to be when you grew up?

I had the vague notion that I'd lead a painter's life.

What artistic training have you undertaken?

I focused on graphic design in the art university that I attended.

How well did this prepare you for life as an illustrator?

Well, since I studied graphic design, it didn't really provide preparation for illustration. However, it was very helpful for me in terms of gaining knowledge and practice for composition, balance, colour schemes.

Do you have an agent? If yes, how does this benefit you?

Yes, by having an agent, I can receive jobs from clients that I wouldn't otherwise have received by myself. (I'm referring to my agents outside of Japan.) Also, my agents can take care of the areas that I am not so good at, such as negotiating fees.

How do clients find out that you and your work exist? How do you promote yourself?

Mainly through my agents' websites and my personal website. The agents handle promotional mailings for my own artwork, and have included my work in promotional calendars with other artists that they represent.

How does your website benefit your career?

Yes, I have a website. I believe it expands my opportunities to receive more jobs.

Do you work in any other areas of illustration, art and design?

Yes. I don't just work for fashion illustrations, but also other different kinds of illustrations. I also enjoyed working in design and wouldn't mind doing that more often.

What is your greatest achievement?

At present, products featuring my artwork are sold in America, Europe, and Japan. I'm hoping for even bigger accomplishments in the future.

What is your one tip for a new fashion illustrator?

Keep doing what you love. Eventually, it will serve you well.

Marcos Chin
www.marcoschin.com / marcos@marcoschin.com

Which media and techniques do you use?
I use a mix of digital with hand-rendered techniques.

How long does it take you to complete an illustration?
It really depends on how large or complicated the image is. When I begin a new drawing, I like to spend a couple of days brainstorming, coming up with some thumbnail sketches in the attempt to come up with an idea and image that solves the (client's) problem. Once I get a sketch approved by the client, it takes another two days to evolve that into a final illustration.

What fashion illustration tool could you not live without?
A pencil.

What artistic training have you undertaken?
I studied illustration at the Ontario College of Art and Design in Toronto, Canada.

How well did this prepare you for life as an illustrator?
I don't think school can fully prepare a student entirely for the professional world that lies beyond; however it did provide me with a strong foundation in the basic skills of drawing and painting, as well as new ways of observing the world and how to (re)present it as a picture. Being in a school that focused only on fine art and design, encouraged me to learn from, and to become inspired by, the creativity of other students around me, which ultimately helped my work to evolve and improve.

Do you have an agent? If yes, how does this benefit you?
Yes, actually I have a couple: one who represents me in America, and another in Europe. In terms of benefits, it's difficult to say as I have only recently begun to work with the both of them. I think there's a misconception that agents can magically make work appear for an illustrator; in order for this to occur there needs to be some sort of demand for the illustrator's work before an agent can sell it to a client. Having said that, a good agent helps to bring and champion his/her artists' work to clients within parts of the industry, such as advertising, which are often difficult for illustrators to access.

How do clients find out that you and your work exist? How do you promote yourself?
Nowadays it is extremely important to have a website – I would say that if an illustrator does not have a website, then s/he does not exist. A website has truly taken precedence over the (physical) portfolio. Although I still receive calls from clients to send my portfolio, for the most part, clients from all over the world have access to my work via the internet. I also send out promotions (i.e. postcards) through the mail to clients in order to grow new/more business. The work that I do begets more work via exposure, especially within the editorial market. I enter illustration competitions annually, such as The Society of Illustrators, *American Illustration*, *3x3 Magazine* and *Communication Arts*, and hope that if some pieces are accepted into the competitions that it will in turn, gain me more exposure.

What is your one tip for a new fashion illustrator?
Work hard. I know that doesn't sound very inspirational, but it's true. I think it's easy to believe that just because a person is talented talent alone will springboard them into success. Being a fashion illustrator means that you are your own business and so have to be aware not only of your talent, but of how to market it to clients. There will be moments when work slows down, or the phone stops ringing, but during these 'down days' it's important to continue to work on personal projects so that your skills and talent will be kept up and your portfolio expanded. Being a (fashion) illustrator is about working even when you are not inspired because in the end you are in a business pact with a client to deliver them your product (i.e. illustration) on time.

Ed Carosia

www.ed-press.blogspot.com / www.ed-book.blogspot.com / ed@el-ed.com /
ed.carosia@gmail.com / www.agent002.com / www.bravofactory.com

Describe your fashion illustration style.
I think I could divide my fashion styles in two: the more formal and classic one with current reminiscences and another 'pop' with reminiscences of the comic.

Which media and techniques do you use?
First of all I use a pencil, then I scan or photograph and start the whole creative process in Photoshop, where I incorporate different textures and colours.

How long does it take you to complete an illustration?
I usually do the illustrations very quickly. I think the time an illustration takes is largely the time taken by the client. Sometimes both the concept and the drawing are approved almost immediately by the client, but often this process takes more time and in the end it takes you more time than you expected at the beginning

Which fabrics are hardest to illustrate?
I don't think any fabric could be really hard to illustrate.

What fashion illustration tool could you not live without?
I can't live without the 'Undo' tool!

As a child, what did you want to be when you grew up?
I wanted to draw and make music!

What was your first illustration job after leaving college?
My first work was designing and creating games for children, then I worked on cartoons, comic strips, illustrations for newspapers and lately I began to work in fashion illustration.

Do you have an agent? If yes, how does this benefit you?
I have two agents (one in France, and one in Spain) and I only have good experiences with them. I've learned so much from the work that we've done together.

How do clients find out that you and your work exist? How do you promote yourself?
Through my website and my blog, and by recommendation.

How does your website benefit your career?
Actually I don't have my website updated, but it takes less time for me to manage with my blogs, and it turned out to be more practical for me too.

Do you work in any other areas of illustration, art and design?
Yes I do illustrations for newspapers and magazines, cover-books and comics too.

Vince Fraser
www.vincefraser.com / vince@vincefraser.com

Describe your fashion illustration style. I'm inspired by seductive female forms and love creating fantasy worlds and abstract characters in surreal settings.

Which media and techniques do you use?
I tend to do everything digitally, using Photoshop as my main tool. I use Illustrator for vectors and 3D Studio Max for creating abstract 3D shapes. If I need to hand draw anything, I use a Wacom Intuos 3 A5 widescreen graphics tablet, great if you work on dual widescreen displays because it has the 16:10 ratio format. I occasionally use my Epson scanner and a Canon EOS 400D SLR digital camera with various lenses ranging from EF 50mm to EF70–200mm.

How long does it take you to complete an illustration?
It can depend on many factors, such as the complexity. Tweaks or final adjustments can be time-consuming. I would say an average illustration can take 1-2 days to complete but I have been known to spend a week or so.

If you could illustrate for any fashion client in the world, who would it be and why?
Armani or Prada because they are household names and known worldwide for their excellent brands.

How do you promote yourself?
Through my website, illustration

forums, design blogs, my agent, word of mouth, postcard mail-outs.

How does having an agent benefit you?
Agents are great when pitching for the bigger jobs like advertising campaigns, which you just couldn't pitch for as a freelancer. Advertising agencies take you more seriously when you have an agent and prefer to work through them for big jobs.

How does your website benefit your career?
It's vital for a fashion illustrator to have a personal website because it enables you to showcase your skills to a wider audience and potential clients. The most popular artists are constantly producing new material and have sketch blogs in addition to the main gallery on their sites.

What do you like most about being a fashion illustrator?
Having extra time to do things I enjoy and spending more time with my family and friends.

What is your one tip for a new fashion illustrator?
Always push the boundaries, be original, be unique, stay focused and do what you do best. Try not to follow trends and watch what everyone else is doing. Stick to developing your own style. Figure out what your strengths are and what adjectives people use to describe the way you draw. You may not want to categorize yourself, but to a certain extent you will need to if you want to focus yourself and find the places that will actually hire you. If you do put in the hard work, you will eventually get recognised.

Alma Larrocca

www.almalarroca.com / www.almalarroca.blogspot.com / alma.larroca@gmail.com

How well did this prepare you for life as an illustrator?
Very well… but I think that the best learning is to work every day enjoying what you do, and to continue researching new things.

What was your first illustration job after leaving college?
For a magazine, a series of portraits of famous people.

What do you like most about being a fashion illustrator?
To live doing something that I enjoy.

What do you like least about being a fashion illustrator?
I don't like it when the client asks for too many changes.

Do you work in any other areas of illustration, art and design?
Yes, I do illustrations for magazines, newspapers and book covers.

What is your greatest achievement?
I think I'm still waiting for it…

Which media and techniques do you use?
Collage, mixed media.

How long does it take you to complete an illustration?
It depends on each work, anything from one hour to many days!

Which fabrics are hardest to illustrate?
I don't think any fabric is really hard to illustrate.

What fashion illustration tool could you not live without?
My scissors.

As a child, what did you want to be when you grew up?
A dancer.

What artistic training have you undertaken?
Graphic design at the University of Buenos Aires, Argentina and some painting workshops.

Sara Singh

www.sarasingh.com / mail@sarasingh.com / stephaniep@art-dept.com / www.art-dept.com

Describe your fashion illustration style.

Happy accidents. My style is more about lines than volume. I like to get the anatomy right.

Which media and techniques do you use?

I use pen and ink and paint with ink washes and Photoshop.

How long does it take you to complete an illustration?

I do many many drawings of the same subject until I get it right. But each drawing takes only minutes. The scanning and post-production take more time.

Which fabrics are hardest to illustrate?

I find rendering fabrics a fun challenge. I like to try different ways and not go for the most obvious solution. I suppose paillettes and tweed can be hard. Knitwear.

What fashion illustration tool could you not live without?

Parker ink and some nice nibs.

As a child, what did you want to be when you grew up?

I wanted to be a painter. I remember being five years old and standing for the first time in front of a real (child-size) easel in school. I had a large paintbrush and it just felt completely right and I thought that I'd like to do that when I grow up.

What was your first illustration job after leaving college?

Rough pencil sketches for an advertising agency. After graduating I did a lot of presentation sketches and storyboards for advertising agencies. I learned to draw everything from VW Beetles to yoghurt containers. And this was all before I had a computer. I even wrote my invoices by hand in pen and ink.

Do you have an agent? If yes, how does this benefit you?

I'm represented by Art Department in the US; by Serlin Associates in London and Paris; and by Agent Bauer in Scandinavia. It's important to have a good agent. Promotion and dealing with prices are a large part of the job. I'm not good at dealing with these things, so I'd be quite lost without an agent.

How do clients find out that you and your work exist? How do you promote yourself?

Through my agent, editorial work for magazines or my website.

How does your website benefit your career?

I find that a lot of people look at the website. I just need to update it more frequently.

What do you like most about being a fashion illustrator?

I really like drawing clothes and bodies and movement.

What do you like least about being a fashion illustrator?

People, especially in advertising, think of illustration in the same way they do photography. For me they are two very different media.

What is your one tip for a new fashion illustrator?

Respect your own creative process. As one evolves one doesn't necessarily evolve in a steady upward curve. Keep some old drawings and have a look at them every so often (perhaps on a bad day) to see your own evolution.

Jeff Nishinaka

www.jeffnishinaka.com / paperart@earthlink.net

Describe your illustration style.
Paper sculpture.

Which media and techniques do you use?
Paper, cut, layered and glued.

How long does it take you to complete an illustration?
Two weeks on average.

If you could illustrate for any fashion client in the world, who would it be and why?
Prada, I dig Prada!

What artistic training have you undertaken?
BFA in illustration from the Art Center College of Design, Pasadena, US.

How well did this prepare you for life as an illustrator?
Art Center pretty much took care of everything for the real world.

What was your first illustration job after leaving college?
A double-page spread in the *Daily Variety* magazine for 20th-Century Fox.

Do you have an agent? If yes, how does this benefit you?
Yes, several. They have direct access to clients who look to and depend on them for illustrators.

How do clients find out that you and your work exist? How do you promote yourself?
Besides my reps, I have my websites, advertise in illustration books, have gallery exhibitions. Of course there's always more I can do.

How does your website benefit your career?
I have two, but one is more current that the other. The benefit is they reach the world.

Do you work in any other areas of illustration, art and design?
Absolutely! I've done book covers, editorial, ads, billboards, TV commercials, public art, and gallery exhibitions in the US, Japan and China.

What is your greatest achievement?
A paper sculpture installation in the ANA Hotel Tokyo, Japan. The paper sculpture was a tree with birds, grass, flowers, fish, and a frog. It measured approximately 6.5 metres square. It was big!

What is your one tip for a new fashion illustrator?
Be unique, different, like none other!

Silja Goetz

www.siljagoetz.com / silja@siljagoetz.com / www.art-dept.com / stephaniep@art-dept.com

Describe your fashion illustration style.
Elegant, harmonious, witty.

Which media and techniques do you use?
Manual techniques and Photoshop.

How long does it take you to complete an illustration?
That depends completely on the style and the client.

Which fabrics are hardest to illustrate?
Fabrics with folds and a pattern are a lot of work.

What fashion illustration tool could you not live without?
None. There's always an alternative technique.

As a child, what did you want to be when you grew up?
Stable hand at a stud farm or illustrator

What was your first illustration job after leaving college?
I already had done some work for a children's magazine during my studies. Afterwards I wanted to get into fashion magazines etc., so I showed my book to several editorials in Germany. My first assignments came subsequently from *Elle* and *Cosmopolitan*.

Do you have an agent? If yes, how does this benefit you?
I am with Art Department. They help me to get new clients and take care of the invoicing, which is a good thing with clients outside of Europe.

How do clients find out that you and your work exist? How do you promote yourself?
The personal website is crucial, it's something that anyone will look at before contacting me. I am also featured in a lot of books and blogs on illustration. Over the years I've gotten to know a lot clients from Germany and Spain personally at go-sees with my portfolio, and of course there's the agency. There's also a snowball effect: people see my published work and find out about me. The important thing is to leave a good impression whenever possible, to be easy to work with, and only to show really good and recent work to possible clients.

Is being a fashion illustrator a good job?
Although it has it's difficulties, it's the best job. Definitely better than stable hand. Mind you, I do not specialize in fashion only, I don't think I could make a living out of that exclusively, and it would also get boring.

What do you like most about being an illustrator?
Being my own boss.

What do you like least about being a fashion illustrator?
Revisions.

What is your greatest achievement?
To get published in *The New Yorker*.

Kate Gibb

www.kategibb.blogspot.com / info@thisisanoriginalscreenprint.com / www.bigactive.com

Describe your fashion illustration style.

I work as an illustrator, not purely for fashion. In fact fashion dictates only a minority of my jobs. Having said that, I reflect on them as some of my favourite pieces of work. To describe my style I would say it has a strong graphic feel, probably because of the nature of silkscreen. My use of colour seems to dominate most prints and often is the strength behind the drawing.

Which media and techniques do you use?

Everything I create is silkscreened, often worked into by hand with brush and ink, paint, pencils.

If you could illustrate for any fashion client in the world, who would it be and why?

That's a tough question, there are so many designers I love. To have worked for Dries Van Noten was amazing and I would work for them at any time. Other labels would include Vivienne Westwood, Eley Kishimoto, Cacharel, Stella McCartney to name but a few.

What artistic training have you undertaken?

Quite a lot really, although I don't think it's a necessary route to creativity. I've completed a degree in textiles and an MA in illustration.

How well did this prepare you for life as an illustrator?

Not as well as taking a leap of faith and renting some studio space, even though work was thin on the ground. College allowed me time to explore different artistic disciplines and materials but I feel it can often lull you into a false sense of security. Having a studio threw me in to being part of a creative, working environment. It's amazing how external pressures (such as paying two rents!) can motivate you and often leads you to produce your best work.

What was your first illustration job after leaving college?

I actually got my first commission while at college, although this was during my MA which was part time so you needed to work to support yourself. I had produced a simple mail-out of pieces of college work and sent them to a few favourite design groups. From this I was commissioned to work on a series of record sleeves for a band called Mono. On reflection I couldn't quite believe it.

Do you have an agent? If yes, how does this benefit you?

Yes, check www.bigactive.com. It benefits me in a big way. Knowing that they are actively looking for and showing people my work while I am at the studio printing away is crucial to making a living.

How do clients find out that you and your work exist? How do you promote yourself?

Most recently it is from starting my blog. With my agent we do regular postcards/mail-outs, globally. They also travel around with all of our portfolios, keep an updated website and also have their own blog. The internet still blows my mind, it makes your work so accessible.

Do you have a website? How does this benefit your career?

Only through my agent. They have spent a lot of time designing it both artistically and to make it user-friendly. It generates a lot of work for the company. Allowing people from all around the world to access work and portfolios at any time of the day.

Do you work in any other areas of illustration, art and design?

Yes, for the majority of the time. Most of my work revolves around the music industry and publishing.

What is your greatest achievement?

I feel I have had many along the way and for many different reasons. But to be making a living doing something I love, on a daily basis, that for the majority of the time feels like play is probably the best.

What is your one tip for a new fashion illustrator?

Keep taking risks, don't always aim to please!

Robert Wagt
www.lindgrensmith.com / www.margarethe-illustration.com

Describe your fashion illustration style.
A graphic, colourful style.

Which media and techniques do you use?
Collage, photography, Photoshop.

How long does it take you to complete an illustration?
It depends on the complexity and the client.

Which fabrics are hardest to illustrate?
I don't have this problem.

What fashion illustration tool could you not live without?
I think any tool could live perfectly well without me.

As a child, what did you want to be when you grew up?
Painter/artist but before that I wanted to be king and a chimney sweeper.

What artistic training have you undertaken?
Art school.

How well did this prepare you for life as an illustrator?
I prepared very badly and thus learned the hard way.

Do you have an agent? If yes, how does this benefit you?
Yes, an intermediate/buffer between me and the client.

How do clients find out that you and your work exist? How do you promote yourself?
Workbook or Showcase and *BlackBook*, mailing, the internet.

Do you have a website?
No.

What is your one tip for a new fashion illustrator?
Never follow anything and do what you believe in; it's in you, whatever you grasp for. You must have love, insight and a strong point of view.

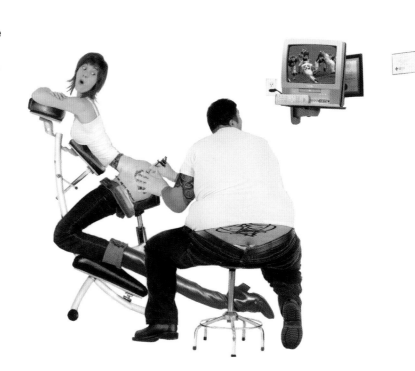

Victoria Ball

www.illustrationweb.com / team@illustrationweb.com

Describe your fashion illustration style.
Eclectic, vintage.

Which media and techniques do you use?
Mixed media, collage and digital.

How long does it take you to complete an illustration?
Depending on complexity, at least a day, often longer.

What fashion illustration tool could you not live without?
A scanner, camera and Photoshop probably.

If you could illustrate for any fashion client in the world, who would it be and why?
Matthew Williamson. I adore his prints, textures and colour palette.

As a child, what did you want to be when you grew up?
I wanted to be an artist.

What artistic training have you undertaken?
Foundation studies in art and design at Cheltenham and Gloucester College of Higher Education and first-class BA Hons in illustration at Falmouth College of Arts

How well did this prepare you for life as an illustrator?
Very well indeed. At Falmouth there was a strong emphasis on professional practice. All the tutors are working illustrators themselves. We all were encouraged to develop our own individual style, whilst being guided on the fundamental techniques of visual communication. Our own interests were nurtured rather than having a 'house style' forced upon us… and we were by the sea, what more could you want?

What was your first illustration job after leaving college?
It was to create 50 illustrations for a children's series called *Ripley and Scuff* for Children's ITV. I found out I had the commission on the day of my graduation!

Do you have an agent? If yes, how does this benefit you?
Yes. Illustration Ltd. They're great because they do a great deal of promotion for me and they deal with lots of the admin that goes with taking on new jobs etc., which gives me more time to illustrate.

How do clients find out that you and your work exist? How do you promote yourself?
Agent website, my website, word of mouth.

How does your website benefit your career?
It gets my name out there more. It's just good to have as much of an internet presence as possible.

What do you like most about being a fashion illustrator?
Sourcing beautiful pieces of vintage fabric and pattern and making pretty pictures out of them.

What do you like least about being a fashion illustrator?
Really short deadlines!

Do you work in any other areas of illustration, art and design?
Yes. Alongside editorials for magazines, I create a lot of imagery for greetings cards, wrap and stationery. Merchandise like aprons, kitchenware, porcelain. Advertising, packaging, book jackets. I also illustrate children's books.

What is your one tip for a new fashion illustrator?
Work hard and don't be put off by constructive criticism, it makes your work better. Most of all, enjoy yourself.

"SO MANY SHOES.... ONLY TWO FEET."
ANON

Annika Wester

www.annikawester.com / www.cwc-i.com / agent@cwc-i.com

Describe your fashion illustration style.

Delicate line work with quite well-shaped silhouettes and much focus on details. Feminine, big eyed-girls.

Which media and techniques do you use?

Ink pens and gouache mainly.

Which fabrics are hardest to illustrate?

Organza and tulle.

What fashion illustration tool could you not live without?

Ink pens.

What artistic training have you undertaken?

Fine art studies, such as painting and print.

What was your first illustration job after leaving college?

It was a cover for *Budapest Week*, a Hungarian-based weekly paper in English.

Do you have an agent? If yes, how does this benefit you?

I am represented by CWC and CWC-i and through them I got to work with clients and with projects that I have always wanted to do. These agents are very good at seeing where I fit in for what I draw.

How do clients find out that you and your work exist? How do you promote yourself?

My agents in New York and Tokyo are well known. From time to time I do send out my own promo cards and e-mail my work to clients in Europe.

Do you have a website? How does this benefit your career?

Yes, and it has been working out very well. I get good responses for my website, which only contains my illustrations and texts. No one else's designs are there and it looks quite personal.

Is being a fashion illustrator a good job?

If one is devoted, yes. If not, it is not a good idea I guess.

What do you like most about being a fashion illustrator?

That I can interpret what I see my way.

What do you like least about being a fashion illustrator?

Perhaps being too niched in many people's eyes. There are a lot of other things I can draw too, such as food, buildings, landscapes.

Do you work in any other areas of illustration, art and design?

I have done more and more jobs for children and teenagers the past years, especially books. I also do handwriting quite well.

What is your greatest achievement?

Early on in my career I went to New York from Sweden to look for jobs and got some great ones as a result of daring to show my work around, travelling far away.

What is your one tip for a new fashion illustrator?

The more you work, the better you get.

Max Gregor
team@illustrationweb.com / www.illustrationweb.com

Describe your fashion illustration style.
I've always been a huge fan of comics and superheroes and that has influenced my work hugely along with photo realism and 50's pin-up art, so I would say my style is idyllic graphic realism.

Which media and techniques do you use?
My work is hand-drawn and then coloured on the computer using Photoshop and a program called Corel Painter.

Which fabrics are hardest to illustrate?
Shiny fabrics tend to take the longest: PVC, lycra, that kind of thing.

What fashion illustration tool could you not live without?
My camera. A lot of my drawings start off with at least some photo reference. This is because there are imperfections in a real person's face that you just can't make up. They are too organic and it's those imperfections that make the subject seem alive I think rather than just looking like a drawing of a mannequin.

If you could illustrate for any fashion client in the world, who would it be and why?
Well, my friend (George Glassby) is about to finish his first collection and I am doing the promo drawings. It's important I think, to have a personal element to your work when you do, it tends to be the more successful and create a greater response when you have some kind of emotional investment in the project, like a friendship.

As a child, what did you want to be when you grew up?
A strong man pulling trucks with my teeth, or an orc.

What artistic training have you undertaken?
I am self-taught. I learnt a lot of the techniques I use from how-to-draw comics books and my father who is a painter and mother who is a designer taught me a lot.

How well did this prepare you for life as an illustrator?
It kept me open to reading about all these different schools of thought on how to construct an image and helped me create my own way of thinking.

Do you have an agent? If yes, how does this benefit you?
Yes and it's great! You get these nice people who ring you up from time to time and say "So and so wants to give you money, if you would like to do a drawing for them". Easily one of the best things to ever happen to me was getting an agent.

How do clients find out that you and your work exist? How do you promote yourself?
Through my agent but I also get a lot of work on more specialist stuff like painting murals and drawing comics through friends I have built up over the years.

Do you have a website? How does this benefit your career?
No, not yet. I am working with a friend to create something for me that is like a piece of work in itself rather than another picture gallery and shop.

Is being a fashion illustrator a good job?
That depends if you like drawing or not and if you are prepared to be on your own in your studio for days on end.

What do you like most about being a fashion illustrator?
It's a hell of a buzz when you see a magazine on a friend's coffee table and its got one of your drawings in it.

What do you like least about being a fashion illustrator?
It's not a social job at all, you have to get used to your own company.

What is your one tip for a new fashion illustrator?
There is always someone who is harder working, better looking, funnier and better dressed than you, who can also draw.

Cecilia Carlstedt

www.ceciliacarlstedt.com / info@ceciliacarlstedt.com / www.art-dept.com

Describe your fashion illustration style.
Eclectic, with a love for contrasts.

Which media and techniques do you use?
It's a mix of traditional media like pencil and ink and modern techniques including Illustrator, Photoshop and photography.

What fashion illustration tool could you not live without?
My pencil.

If you could illustrate for any fashion client in the world, who would it be and why?
Someone who really experiments and stretches the borders between fashion and art would interest me… someone like Victor & Rolf or Hussein Chalayan.

What artistic training have you undertaken?
I began my formal studies in Art and Design at Södra Latins Gymnasium. After A-levels I studied art history for a year at Stockholm University. In 1998 I was accepted into the graphic design foundation course at London College of Printing. This led to a BA in the same subject specializing within experimental image-making. The course also offered a five-month exchange programme at The Fashion Institute of Technology in New York.

How well did this prepare you for life as an illustrator?
I think it was great to have a few years to really have the opportunity to experiment and explore illustration. It gave a good base and an overall knowledge of the field. What was hard and could have been better prepared for is how the industry works, how to promote yourself when you first start and how to work to very tight deadlines!

As a child, what did you want to be when you grew up?
It's always been illustration.

What was your first illustration job after leaving college?
My first commission was for Swedish *Elle* and was a fashion illustration for the upcoming trends.

Do you have an agent? If yes, how does this benefit you?
I have a few agents that represent me in different countries. They benefit me in many ways by promotion and getting my work out there, getting new commissions and negotiating fees, making sure contracts are kept, etc. Basically everything that I'm not so good at doing or don't have the time to handle myself.

Do you have a website? How does this benefit your career?
Yes, I think it's a must these days. It's the simplest and most efficient way of broadcasting your work.

Do you work in any other areas of illustration, art and design?
I do all types of illustrations and aim to move more towards art.

What is your one tip for a new fashion illustrator?
Create a strong personal style, keep up to date with what's going on in the field to stay contemporary. Get a website, be part of networking sites, make a business card, produce a portfolio and contact everyone you would like to work for. Agents, magazines, advertising agencies, there's no way round it. At first you have to show your work as much as possible and even if you don't always get a response it doesn't mean that the people you've contacted haven't looked at your work and kept you in mind for future projects!

Tina Berning
www.tinaberning.de / www.cwc-i.com / agent@cwc-i.com

Which media and techniques do you use?
Everything suitable.

How long does it take you to complete an illustration?
Sometimes it takes five minutes, sometimes it takes days. It depends on mood and ideas.

What artistic training have you undertaken?
I studied design, focusing on illustration, and I kept drawing and drawing and drawing.

What was your first illustration job after leaving college?
I was still at college and did drawings for bakery paper bags of happy people with pretzels and baguettes in their hands in front of timber-frame houses. They still sell pretzels in these bags in Bavaria where I studied.

Do you have an agent? If yes, how does this benefit you?
I have agents in the US, Asia, Germany, Benelux and Britain. Agents approach bigger markets than you can sitting in your studio. If an agent takes your work seriously and you take your agent's work seriously, the agent will be a big benefit.

Do you have a website? How does this benefit your career?
A website is essential and it should be maintained very well, which I do not always manage due to lack of time. Your website is where you show what you can offer to a client. You should not only show what you have done but also what you would like to do. To keep your career running for a long time you need to invest a lot of time in experiments and new ideas. Your art is a matter of development every day. If you start repeating yourself, you get stuck. The website, as a display of your work is the perfect place to show your newest ideas that do not neccesarily have something to do with a job.

What do you like most about being a fashion illustrator?
Automatically being informed about the latest fashion. Drawing is understanding: when you draw, you see through the surface. For fashion, that means you don't see brands anymore but an evolution or morphing of volume and shape, lines, patterns and silhouettes season by season.

What do you like least about being a fashion illustrator?
Having to think about the superficiality of it every day.

What is your greatest achievement?
As a fashion illustrator: a publication in *Vogue Italia*. As an artist in general, every job I am able to do without any compromises to my art.

What is your one tip for a new fashion illustrator?
You will always be best at what you love to do most, and do not steal; it won't help you.

Amelie Hegardt

www.ameliehegardt.com / info@ameliehegardt.com / www.trafficnyc.com / www.darlingmanagement.com

Describe your fashion illustration style.
I would describe it as rather sensitive and sometimes autobiographical. Over the years I have come across people's comments (the ones that I prefer to remember) that use words such as sensual, timeless and suggestive. I find them all incredibly flattering.

Which media and techniques do you use?
Pastel, ink, water and graphite on paper.

How long does it take you to complete an illustration?
Sometimes it takes weeks, others take a day or seconds.

What fashion illustration tool could you not live without?
Eraser and levels in Photoshop.

If you could illustrate for any fashion client in the world, who would it be and why?
Alexander McQueen is an incredible craftsman that I admire for mixing beauty with the ugly and scary. I love the dark and mysterious aspects of his work and would love to work with those.

As a child, what did you want to be when you grew up?
I think I was very unaware of what I wanted to do. But in a way that was itself a great awareness to have.

Looking back it seems like I had it all planned but that is of course not true.

What artistic training have you undertaken?
Stockholm Art School, Art History at the University of Stockholm, Saint Martins, London.

How well did this prepare you for life as an illustrator?
I would say that life itself took care of my education. My first foundation year was the most revealing period in my life. I had a lot to learn technically but somehow I felt that I had something to contribute. It was this feeling more than the actual education which spurred me on.

What was your first illustration job after leaving college?

I remember that I did a job for *Vogue Gioiello*, Italy, during my studies. It is safe to say that I would have done a better job today. When I came to New York I was selected as one of nine other artists to do six pages each for *BlackBook Magazine*. I signed with my first agent a few weeks after that.

How do clients find out that you and your work exist? How do you promote yourself?
My agents promote me but clients also find me through published work.

Do you have a website? How does this benefit your career?
It has yet to be completed. I've managed without one but I suppose it is a good idea to get one.

What do you like most about being a fashion illustrator?
Late mornings. My studio. The fact that it is a very traditional profession. I find the handcraft in itself very beautiful and poetic. Above all it allows me to be me. Most of the time.

What do you like least about being a fashion illustrator?
The situations which I think we are all exposed to when you cannot deliver and there is a deadline.

What is your one tip for a new fashion illustrator?
Listen to yourself. Never stop daydreaming.

:puntoos

www.trafficnyc.com / info@trafficnyc.com

Describe your fashion illustration style.

Our illustrations are contemporary scenes in which silhouettes are drawn over colourful backgrounds, stated with extreme clarity and simplicity. We do photography-based, vector illustration; it allows us to make changes and improve our illustration at any time.

Which media and techniques do you use?

We use Illustrator, running on iMac 24", with a Wacom tablet and a Nikon D90. First, we look for related information in magazines, internet, personal photos. The information phase is the most important for us. Then we select pictures (personal photographs, magazines, books), shoot our photos, and start drawing over them in Illustrator. We love working on a big screen. When you're working long hours in front of a computer, the more comfortable you are, the better, and the sooner and the smoother your work flows.

Which fabrics are hardest to illustrate?

The difficult point for us is not in the fabrics. We do create flat colour pictures, and it's not usual for us working with shading, gradations, and realistic textures. Anyway, we would like to think that we are quite professional to adjust our style to what the client is looking for.

What artistic training have you undertaken?

We both studied Fine Arts at Universidad Politécnica de Valencia (Spain), and met each other doing a photography BA (Hons) at Southampton Solent University, UK.

How do you promote yourself?

It depends. Our agent in the US does a great job and finds new clients for us. Depending on the job, we've been insistent when we wanted to work for a magazine, and get in contact with them again and again. But most of the time, people call us and we don't do so many commercial jobs.

Do you work in any other areas of illustration, art and design?

Yes, we make graphic design as well, and collaborations with interior architecture. We also create our own illustrations for a fine art printing and textile company, and we receive royalties from their sales. Illustration can be applied in so many supports: fabrics, paper, vinyl, mobiles…

Is being a fashion illustrator a good job?

It is, of course. It has good and bad moments, as every job, but we do enjoy it. You must be disciplined when you work on your own, it can be hard to organise your time. But anyway, it's a way of life. We can listen to music we love during work hours, and have no dress code – isn't it fabulous?

What is your greatest achievement?

We like to think that the best is yet to come. But working on this is a cool, great achievement by itself. The feeling of creating new things keeps us alive. Every day is a new beginning.

Louise Gardiner

www.lougardiner.co.uk / loulougardiner@hotmail.com

Describe your fashion illustration style.
Quirky, fun, more about people and what they wear than fashion.

Which media and techniques do you use?
Drawing, painting and embroidery with a sewing machine.

What fashion illustration tool could you not live without?
A pen.

As a child, what did you want to be when you grew up?
A farmer or an actress.

What artistic training have you undertaken?
A foundation, a degree and a masters in textiles and illustration.

How well did this prepare you for life as an illustrator?
I learnt to draw and get drunk.

What was your first illustration job after leaving college?
It was years later for the *Guardian* newspaper when I had almost given up on illustration.

Do you have an agent? If yes, how does this benefit you?
I do have an agent but generally I represent myself because I love dealing with people. I only like giving away big commission chunks to galleries and agents who shout your name from the rooftops. These are rare – especially when you specialise in embroidery!

How do clients find out that you and your work exist? How do you promote yourself?
I do talks, teaching and exhibitions all over the country and abroad. Now it is mainly word of mouth. I design and sell cards with a mini artist's statement on the back. I say yes to opportunity as much as I can and I work a lot.

Do you have a website? How does this benefit your career?
Yes – it makes life easier and people can look at what you do without you having to lift a finger. The only problem is it needs updating so often so get a website you can update yourself.

Is being a fashion illustrator a good job?
It can be absolutely brilliant and sometimes it can be utterly frustrating and stressful. Big ups and big downs. Not an easy ride.

What do you like most about being a fashion illustrator?
I am my own boss and I don't have to answer to anyone (except my mother).

What do you like least about being a fashion illustrator?
Doing my own accounts and paying tax in big lumps.

Do you work in any other areas of illustration, art and design?
Yes – my main area of work is private commission and I exhibit regularly. I also do commissions for hospitals and book illustration. I like variety.

What is your greatest achievement?
To now be able to politely say "no" to the jobs I don't want to do or don't pay enough. Or "yes" to the jobs that don't pay enough but I want to do. To have realized that you must always be honest and work with integrity.

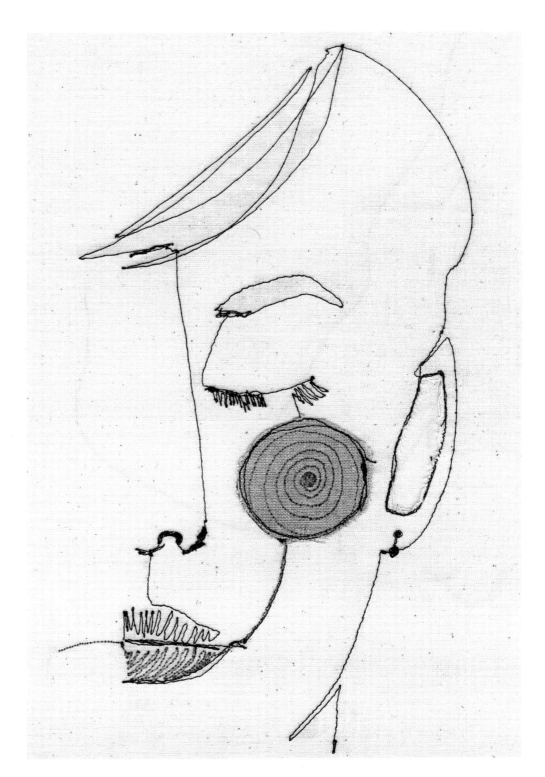

Montana Forbes

www.montanaforbes.com / me@montanaforbes.com

Describe your fashion illustration style.
Strong lines, vivid colours and abstracted concepts.

Which media and techniques do you use?
Pen and pencil sketches transferred into Photoshop.

What fashion illustration tool could you not live without?
Pencils.

As a child, what did you want to be when you grew up?
An artist or a modern ballet dancer.

How long does it take you to complete an illustration?
About 1-3 days, depending on the detailing.

Which fabrics are hardest to illustrate?
Brocade, check and intricate lace.

What was your first illustration job after leaving college?
It was to produce hair and beauty illustrations for a hair salon in central London.

If you could illustrate for any fashion client in the world, who would it be and why?
I'm currently obsessed with Chloé as I'm inspired by the brand's creative spirit. It has vintage craftsmanship influences with modern and inventive designs.

Do you have an agent? If yes, how does this benefit you?
Yes and they liaise with clients on job details and promote my work to a wider audience.

How do clients find out that you and your work exist? How do you promote yourself?
I get a lot of clients through my agency and I have art prints for sale at a London-based gallery (Eyestorm, www.eyestorm.com), as well as an upcoming personal website.

Do you have a website? How does this benefit your career?
I'm developing a personal website (www.montanaforbes.com), where I'll feature my illustrations and fine art along with current interests.

What do you like least about being a fashion illustrator?
Working in an isolated environment with minimal socializing.

Do you work in any other areas of illustration, art and design?
Yes, I'm also a fine artist.

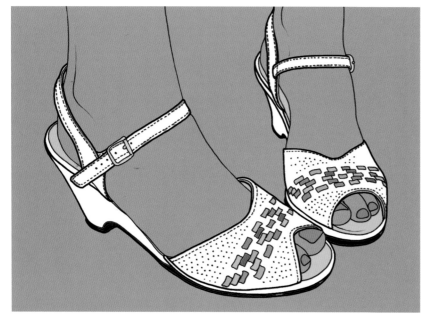

Edwina White

www.edwinawhite.com / fiftytwopickup@gmail.com

Describe your fashion illustration style.
Hand-generated, narrative, character-driven, injected with humour.

Which media and techniques do you use?
Pencil, ink, paint, tea, collage, old papers.

What fashion illustration tool could you not live without?
A sharp pencil.

If you could illustrate for any fashion client in the world, who would it be and why?
House of Prada.

As a child, what did you want to be when you grew up?
A parachutist or a cartoonist.

What artistic training have you undertaken?
Design school classes and consistent practice.

Do you have an agent? If yes, how does this benefit you?
Yes. It allows me to live in New York, clients from around the world can find me, and she talks business and handles contracts.

How do clients find out that you and your work exist? How do you promote yourself?
My agent's website, my own fine art projects and word of mouth.

Do you have a website? How does this benefit your career?
Am building it now! It will make me a grown-up.

Is being a fashion illustrator a good job?
Sure, I make all sorts of images. It's very satisfying if I can inject some flavour and character. Then it's compelling and great fun.

Do you work in any other areas of illustration, art and design?
Absolutely. I am a fine artist, animator, product designer and editorial illustrator.

What is your greatest achievement?
Making a living, while loving what I do.

What is your one tip for a new fashion illustrator?
Be yourself, develop your own signature after a good deal of experimentation and adapting to the work.

Wendy Plovmand

www.wendyplovmand.com / mail@wendyplovmand.com / www.centralillustration.com / info@centralillustration.com / www.trafficnyc.com / info@trafficnyc.com

Which media and techniques do you use?

My technique is multi-layered with a mix of hand-drawn images and textures and digital drawings in Photoshop. I love to develop my style continuously and experiment a lot! Sometimes I even use details from my acrylic paintings in an illustration.

How long does it take you to complete an illustration?

Hmm, it depends on size, theme, restrictions, level of details, etc. But in general between eight hours to a week!

Which fabrics are hardest to illustrate?

I don't do much fabrics – I focus more on the pattern.

What fashion illustration tool could you not live without?

Aquarelle and my computer!

If you could illustrate for any fashion client in the world, who would it be and why?

I'm a huge fan of Balenciaga, Chloé, Anna Sui and Marc Jacobs, so any of these would be wonderful to work with. I like their personal style, the patterns they use and they always impress and surprise with their collections. Their clothes inspire me!

As a child, what did you want to be when you grew up?

I wanted to be a fashion designer, I sewed many strange outfits and got my classmates to wear them while videotaping a complete self-generated fashion show! Really absurd results came out of this. Later on when I attended the Danish Design School, Fashion Line, I realized I didn't like sewing and much preferred telling stories, so I decided to study graphic design instead.

What was your first illustration job after leaving college?

My first client was actually a huge one, when I was still in art school I did a school project to design the 250-year anniversary poster for the Royal Theatre of Denmark and the 550 years anniversary poster for the Royal Chapel of Denmark. I decided to show it to the Royal Theatre and Chapel and they hired me to do the job! After establishing my own studio, my first client was a Danish fashion magazine, I still work for them today.

How do clients find out that you and your work exist? How do you promote yourself?

A couple of times a year I send out a news e-mail, like highlights from a couple of months. I only send it to people I know or have at least seen and had a meeting with. My work has been in several really nice publications around the world, from all the big book publishing houses and also I gave interviews to many magazines – I think that's how people find out about my work today, and of course through my agent as well.

Do you have a website? How does this benefit your career?

Yes I do, it's like a business card. It's good if it represents your work in a nice way and if you remember to update it once in a while! All my clients visit it to see my work before they hire me I think, so it's an important tool to have when you work as an illustrator.

What do you like most about being a fashion illustrator?

I love to arrive in my studio, turn on my favourite music very loud and dive into a new, exciting project.

What do you like least about being a fashion illustrator?

That it's really difficult to go on holiday and turn off your phone and e-mail because you've got to be available at all times.

What is your one tip for a new fashion illustrator?

Be unique, don't try to figure out what sells, better develop your own style as an illustrator, then one day, the clients will come to you because you are unique!

Yuko Shimizu
www.yukoart.com / yuko@yukoart.com

Describe your fashion illustration style.
I think the best way is if the viewer describes it. It is always hard to describe your own work.

Which media and techniques do you use?
I draw by ink with brush on watercolour paper, and the colour is done in Adobe Photoshop.

Which fabrics are hardest to illustrate?
I am pretty good at drawing any fabric. You may think that is a skill of fashion illustrators, but all illustrators in any field should know how to draw different textures. It just makes the work richer. My favourite is drawing sweaters. I love knitting but I don't really have time to knit right now.

What fashion illustration tool could you not live without?
Drawing. I can live without Photoshop, or colour, but I love drawing. Ink, pencil, you name it. As long as I have a material I can draw with, I am OK.

If you could illustrate for any fashion client in the world, who would it be and why?
There are a lot of designers I really love, but if I were to narrow down, I go for the more artistic type; those who treat fashion almost like fine art or conceptual art. Jean Paul Gaultier, Hussein Chalayan, Thierry Mugler, Azzedine Alaia, Alexander McQueen, John Galliano, Martin Mengele, to name but a few.

As a child, what did you want to be when you grew up?
I wanted to become an artist!

What artistic training have you undertaken?
An MFA in illustration from the School of Visual Arts, New York.

How well did this prepare you for life as an illustrator?
I also majored in marketing and advertising for my BA, and worked in corporate Japan before moving to New York and going back to school. With both of them together, I think it really made me get ready to be working as an artist as well as a small business.

What was your first illustration job after leaving college?
I started getting work while I was still in the masters programme, so my first job was not after college. But anyway, I got a portrait illustration job for *The Village Voice* and also a small illustration for *The New York Times*, both of which got published on the same day.

Do you have an agent? If yes, how does this benefit you?
For the longest time I didn't, but I do now. Both in London and in New York. There are certain fields in illustration it is really difficult for an individual illustrator to approach and promote, mainly advertising clients. This is when a reliable agent who has a good sense of business and a good group of artists can really help. If you decide to get an agent, it cannot be just any agent, you have to choose the one you really feel the connection to, as well as them being a good agent.

How do you promote yourself?
Mainly through my website, combined with existing work that's around, including illustration annuals, magazines, books, etc. Also, of course, my agents do promote their artists a lot. I think the web is the promotional tool of choice for the 21st century.

What is your one tip for a new fashion illustrator?
Absolutely love what you do, and work hard. Life is never easy regardless of what you choose to do, so pick 'the one' that makes you happiest. As long as you are happy, you are good!

James Dignan
www.jamesdignan.com / james@jamesdignan.com

Describe your fashion illustration style.

Hopefully it speaks for itself, but either liney and graphic or painty and graphic. A touch of irony, humour and lots of length in the limbs.

Which media and techniques do you use?

Painty-acrylic paint or gouache and coloured inks. Liney-Rotring pens, my lucky Montblanc Meisterst CK, brushes and ink, and Mr Photoshop.

Which fabrics are hardest to illustrate?

Unattractive ones! Men's suit fabrics are a bit tricky too.

What fashion illustration tool could you not live without?

My imagination.

If you could illustrate for any fashion client in the world, who would it be and why?

Christian Dior Haute Couture, it always knocks my socks off and makes me happy for the whole season. It's Fashion writ large and unapologetic.

As a child, what did you want to be when you grew up?

An archaeologist.

What artistic training have you undertaken?

I studied fashion design and illustration at Studio Berçot in Paris.

How well did this prepare you for life as an illustrator?

Well it threw me in to the Parisian fashion business at the deep end. Studio Berçot is run like an intense fashion laboratory full of big personalities. They were pretty critical at first, especially as I'd come from somewhere that wasn't really fashion forward (Australia). So it was a bit of a deconstruction and rebuilding process. All good life lessons for a freelancer, you need to be pretty thick-skinned and resourceful.

What was your first illustration job after leaving college?

I made the press kit illustrations of the Autumn/Winter collections for both Chloé and Jil Sander. So it was quite a good start when I think about it in retrospect.

Do you have an agent? If yes, how does this benefit you?

I have four agents: in New York, Amsterdam, Tokyo and Hamburg. They do amazing work on my behalf, I just wouldn't have the time or the skill for all the work they do in promotion, bridge-building and negotiations. I love my agents! They really make it all happen.

What do you like most about being a fashion illustrator?

Inspired and inspiring clients and everybody happy with the results.

What do you like least about being a fashion illustrator?

That there's not more of it. I think we're poorer for not being exposed to more ways of seeing the world. So many wonderful illustrators and so few formats for them. I also don't like scanning.

Is being a fashion illustrator a good job?

It's a very particularly fantastic job if you're up for it. There really should be much more demand, but that does vary a lot between different cultures and sensibilities.

Do you work in any other areas of illustration, art and design?

Yes, a lot of editorial illustration work, advertising, print design and ceramics. Basically if there's a surface, I'll paint or draw on it. I make some art every day.

Petra Dufkova
www.illustrationweb.com

Which media and techniques do you use?
My favourite drawing medium is watercolour, particularly gouache. These traditional techniques are stamped on my style and allow me always to experience, make new effects and combinations with other drawing media like ink or lacquer.

As a child, what did you want to be when you grew up?
Fashion designer or artist.

What artistic training have you undertaken?
First I studied art at a technical school for applied arts in the Czech Republic. In 2008 I graduated as a modelist/stylist at the international fashion school ESMOD in Munich, Germany.

How well did this prepare you for life as an illustrator?
During my education I participated in many projects and competitions in Germany, Spain and China. I illustrated a children's book and a few pages in *Snowboarder Magazine*.

What was your first illustration job after leaving college?
I made fashion illustrations for a website.

Do you work in any other areas of illustration, art and design?
I also work as a stylist and fashion designer for the label Marcel Ostertag.

7.

The purpose of this book is to help you move through the artistic journey of fashion illustration by learning imaginative techniques and thinking creatively about fashion presentation. Alone, this is not enough to succeed in your chosen career – there are practical steps to take to secure a foothold in the fashion industry. Whether you are applying to study fashion design, with illustration only a small element within the course, or you are choosing fashion illustration as a career, this final chapter aims to guide you through the issues that may be causing you concern. It also features advice and practical recommendations from industry specialists to help you face the future confidently in this competitive world.

Portfolio presentation

Whether you are applying to study at university, or seeking employment as an illustrator, you need a portfolio – a flat, portable case for presenting your artwork. Your portfolio is like a curriculum vitae showing the viewer what you are capable of achieving. Effective visual communication is vital in the fashion world and first impressions count, so your portfolio should be a powerful self-marketing tool.

Portfolios range from A4 to A1 in size, but A3 (42 x 29.7 cm) or A2 (59.4 x 42 cm) types are most suitable for fashion artwork. These sizes ensure that the work is large enough to view but still portable. Unless you can afford more than one portfolio, it is probably best to decide at an early stage which size suits your personal working style. This allows you to plan your artwork to fit your portfolio. However, don't let portfolio size restrict your creativity – add fold-out sections for larger pieces, or reduce them to fit on a colour photocopier.

FINAL COLLECTION 2008 'Constrictor Clarence'

Taking inspiration from the tough, empowered models and icons of the eighties and early nineties, Poppy Dover (winner of Portfolio Award at London Graduate Fashion 2008) aimed to create a collection that draws upon their gender-crossing sensuality, but that for the empowered woman of today complements her cooler, laid-back approach to life. The silhouettes of the garments are cut close to the lower body in contrast with varying volumes on the upper body that also focus on protecting the neck area. Longer layers underneath cropped tops create a modern-day version of the classic eighties crop shape. This example of a portfolio collection line-up shows the six-piece collection in detail.

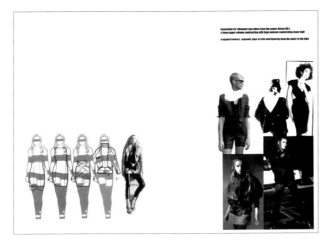

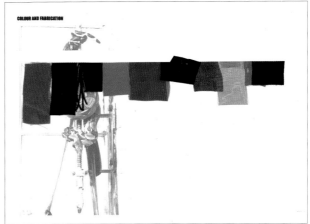

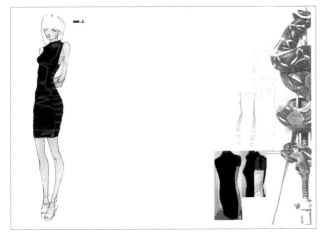

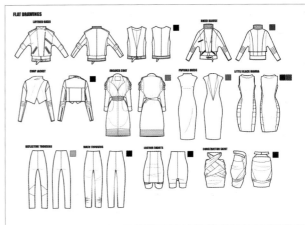

A strong portfolio case enables you to keep work neat and flat. Take pride in your artwork by looking after it properly. In the highly visual world of fashion, curled edges or tatty, smudged sheets do not create a good impression. Protect your work by presenting it in transparent plastic sleeves that clip into the spine of the portfolio case.

The running order of the artwork in your portfolio needs to flow smoothly. The aim is to encourage the viewer to keep turning the pages in anticipation of impressive work. It is often a good idea to put your best pieces at the start and end of the portfolio, as they will become the most memorable. These are often known as "conversation pieces" – artwork that the viewer may want to discuss further. It is important to note that you should only choose to show work that you feel comfortable talking about. If you are not particularly confident about a piece, leave it out of the portfolio entirely.

You can group your work in assorted ways. Chronological order will show development, while varying project themes and styles will add diversity to the running order. Remember that the viewer will be looking at the work for the first time, so your portfolio should tell the story of how you researched and resolved a brief clearly. It should not be necessary to question you. Likewise,

Above

Dover has used references to the symbol of the snake in the contortion and the texture of the fabrics, to give the wearer that heightened sense of sensuality. The burnt-out shades of red and black also draw upon that feeling. Key pieces include a linear organza coat with puffy sleeves under pull-tie epaulets, a wet-look lycra skirt of contouring fabric and a layered leather biker jacket enveloped by a mass of nylon thread zipped onto parts of the jacket. These portfolio pages show Dover's inspiration, fabric choices, fashion figures and garment flats.

Overleaf

In her fashion illustration and photographs Dover keeps a coherent, professional layout throughout with a clean, white background and the same basic colour palette taken from the collection.

the viewer should not have to turn your portfolio at all angles to see the work – keep the orientation of your pages the same. For continuity, organize your work logically, grouping projects together for clarity.

Further education portfolio

If you are applying to further your education (after an art foundation course, for example), on a fashion-based course, assemble a portfolio that shows your strengths and abilities. Much of the advice above is applicable, but focus on showing the course interviewer the development of your creative work, so that your future potential is evident. Display a range of visual studies, including life drawing, still-life studies, textile sampling and imaginative observational work. Although the portfolio should have a slight fashion focus, you will be learning fashion skills on the course. The interviewer will want to see wide-ranging artistic abilities in your portfolio that can be developed in a fashion environment. At this stage, it is not your technical expertise or fine-tuned fashion illustrations that are important, but your ideas. With this in mind, keep a few sketchbooks in the back of your portfolio, and possibly some examples of written work, so the interviewer discovers as much as possible about your creative talents.

Graduate portfolio

When selecting artwork for your portfolio, remember that professionalism is key. You will not be able to carry garments to interviews, so you are reliant on your portfolio to impress clients. If you are seeking employment as a graduate, include any live projects that you have completed. These are often projects linked to reputable businesses, companies or industry specialists that have sponsored a university or college fashion course, usually donating

PAPRIKA DRESS
Paprika viscose diamond back dress

...6

Above and left
When asked to give advice to other graduates Dover says the following: "The main question I ask myself when working on my portfolio is 'does this read easily?' An interviewer is learning about your work for the first time, and unless it is clear, they may struggle to understand processes and miss things. So keep the pages clear and be selective about images. Be confident about who you are as a designer and maintain a personal style throughout. The individuality of the projects should speak for itself without varied graphics and fancy fonts. Finally, don't be afraid to title images or use brief annotations to make your thoughts and development even more coherent."
Dover currently works as a designer for Max&Co, a diffusion range of MaxMara.

fabrics or offering appropriate payment and prizes. Many fashion companies also reward students with work placements or internships. By including live work in your portfolio, you demonstrate that you are aware of the industry you are entering. An interviewer will be interested to know how you coped with meeting deadlines, working to a brief, and presenting your final ideas. This creates a valuable snapshot of you as a potential employee. Display in your portfolio national and international competition entries, too, because they provide evidence that you are ambitious, enthusiastic and keen to be the finest in your chosen field. A fashion-design graduate should also include promotional photographs of garments, setting up photo shoots on location or in a studio.

Professional portfolio

Your portfolio will have gone through many changes by the time you reach professional status. Now you should have a clear direction and focus, reflected in your portfolio. You can be more selective about the pieces you include and you will be able to organize your portfolio to appeal to a specific employer. Your portfolio will be either predominantly fashion design or promotional illustration. Like many professionals, you might show a portfolio of work on your own website.

There are many ways of presenting fashion artwork. The images in this section are all portfolio pieces produced by students on various fashion courses ranging from diploma to degree level. In your portfolio, aim for continuity, diversity, stunning imagery and a professional approach to organization and presentation. Then be proud of what your portfolio holds and your confidence will communicate itself.

Above
A digital portfolio is the fastest way of letting interested clients view your work. Here Vince Fraser shows his self-promotion as a professional illustrator. He includes snapshots of his artwork and essential practical information such as contact details and a biography. Scan the contents of your portfolio at high resolution and save it onto a disk. This can be sent through to clients or shared online. You can also e-mail work-sample files instantly if requested, making your work even more accessible. Creating a convenient digital portfolio can save you from carrying the real thing to interviews. However, always check what clients prefer as some would rather look through the original than through digital copies.

The future: making choices

Further education

Fashion is a 'glamorous' industry that many find attractive, resulting in much competition for places on fashion courses. Before applying, research the type of course that will suit you best. The aim of a university course is to make your training as relevant as possible to a job in the fashion industry, so the correct course choice at this stage is vital. It is no longer as simple as choosing to study 'fashion'; courses with similar-sounding titles vary considerably. Fashion design and garment construction dominate many degree courses, but fashion illustration and promotion are also often key areas. The following list demonstrates the variety of fashion degree courses offered:

- Costume Design
- Fashion Accessories
- Fashion Art
- Fashion Brand Promotion and Journalism
- Fashion Design
- Fashion Design with Business Studies
- Fashion Design with Retail Management
- Fashion Enterprise
- Fashion Promotion and Illustration
- Fashion Photography
- Fashion Knitwear
- Product Development for the Fashion Industry

When you have narrowed your field, a good starting point is to search the internet for possible study locations. Most institutions offer a prospectus that you can order online or by telephone. Prospectuses and brochures are the marketing tools that universities and colleges use to sell their courses to you. They provide a wealth of information about course outlines, educational procedures, university location and success rates. Many prospectuses also include student opinions about what it is like to study at the university, and information about social activities and nightlife. Some cities hold annual careers fairs in large exhibition centres, packed with stands from major institutions offering art and design courses. Visiting such an event is an ideal opportunity to talk to members of staff and collect prospectuses.

The next step, and probably the most important in the decision-making process, is to visit the institutions that you are interested in. Attend their open days, taking the following checklist with you on the visit and noting the answers to help you decide on your future.

- What is it like to be a student at the institution?
- What is the structure of the course?
- What proportion of the course is dedicated to written work and contextual studies?

- Is there up-to-date machinery, technology and facilities?
- Will I have my own work space?
- What are the studio and workshop hours?
- Are the staff team skilled and inspiring?
- What is the student-to-staff ratio?
- Are there links with other departments?
- Are there links with industry?
- Are study visits organized to major cities at home and abroad?
- Where is the degree show held?
- What have previous graduates from the institution achieved?
- Which key elements will the interviewer be looking for in a portfolio?
- How many candidates applied last year?
- Do I like the location and atmosphere of the institution? Is its surrounding area somewhere I would enjoy living? Is there student accommodation? What are the opportunities for socializing?

With all your queries answered and the decision made, it is time for your university selection interview. Try not to think of this as a terrifying ordeal, but as an opportunity to impress. Practise your interview technique beforehand. Ask a tutor to set up mock interviews, or get your family to test you with suitable questions. Interviewing differs greatly from one institution to another. Some review portfolios before deciding whether to interview a student, while others ask you to bring your portfolio to the interview and dedicate time to the questioning and answering process. Questions vary, too, so prepare answers on a wide range of subjects. Remember that questions are not meant to trick you, but are asked to discover more about you. The interview is not an examination, so there are no right or wrong answers. Before making a selection, the interviewer wants to learn about your personality and your commitment. The following list shows a small range of questions that you may be asked at interview:

- Why have you chosen this course?
- Why do you want to study in … (name of town or city)?
- Did you come to the open day?
- Where do you see yourself in five years' time?
- Have you completed any work experience?
- Which is your strongest piece of work and why?
- Which fashion designers do you admire?
- Which fashion illustrators inspire you?
- What do you like/dislike about the fashion industry?
- Which is your favourite high-street retailer?
- Which television programmes do you enjoy watching?
- What are you reading at the moment?
- What is your favourite piece of clothing and why?
- Which magazines do you read?

Above and overleaf
Photographs of Nottingham Trent University's Graduate Fashion Week stand. The area is a showcase for graduates' portfolios, garments, promotional postcards, business cards and literature about the fashion courses run by the university. GFW is an ideal opportunity for a new designer or illustrator to launch their career.

- Where do you wish to travel?
- What was the last exhibition you saw?
- What do you like best about your personality?
- Do you have any weaknesses?
- What is your greatest achievement to date?

Another issue for students attending a fashion-based interview is what to wear. Selecting the right outfit is difficult if you are worried about the scrutiny of the interviewer. It is fair to say that the interviewer's main objective is to scrutinize your work rather than your dress, but a little effort in this area will not go unnoticed. Choose something you feel comfortable wearing – your clothes should reflect your personality. Don't try to be someone you are not just to impress. It can be a good idea to wear a garment or accessory that you have made yourself to underline your creativity.

Most importantly when attending interviews at this level, remain calm and confident. Think about the questions carefully and answer with considered sentences. Your main aim is to make the interviewer think they would be making a mistake if they were to reject you. Believe in yourself and others will believe in you.

The big wide world

Many students embark on their education as a clear route to a career, while for others it is more of a personal challenge – they enjoy a subject, such as fashion, and want to develop their work as far as possible. After many years of study, and probably a great deal of expense, you are no longer a student but a graduate ready to enter the big wide world. At this stage, you will probably ask yourself: "How do I decide what to do next?"

There will be many others in a similar position when you leave the safety of the study environment. Most courses showcase graduate work in annual, specialized graduate exhibitions attended by members of the fashion industry and the press. This is a wonderful opportunity for graduates to network and establish contacts for possible future employment. It is also a chance to receive feedback about your work and observe the work of others. Fashion scouts visit these events to hunt for emerging talent, so label your work clearly with your name and contact details. Printing memorable postcards or business cards for possible employers to take away is worthwhile to try to ensure you make a lasting impression.

A degree course is not the only route to a career in fashion illustration. Many people become self-taught illustrators or attend night classes to gain extra artistic skills to build a suitable portfolio. To succeed in this way, you need to be committed and passionate about your future. You should network actively and sell yourself, as you will not have the support of an educational establishment. This is probably a slightly tougher journey, but not an impossible one if you are dedicated.

Many jobs in the creative field are not advertised, but found through

personal contacts, networking or by approaching an employer directly with a curriculum vitae. If you are seeking employment, you need to sell yourself. Just like in the university selection interview, encourage employers to think they will be making a mistake if they do not hire you. Conduct a thorough and organized search for an appropriate job vacancy, attending careers fairs and consulting websites, national, regional and local newspapers, industry-specific journals and publications, job centres and, most importantly, specialist fashion-recruitment agencies. Listed on page 231 are some useful addresses giving information on finding employment.

Self-employment, or freelancing, is another avenue to explore. Many fashion illustrators work on a freelance basis, being employed for a specific job then moving on to the next when that is complete. For an illustrator, this is an excellent way to build a diverse portfolio with a varied range of clients. You need to be highly motivated to work in this way, and may require an agent to help promote your skills.

Postgraduate study is an opportunity to further your education. Many graduates return to college or university to continue studying the subject they enjoy, or to gain higher-level training and qualifications to increase their employment opportunities. This is a costly process so, before applying, find out about any available funding such as scholarships. Postgraduate study can be undertaken at any time. Some employers may fund your study on a part-time basis if your new qualifications and skills will also be advantageous to them.

Residencies offer an income and work space in return for producing a work of art that meets a particular brief. Clients can range from schools, hospitals, galleries and community spaces to industrial and commercial settings. Becoming a resident at an appropriate location is an excellent way to gain experience and enhance your development as an artist.

The stand at Graduate Fashion Week has a seated area and refreshments to encourage perspective employers and recruitment agents to view the graduate portfolios.

Taking time out to travel in between graduating and joining the workforce can also be a valuable learning experience, giving you inspiration and confidence. Travel with a camera, sketchbook and diary to record different cultures and lifestyles. When you return to the job market, you will be competing against a new set of graduates, so use your travelling observations to demonstrate the connection between this experience and your work.

Selling yourself

Your curriculum vitae (CV) is a personal marketing tool presenting qualifications, skills and attributes that demonstrate your suitability for a job. It must be accurate, interesting and up-to-date to make the best impression possible and get you noticed. Frequently asked questions include: How many pages should it be? Which font size should I use? Should I list my interests? The final decisions rest with you. Make your curriculum vitae a personal record of your life that promotes you to your best advantage. Start by analyzing the skills and interests you have to offer in relation to your career choice. Your experience in higher education is not just about what you learned from studying, but about your life. Consider your academic achievements, social life, work experience, hobbies and responsibilities. All provide evidence of the qualities sought by employers. The following is a useful checklist:

- Name
- Contact details
- Personal profile/statement
- Education
- Qualifications
- Employment/work experience
- Responsibilities

- Skills/abilities/specialist areas
- Achievements/competitions/awards
- Interests/hobbies
- Referees

As an artist, consider the visual aspect of your curriculum vitae. Including images of your work will make you memorable to an employer. Think of ways to promote yourself further, perhaps creating a marketing pack that includes a curriculum vitae, business card with contact details, and postcards or photographs of your artwork. Some people send digital visual curriculum vitaes online in the form of a PDF file. Most importantly, always follow up with a phone call to a potential employer. There are many ways of selling yourself effectively and making sure that you stand out from the crowd.

When it is time to enter the world of employment, it may take you a little while to know exactly what you want to do. The following interviews with industry professionals may help you to decide the path you wish to take. Stephanie Pesakoff, from Art Department, describes the role of an illustration agent. David Downton tells of his fascinating life as a fashion illustrator. Lysiane de Royère, from Promostyl, discusses how to illustrate future fashion trends, and Jeffrey Fulvimari tells of his growing empire as a commercially led fashion illustrator.

Illustration agent

Art Department
www.art-dept.com

Fashion illustrators often work on a self-employed, freelance basis whereby they are hired to illustrate specific assignments. Working as a freelancer involves learning to juggle several commissions at once, invoicing clients and managing all administration. Many freelancers gain the representation of a reputable agent, who promotes them. The services of an agent vary depending on the individual illustrator but, in general, they handle all enquiries, portfolio requests, negotiations, scheduling and invoicing. In addition, a good agent maintains portfolios and an agency website with samples of illustrators' work, and perhaps orchestrates agency promotions.

Stephanie Pesakoff is an illustration agent at Art Department, based in New York. Art Department also represents photographers, fashion stylists, hair and make-up artists, and prop and set designers. Stephanie suggests: "An illustrator should have some professional experience under their belt before approaching an agent, as they then have a better idea of the agent's job and more realistic expectations and appreciation of the agent."

It is not easy to get onto the books of Art Department. They receive enquiries from an average of five illustrators a week, yet take on only approximately four new illustrators a year. However, Stephanie says she is "always happy to see new work" and suggests "e-mail contact with jpeg samples is the best way to approach an agency". When looking for the right agent Stephanie advises: "It's a really personal thing. First and foremost, the illustrator should do their homework and learn about various agencies. The illustrator should like the work that an agency represents and also the branding or positioning of the agency. I also think it is really important to meet the owner, or agent, and get a sense of whether you like and trust them as a person. This is someone you might well be speaking with on a daily basis, so I think it's necessary to like each other. I think it is appropriate to check around and enquire about the reputation of the agency; you can ask industry people, or even ask the agent if you can speak directly with some artists already on their roster."

When Stephanie is selecting an illustrator to be represented by Art Department, she says: "They must first be nice, communicative and professional people; I then have to love their work. And finally, I think it's important that their style fits in with the look and client base of our agency."

So, how important is fashion illustration in the commercial world? Stephanie states adamantly: "Not important enough! Historically, there is a very rich and varied legacy of fashion illustration, so it seems ironic that, today, illustration is often considered a 'risky' or 'edgy' option. Look at any issue of *Vogue* from the 1940s and you will find it's all illustration. I still consider a big part of my job to be education."

Fashion illustrator

David Downton
www.daviddownton.com

Although David Downton describes his role in the fashion industry modestly as "peripheral", it could be argued that it is set firmly in the centre. Born in London, he trained at Canterbury and Wolverhampton Art Colleges in graphics and illustration. On graduating, David's first commission was to illustrate a cover for *Which Computer?* magazine, but it didn't take long for his distinctive style of portraying figures to be recognized, transporting him into a very different environment. "I didn't set out to become a fashion illustrator, and came at it via a circuitous route," says David. "The job that changed everything for me was in 1996, when I was sent to Paris by a magazine to cover the couture shows. I'd dabbled in fashion illustration prior to this, but then I'd also done all the usual jobs that an illustrator tackles, from educational books to packaging design." David became a familiar face, back stage and front of house, in the lavish and illustrious Paris haute couture shows. His reports from the collections have appeared in *The Times, The Daily Telegraph, The Independent* and *Harper's Bazaar* (Australia).

David has spent time in Paris drawing the world's greatest models wearing couture clothes from Dior, Chanel and Valentino. Following a seven-hour sitting with Linda Evangelista at the George V Hotel for *Visionnaire* magazine, he said: "I could retire now – it doesn't get any better than this."

But retirement is really far from the thoughts of one of the world's most glamorous and busy fashion illustrators. When asked to describe his most recent work commitments, the list wasn't exactly short. He designed a poster for the V&A exhibition *The Golden Age of Couture*, collaborated on a project with Dita Von Teese, illustrated the famous 'Twiggy' bags for M&S, worked with Philip Treacy on images for his hotel in Galway, created a range of greetings cards, had a solo exhibition (*Couture Voyeur* charting ten years of his prestigious and hugely successful career), is writing his own book and has just been made a visiting professor at the London College of Fashion before receiving an honorary doctorate in San Francisco later in the year.

Like René Gruau, René Bouché and Antonio Lopez before him, drawing beautiful women has become second nature to David, who has captured the likenesses of some of the world's most striking women. He has created portraits of Jerry Hall, Carmen, Elizabeth Hurley, Iman, Paloma Picasso, Joely Richardson and Anna Piaggi. His friendship and many collaborations with the model Erin O'Connor has brought him further recognition. In an article for The Association of Illustrators, David says of Erin: "I can never decide whether she looks like a drawing, or whether she is how a drawing ought to look." David also advises: "Drawing from a model (famous or not) is vital; in many ways the model is the drawing." Asked how he achieves the perfect fashion illustration, David answers simply: "I don't think it is possible to achieve

Above
The front cover of Downton's acclaimed fashion illustration magazine *Pourquoi Pas?* The magazine is a celebration of drawing in a digital age.

Opposite top
Pourquoi Pas? features an article entitled 'Whatever Dita wants…' and is illustrated with an exclusive sitting by Dita Von Teese from which this illustration is taken.

Opposite bottom left
In 2003, David Downton drew Carmen at the Hardy Amies Couture House in Savile Row, London. This watercolour image was also featured as a cover for the *Telegraph* magazine. Carmen has modelled for more than 60 years. Downton says: "She understands how to edit herself for the page. She is so wonderful to draw, because she understands what it is that you see and knows how to make pictures."

Opposite bottom right
Another illustration from Downton's first solo exhibition shows a Thierry Mugler couture dress portayed in flat colours, cut paper and acetate overlay. This image became iconic, selling instantly. It is still well-remembered and is pictured on cards for The Art Group and IKEA.

a perfect illustration. But hope springs eternal. I think it involves a lot of work and a lot of drawing and my mantra is always 'keep working until it looks effortless'." It is fair to say that David Downton's working process is far from effortless. For The Association of Illustrators, he describes how he captures the moment with a model such as Erin O'Connor: "Between us we come up with a pose that will look good on the page and will show whatever is interesting or important about the clothes. I then take maybe half a dozen photographs. Then I make between 10 and 20 drawings of each pose during the sitting, using pen or graphite on cheap cartridge or layout paper." When the preparatory stage is complete David begins again, this time working on watercolour paper, "refining the image, while trying to maintain the spontaneity of the first drawing".

The importance of practice cannot be emphasized enough for David: "To get one good fashion illustration, I have often completed 20 sketches beforehand. Forests have perished in the name of this! As an illustrator, you should be constantly learning and striving to get better." The art materials and techniques he uses vary: "It depends on the situation, the job, or my mood. I use watercolour, gouache, Dr. Martin's inks, cut paper, pencil and lots of Rotring black ink – I am keen to develop my skills and would like to try oils and I am going to take a screen-printing course."

Left
Illustration of Erin O'Connor backstage at a Galliano/Christian Dior Haute Couture summer show.

Above
For this image for a Topshop advertisement, David Downton spent days drawing Lily Cole and Erin O'Connor. He describes it as: "A perfect job – when you draw from models like these, so much of your work is done. They wear the clothes so well, creating a fashion illustration came easily."

Opposite
This long, black dress is a YSL couture creation that David illustrated for his 2006 exhibition. It is created with ink, gouache and charcoal. The lucky owner of this illustration is Colin McDowell, one of the world's most authoritative fashion commentators.

When talking about different styles and techniques for fashion illustration, David says: "There are no rules." Although computer-generated work is not for him, he explains: "It's great if used with skill and imagination. Jason Brooks showed us all how it could be done." Aspiring illustrators are often concerned about capturing their own style, but David advises: "Don't worry about it. Very few people start out with a 'style' as such. It will evolve the more you work – in fact, most illustrators work in several styles. Above all, I think drawing is at the centre of it, whether you finally end up producing work digitally or not. So, my advice would be to keep drawing, and be very persistent."

As well as looking to the future, David has an eye on the past. He admires the work of René Gruau for his peerless graphic sense and glamour; Eric for his draughtsmanship and consistency; and René Bouché for his way with a likeness. Today, David thinks Mats Gustafson is the illustrator's illustrator. When speaking of his own fashion illustration career, David believes: "It is important to never really be in fashion. I was never really the illustrator of the moment, and never having been exactly 'in', I've also never really gone 'out'." This theory has made for a successful career spanning over two decades. David recognizes his many achievements and says: "I have been lucky enough to work with some extraordinary people – designers, models, some of the most iconic faces of our time – but I think probably my greatest achievement is to have had solo exhibitions in London, Paris and New York."

David is keen to point out that, following a brief interlude when fashion illustration fell out of favour, the industry is growing again. He acknowledges: "There are a lot of illustrators out there – but, thankfully, there is also a lot of work today. You can work editorially in newspapers, magazines and publishing; for card companies; in advertising – in conjunction with designers or fashion houses; or alternatively pursue fashion as 'art' rather than illustration, and work with galleries and on limited-edition prints."

In 2008 David launched the first international magazine dedicated to fashion illustration, *Pourquoi Pas?* Its aim? To celebrate drawing in our digital, disposable, point-and-shoot world. It features articles on the greats, like Bouché, Berthoud and Viramontes to name but a few. "I wanted to celebrate drawing in an industry almost completely dominated by photography. The reason I became a fashion illustrator was not fashion *per se*, but the work of these great artists, and the reason I started the magazine was in order to pay tribute to them," explained the legendary illustrator. The precious 1,500 limited-edition copies of *Pourquoi Pas?* are stocked in exclusive stores such as Browns, Harrods and the V&A. (Find out more at www.pqpmagazine.com.)

Finally, what for David Downton is the best thing about his job as a fashion illustrator? "I don't have to shave. Independence. Drawing every day. But most of all having a window onto the world of couture and all its craziness, and then going home to a real family situation. As I said before, 'it's peripheral.'"

Trend forecaster

Promostyl
www.promostyl.com

In the constantly changing world of fashion, trend-forecasting companies offer a prediction service to members of the retail industry. Promostyl is an independent company specializing in style, design and trend research. Created in 1967, Promostyl now has a large international client base, including companies such as Adidas, Chanel, Coca-Cola, L'Oréal, Orange, Swarovski, Waterman and Zara on their books. Promostyl employs fashion illustrators on a regular basis to help sell its trends.

Launched in the early seventies by Danielle de Diesbach, of Promostyl, the *Trend Book* has become an indispensable tool for fashion and textile professionals. Today the *Trend Book* is a full-colour publication created using computer graphics with many colour fashion illustrations, in volume and in flats. These show clearly the accessories, colour ranges and garment shapes, prints, badges and logos of the future. Each fashion trend is divided into various stories as outlined in the images (facing page). The pages are filled with themed fashion illustrations, fabrics and colour details destined for the future.

Promostyl creates 15 different illustrated *Trend Books* per season, including *Colours, Fabrics, Influences, Home, Baby-Layette, Sport and Street, Lingerie, Women, Ultimates* (for young women), *Men, Children, Junior, Shoes, Knit* and *Beachwear*. Promostyl's *Trend Books* are published 18 months in advance of the season they are predicting, and are compiled for spinners and weavers, garment-makers, fashion designers, accessory brands, cosmetic and sports companies, industrial designers, marketing people, and all those whose products must be in step with changing trends and lifestyles.

The Head of Communications at Promostyl, Lysiane de Royère, says: "Curiosity and intuition are very important qualities in this business. It is very important to know as early as possible everything that is new on our planet. At Promostyl, we have a network of agents, and information is continually gathered through travel, the international press and by consulting the internet."

To make these books as original as possible, Promostyl employs just over ten fashion illustrators. "They are employed on a freelance basis, with some illustrators working three to four months every year for us," states Lysiane. "We select an illustrator because of the allure or the modernity of their sketches, as well as the legibility of the items," she explains. "A Promostyl fashion illustration needs to be nice to look at but easy to understand and translate into a garment." The illustrators are given as much information as possible to complete their work: a brief, rough sketches, colours and the names of the trends. "They use a range of materials including pens, pencils, markers and the computer. Very often, we ask them to scan their sketches and add fabric and colours onto them using Photoshop," says Lysiane.

Above
A selection of womenswear fashion illustrations that feature in Promostyl's *Trend Book* pages. The illustration styles vary according to the story of the season.

Opposite
Promostyl's *Trend Book* pages for womenswear and menswear display future trends for fashion, fabrics and accessories. Colourways for future seasons are also outlined.

When asked which qualities Promostyl look for when employing a fashion illustrator, Lysiane replies: "They need to have a good sense of themselves, be fashion-orientated and passionate about their work!" Lysiane also explains: "Our illustrators come from all over Europe. It is important to speak languages in order to be able to work with various countries around the world." With its offices in Paris, New York and Tokyo – and its widespread network of exclusive agents spanning Europe, Brazil, Asia, Australia – Promostyl's influence is truly felt around the world.

Commercial fashion illustrator

Jeffrey Fulvimari
www.jeffreyfulvimari.com

"I overstep gallery structures and head straight for the shopping mall," says Jeffrey Fulvimari, creator of the doe-eyed fashionable girls that grace numerous products worldwide. Jeffrey's highly successful fashion illustrations have appeared on everything from Stila cosmetics and Louis Vuitton scarves to a Grammy award-winning CD cover for *The Complete Ella Fitzgerald Songbooks*.

Even as a child Jeffrey was always enthusiastic about art. He says: "I was encouraged by my teachers to express opinions, and they often held up my work as an example for other pupils. I won a big art award when I was very young, so I guess you could say I had a following since first grade!" Jeffrey continued his education at The Cooper Union, New York, and Cleveland Institute of Art in the US. He originally trained as a fine artist, producing conceptual art. However, to generate an income, he decided on illustration as a career. "Fashion illustration drew me in because it was not museum art. I wanted to do something that was as far removed from my education as possible. I am very proud of my fashion illustration career. In the art world, everybody should be different, we do not all have to be on the same page."

Fulvimari has made his name by embracing the commercial world with open arms. He has launched his own range of illustrated clothing, bags and wallets across the UK and US. His fashion brand has been steadily building in Japan since 1998, and his "Bobbypin" girls feature on teenage cosmetics, nightwear and greetings cards in large department stores worldwide. "My work is both my career and my hobby. I like to make statements with the jobs I take," says Jeffrey. "I was at my happiest when a magazine wrote about my merchandise from both ends of the spectrum in the same article. I don't ever want to be labelled as 'prejudiced' in the fashion world. I want my audience to be from all walks of life. So, to have both top-end and cheaper fashion ranges featuring alongside one another really told my story."

Long before he became a successful fashion illustrator, Jeffrey was given a piece of advice that has guided his life since: "Aim high – and you'll go straight to the top." His first job was illustrating a nightclub invitation for a

Above
An advertisement for American department store Neiman Marcus. It stocks fashion's premier designers and the best beauty brands, making Jeffrey Fulvimari's illustrated models the perfect advertising choice.

Below
A selection of Jeffrey Fulvimari's illustrated products. His trademark doe-eyed girls feature on bags, purses, clocks and crockery.

weekly event called "Smashing". It was a folded card with each illustrated panel telling a story. The intriguing invitations became a talking point, and people in the fashion world, such as Anna Sui, started to collect them. Soon he was working for *American Vogue* and the department store Barneys without the aid of an agent. Unafraid to voice his own talents, he had guts and a determination to succeed.

He advises: "Launch your career in a big city. Go to the top, and don't be afraid. I had confidence and self-belief and just willed everything to happen. I've never stopped working since."

Jeffrey describes fashion illustration as "a notion of blank pages being filled with notes. It is a starting point that some people take and turn into a career". He also warns: "I chose illustration because 15 years ago it seemed to be a dead medium. It was easier to get to the top and make some money. Now, you have to be individual as there are so many illustrators out there." When discussing his inspiration, he replies: "I don't really look at other fashion illustrators much, as I don't want to be influenced by their styles. I limit the amount of art I look at because I want to make new art for myself."

Admiring the simple lines of Charles M. Schulz – the creator of Snoopy and Charlie Brown – Jeffrey explains, "Schulz's artwork is perfection – there is not a leaf out of place in Snoopy's world." Another creative influence was the work of Maxfield Parrish, who was one of the best-known illustrators in America. Parrish's first work, created specifically for reproduction as an art print in 1922, became his signature piece. The atmospheric, sun-drenched *Daybreak*, which depicted a reclining classical female figure in a toga, with a nude child standing over her on a columned portico, looking out onto a rich landscape of flowering trees and purple mountains, became an almost instant icon, found on many American families' walls. "I love his work so much that I sign my illustrations with just simple initials, as Maxfield Parrish once did. I admire how many people Parrish's art has touched."

Fashion illustrations by Jeffrey Fulvimari featuring his distinctively featured girls and his hallmark quirky captions.

Jeffrey caught the world's attention in 2003, when Madonna asked him to illustrate her children's book, *The English Roses*. Madonna's team conducted a Cinderella-style search for the person who could bring her *The English Roses* to life. In a top-secret mission, they sent people all over the globe to see if the "illustrator slipper" fitted. When Jeffrey was first approached, he remembers that he was initially unsure: "I had held off illustrating children's books for so long because one day I would like to produce my own. But, how could I refuse? This was Madonna asking! I thoroughly enjoyed working with Madonna. I was involved in the creation of the book at all levels and the art director for the project was excellent. The best thing for me was my grandmother was named Rose, so I hope my involvement with the book would have made her very happy."

In 2006, Jeffrey contributed artwork to Belgian fashion designer Verlaine for the Fall and Spring Fashion weeks in New York. The following season, Verlaine used his illustration as a print for beautiful silk dresses. They whipped up a storm among the fashion set, and Fulvimari was the name on everyone's lips. However, Jeffrey has been a star in Japan for a long time, since his debut exhibition at The Parco Gallery in Tokyo. In 2008 in celebration of the ten-year anniversary of his career launch in Japan, he opened a Superstore in Tokyo's trendy Daikanyama district. The store is dedicated to all things Jeffrey, allowing his fans to access all of his products under one roof for the first time!

When asked about the greatest element of his job, he answers: "I get all the credit, because I did it myself – it is an intensely satisfying role." He also points out: "I am very lucky that I need do very little self-promotion or marketing. I do not have a portfolio as I am approached personally through my agent for new projects. I have worked very hard to be in this position, though it has not been an easy ride." So, is there anything Jeffrey Fulvimari doesn't like about being a fashion illustrator? "Oh, yes", he states "the isolation is so hard. Sometimes I work for days on a project without seeing a single soul. The frustration when things are out of your control is also difficult. My advice is to try and turn any negativity around. Collect rejections and disappointments, because with every ten rejections comes one acceptance. Having a positive attitude is vital in this game!"

With so many commercial fashion-illustration projects under his belt, you wouldn't be alone in thinking Jeffrey lives a glamorous lifestyle but, when questioned about his role in the industry, he argues: "I rarely go to fashion shows. I'm a total outsider really – a fly on the wall. I just enjoy watching people and then using the characters in my illustrations. The truth is I often find my characters very close to home. I live in an imaginative Woodstock house that can only be described as the Hobbit meets Heidi's grandfather! There is even a friendly bear living in my yard!"

The English Roses book, written by Madonna and illustrated by Jeffrey Fulvimari.

Jeffrey's store in the trendy Daikanyama district in Tokyo, which for the first time allows his fans to access all of his products and artwork under one roof.

In summary

Fashion Illustrator *is intended as a rewarding reference book of practical advice and inspirational ideas to form a basis from which individual creativity can develop, and not as a bible to be followed word for word. As Coco Chanel is reputed to have said, "To be irreplaceable in life, one must be different"— excellent advice for your sketchbooks and portfolio, and for life in general! The following pages offer useful information to help you on your journey. You will find recommended further reading, addresses and websites of institutions and other worthwhile contacts, and a glossary of important words.*

Further reading

1 Inspiration

Paul Arden, *It's Not How Good You Are, It's How Good You Want To Be*, Phaidon, 2003

Richard Brereton, *Sketchbooks: The Hidden Art of Designers, Illustrators and Creatives*, Laurence King Publishing, 2009

Gerald Celente, *Trend Tracking*, Warner Books, 1991

Leonardo Da Vinci *The Notebooks of Leonardo Da Vinci: Selections*, Oxford World's Classics, 1998

Gwen Diehn, *The Decorated Page: Journals, Scrapbooks & Albums Made Simply Beautiful*, Lark Books, 2002

Alan Fletcher, *The Art of Looking Sideways*, Phaidon Press, 2001

Carolyn Genders, *Sources of Inspiration*, A&C Black, 2002

Bill Glazer, *The Snap Fashion Sketchbook: Sketching, Design, and Trend Analysis the Fast Way*, Prentice Hall, 2007

Kay Greenlees, *Creating Sketchbooks for Embroiderers and Textile Artists: Exploring the Embroiderer's Sketchbook*, Batsford, 2005

Danny Gregory, *An Illustrated Life: Drawing Inspiration from the Private Sketchbooks of Artists, Illustrators and Designers*, How Books, 2008

Holly Harrison, *Altered Books, Collaborative Journals and Other Adventures in Bookmaking*, Rockport Publishers Inc., 2003

Dorte Nielsen and Kiki Hartmann, *Inspired: How Creative People Think, Work and Find Inspiration*, Book Industry Services, 2005

Timothy O'Donnell, *Sketchbook: Conceptual Drawings From The World's Most Influential Designers and Creatives*, Rockport, 2009

Lynne Perrella, *Journal and Sketchbooks: Exploring and Creating Personal Pages*, Rockport Publishers Inc., 2004

Simon Seivewright, *Basics Fashion: Research and Design*, AVA Publishing, 2007

Jan Bode Smiley, *Altered Board Book Basics and Beyond: For Creative Scrapbooks, Altered Books and Artful Journals*, C & T Publishing, Inc., 2005

Paul Smith, *You Can Find Inspiration in Everything*, Violette Editions, 2001

Petrula Vrontikis, *Inspiration Ideas: Creativity Sourcebook*, Rockport, 2002

2 The Figure

100 Ways to Paint People and Figures (How Did You Paint That?), North Light Books, 2004

Bina Abling, *The Advanced Fashion Sketchbook*, Fairchild Group, 1991

Anne Allen and Julian Seaman, *Fashion Drawing: The Basic Principles*, Batsford, 1996

Sandra Burke, *Fashion Artist: Drawing Techniques to Portfolio Presentation*, Burke Publishing, 2003

Giovanni Civardi, *Drawing the Clothed Figure: Portraits of People in Everyday Life*, Search Press, 2005

Diana Constance, *An Introduction to Drawing the Nude: Anatomy, Proportion, Balance, Movement, Light, Composition*, David & Charles, 2002

Elisabetta Drudi and Tiziana Paci, *Figure Drawing For Fashion Design*, The Pepin Press, 2001

Gustavo Fernandez, *Illustration for Fashion Design: Twelve Steps to the Fashion Figure*, Prentice Hall, 2005

Robert Beverly Hale, *Master Class in Figure Drawing*, Watson-Guptill Publications Inc., 1991

Patrick John Ireland, *Figure Templates for Fashion Illustration*, Batsford, 2002

Patrick John Ireland, *New Fashion Figure Templates*, Batsford, 2007

Maite Lafuente, Aitana Lleonart, Mireia Casanovas Soley, and Emma Termes Parer, *Fashion Illustration: Figure Drawing*, Parragon, 2007

Andrew Loomis, *Figure Drawing For All It's Worth*, The Viking Press, 1943

Kathryn McKelvey and Janine Munslow, *Illustrating Fashion*, Blackwell Science (UK), 1997

Jennifer New, *Drawing from Life: The Journal as Art*, Princeton Architectural Press, 2005

Sharon Pinsker, *Figure: How to Draw & Paint the Figure with Impact*, David & Charles, 2008

John Raynes, *Figure Drawing and Anatomy for the Artist*, Octopus Books, 1979

John Raynes and Jody Raynes, *How to Draw The Human Figure: A Complete Guide*, Parragon Books, 2001

Nancy Riegelman, *9 Heads*, Prentice Hall, 2002

Julian Seaman, *Professional Fashion Illustration*, Batsford, 1995

Mark Simon, *Facial Expressions: A Visual Reference for Artists*, Watson-Guptill Publications Inc., 2005

Ray Smith, *Drawing Figures*, Dorling Kindersley, 1994

Ron Tiner, *Figure Drawing Without a Model*, David & Charles, 2008

Bridget Woods, *Life Drawing*, The Crowood Press, 2003

3 Artistic Techniques

Bina Abling, *Fashion Rendering with Color*, Prentice Hall, 2001

Jennifer Atkinson, Holly Harrison and Paula Grasdal, *Collage Sourcebook: Exploring the Art and Techniques of Collage*, Apple Press, 2004

EL Brannon, *Fashion Forecasting*, Fairchild, 2002

Steve Caplin, *How to Cheat in Photoshop: The Art of Creating Photorealistic Montages – Updated for CS2*, Focal Press, 2005

Tom Cassidy and Tracey Diange, *Colour Forecasting*, Blackwell Publishing 2005

M. Kathleen Colussy, *Rendering Fashion, Fabric and Prints with Adobe Photoshop* (CD-ROM), Prentice Hall, 2004

David Dabner, *Graphic Design School: The Principles and Practices of Graphic Design*, Thames & Hudson, 2004

Brian Gorst, *The Complete Oil Painter*, Batsford, 2003

Hazel Harrison, *The Encyclopedia of Drawing Techniques*, Search Press Ltd, 2004

Hazel Harrison, *The Encyclopedia of Watercolour Techniques: A Step-by-step Visual Directory, with an Inspirational Gallery of Finished Works*, Search Press Ltd, 2004

John Hopkins, *Basics Fashion Design: Fashion Drawing: 5*, AVA Publishing, 2009

David Hornung, *Colour: A Workshop for Artists and Designers*, Laurence King Publishing, 2004

Wendy Jelbert, *Collins Pen and Wash* (Collins Learn to Paint Series), Collins, 2004

Maite Lafuente, *Fashion Illustration Techniques*, Taschen, 2008

Bonny Lhotka, et al, *Digital Art Studio: Techniques for Combining Inkjet Printing with Traditional Art Materials*, Watson-Guptill Publications Inc., 2004

Vicky Perry with Barry Schwabsky (Introduction), *Abstract Painting Techniques and Strategies*, Watson-Guptill Publications Inc., 2005

Melvyn Petterson, *The Instant Printmaker*, Collins & Brown, 2003

Nancy Riegelman, *Colors for Modern Fashion: Drawing Fashion with Colored Markers*, 9 Heads Media, 2006

Sarah Simblet, *The Drawing Book*, Dorling Kindersley, 2005

Kevin Tallon, *Digital Fashion Illustration*, Batsford, 2008

Naoki Watanabe, *Contemporary Fashion Illustration Techniques*, Rockport, 2009

Lawrence Zeegen, *The Fundamentals of Illustration*, AVA Publishing, 2005

4 Tutorials

Jemi Armstrong, et al, *From Pencil to Pen Tool: Understanding and Creating the Digital Fashion Image*, Fairchild Books, 2006

Marianne Centner and Frances Vereker, *Adobe Illustrator: A Fashion Designer's Handbook*, WileyBlackwell, 2007

M. Kathleen Colussy, Steve Greenberg, *Rendering Fashion, Fabric and Prints with Adobe Illustrator*, Prentice Hall, 2006

M. Kathleen Colussy, Steve Greenberg, *Rendering Fashion, Fabric and Prints with Adobe Photoshop 7*, Prentice Hall, 2003

Val Holmes, *Encyclopedia of Machine Embroidery*, Batsford, 2003

Susan Lazear, *Adobe Illustrator for Fashion Design*, Prentice Hall, 2008

Susan Lazear, *Adobe Photoshop for Fashion Design*, Prentice Hall, 2009

Janice Saunders Maresh, *Sewing for Dummies*, Hungry Minds Inc., 2004

Carol Shinn, *Freestyle Machine Embroidery: Techniques and Inspiration for Fiber Art*, Interweave Press, 2009

Kevin Tallon, *Creative Computer Fashion Design: With Abobe Illustrator*, Batsford, 2006

Mary Thomas's Dictionary of Embroidery Stitches, new edition by Jan Eaton, Brockhampton Press, 1998

Elaine Weinmann and Peter Lourekas, *Visual QuickStart Guide: Illustrator CS For Windows and Macintosh*, Peachpit Press, 2004

Elaine Weinmann and Peter Lourekas, *Visual QuickStart Guide: Photoshop CS For Windows and Macintosh*, Peachpit Press, 2004

5 Presentation for Fashion Design

Anvil Graphic Design Inc. (compiler), *Pattern and Palette Sourcebook: A Complete Guide to Using Color in Design*, Rockport Publishers Inc., 2005

Terry Bond and Alison Beazley, *Computer-Aided Pattern Design and Product Development*, Blackwell Science (UK), 2003

Janet Boyes, *Essential Fashion Design: Illustration Theme Boards, Body Coverings, Projects, Portfolios*, Batsford, 1997

Sandra Burke, *Fashion Computing: Design Techniques and CAD*, Burke Publishing, 2005

Elisabetta Drudi, *Wrap and Drape Fashion: History, Design and Drawing*, Pepin Press, 2007

Akiko Fukai et al, *Fashion in Colors*, Editions Assouline, 2005

Richard M. Jones, *The Apparel Industry*, Blackwell Science (UK), 2003

Maite Lafuente, *Details*, Rockport, 2007

Oei Loan and Cecile de Kegel, *The Elements of Design*, Thames & Hudson, 2002

Kathryn McKelvey and Janine Munslow, *Fashion Design: Process, Innovation and Practice*, Blackwell Science (UK), 2003

Kathryn McKelvey and Janine Munslow, *Fashion Source Book*, Blackwell Publishing, 2006

Carol A. Nunnelly, *Fashion Illustration School: A Complete Handbook for Aspiring Designers and Illustrators*, Thames & Hudson, 2009

Mireia Casanovas Soley, Daniela Santos Quartiino, Catherine Collin, and Maite Lafuente, *Fashion Illustration: Flat Drawing,* Parragon Inc, 2007

Richard Sorger and Jenny Udale, *The Fundamentals of Fashion Design*, AVA Publishing, 2006

Steven Stipelman, *Illustrating Fashion: Concept to Creation*, Fairchild, 1996

Linda Tain, *Portfolio Presentation for Fashion Designers*, Fairchild Books, 2004

Sharon Lee Tate, *The Complete Book of Fashion Illustration*, Prentice Hall, 1996

Caroline Tatham and Julian Seaman, *Fashion Design Drawing Course*, Thames & Hudson, 2004

Estel Vilaseca, *Essential Fashion Illustration: Color*, Rockport, 2008

Chidy Wayne, *Essential Fashion Illustration: Men,* Rockport, 2009

6 Historical and Contemporary Fashion Illustration

François Baudot, *Gruau*, Editions Assouline, 2003

Cally Blackman, *100 Years of Fashion Illustration*, Laurence King Publishing, 2007

Laird Borrelli, *Fashion Illustration by Fashion Designers*, Thames & Hudson, 2008

Laird Borrelli, *Fashion Illustration Now*, Thames & Hudson, 2000

Laird Borrelli, *Fashion Illustration Next*, Thames & Hudson, 2004

Laird Borrelli, *Stylishly Drawn*, Harry N. Abrams, 2000

CameraWork, *Unified Message In Fashion: Photography Meets Drawing*, Steidl Publishers, 2002

Paul Caranicas and Laird Borrelli, *Antonio's People*, Thames & Hudson, 2004

Bethan Cole, *Julie Verhoeven: FatBottomedGirls 003*, Tdm Editions, 2002

Martin Dawber, *Big Book of Fashion Illustration: A World Sourcebook of Contemporary Illustration,* Batsford, 2007

Martin Dawber, *Imagemakers: Cutting Edge Fashion Illustration*, Mitchell Beazley, 2004

Martin Dawber, *New Fashion Illustration*, Batsford, 2005

Delicatessen, *Fashionize: The Art of Fashion Illustration*, Gingko Press, 2004

Delicatessen, *Mondofragile: Modern Fashion Illustrators From Japan*, Happy Books, 2002

Simon Doonan, *Andy Warhol Fashion*, Chronicle Books, 2004

Hendrick Hellige, *Romantik*, Die Gestalten Verlag, 2004

Angus Hyland, *Pen and Mouse*, Laurence King Publishing, 2001

Angus Hyland and Roanne Bell, *Hand to Eye: Contemporary Illustration*, Laurence King Publishing, 2003

Yajima Isao, *Fashion Illustration in Europe*, Graphic-sha Publishing, 1988

Robert Klanten, *Illusive: Contemporary Illustration and Its Context*, Die Gestalten Verlag, 2005

Robert Klanten, *Wonderland*, Die Gestalten Verlag, 2004

Alice Mackrell, *An Illustrated History of Fashion: 500 Years of Fashion Illustration*, Costume and Fashion Press, 1997

Francis Marshall, *Fashion Drawing*, The Studio Publications, 1942

William Packer, *The Art of Vogue Covers: 1909–1940*, Octopus Books, 1983

William Packer, *Fashion Drawing in Vogue*, Coward-McCann Inc., 1983

Pao & Paws, *Clin d'oeil: A New Look at Modern Illustration*, Book Industry Services, 2004

Pater Sato, *Fashion Illustration in New York*, Graphic-sha Publishing, 1985

M. Spoljaric, S. Johnston, R. Klanten, *Demanifest*, Die Gestalten Verlag, 2003

Victionary, *Fashion Wonderland*, Viction Design Workshop, 2008

Anna Wintour, Michael Roberts, Anna Piaggi, André Leon Talley and Manolo Blahnik, *Manolo Blahnik Drawings*, Thames & Hudson, 2003

Steve Shipside and Joyce Lain Kennedy, *CVs for Dummies: UK Edition*, John Wiley and Sons, Ltd, 2003

M. Sones, *Getting into Fashion: A Career Guide*, Ballatine, 1984

Linda Tain, *Portfolio Presentation for Fashion Designers*, Fairchild, 1998

Robert A. Williams, *Illustration: Basics for Careers*, Prentice Hall, 2003

Theo Stephen Williams, *Streetwise Guide to Freelance Design and Illustration*, North Light Books, 1998

Peter Vogt, *Career Opportunities in the Fashion Industry*, Checkmark, 2002

7 The Future: Guidance

Noel Chapman and Carole Chester, *Careers in Fashion*, Kogan Page, 1999

David Ellwand, *Fairie-ality: The Fashion Collection*, Candlewick Press, 2002

Mary Gehlhar, *The Fashion Designer Survival Guide: An Insider's Look at Starting and Running Your Own Fashion Business*, Kaplan Publishing, 2005

Helen Goworek, *Careers in Fashion and Textiles*, WileyBlackwell, 2006

Debbie Hartsog, *Creative Careers in Fashion*, Allworth Press, 2007

Sue Jenkyn Jones, *Fashion Design*, second edition, Laurence King Publishing, 2005

Astrid Katcharyan, *Getting Jobs in Fashion Design*, Cassell, 1988

Anne Matthews, *Vogue Guide to a Career in Fashion*, Chatto & Windus, 1989

Margaret McAlpine, *So You Want to Work in Fashion?*, Hodder Wayland, 2005

Kathryn McKelvey and Janine Munslow, *Fashion Design: Process, Innovation and Practice*, Blackwell Science, 2008

Trade publications and magazines

Another Magazine
Arena Homme
Bloom
Bridal Buyer
California Apparel News
Computer Arts
Daily News Record (DNR)
Dazed and Confused
Drapers: Drapers Record and Menswear
Elle
Elle Decoration
Embroidery
Fashion Line
Fashion Reporter
Girls Like Us
Graphic magazine
ID
In Style
International Textiles
Juxtapoz
Living etc
Marie Claire
Marmalade
Numero
Oyster
Pop
Purple Fashion
Retail Week
Self Service
Sneaker Freaker
Tank
10
Textile View
Tobe Report
V
View on Colour
Victor & Rolf
Visionaire
Vogue
W
Women's Wear Daily (WWD)
World of Interiors

Useful addresses

UK

The Association of Illustrators
2nd Floor, Back Building
150 Curtain Road,
London EC2A 3AR
tel: +44 (0)20 7613 4328
www.theaoi.com

The Association of Illustrators was established to promote illustration, advance and protect illustrators' rights and encourage professional standards. The website contains professional resources for illustrators and for those commissioning illustration. It carries a growing catalogue currently consisting of nearly 8,000 images, including self-managed illustrators' portfolios.

The British Fashion Council (BFC)
5 Portland Place
London W1N 3AA
tel: +44 (0)20 7636 7788
fax: +44 (0)20 7636 7515
www.londonfashionweek.co.uk

The BFC supports British fashion designers and manufacturers, especially with export enterprises. It encourages new talent through annual awards to students, such as the 'Innovative Pattern Cutting Award' as well as awards for Graduate Fashion Week presentations.

The Crafts Council
44a Pentonville Road
London N1 9BY
tel: +44 (0)20 7806 2500
fax: +44 (0) 20 7837 6891
www.craftscouncil.org.uk

In addition to having an excellent contemporary gallery and crafts bookshop at this address the Crafts Council offers many services, such as advice, a reference library and development grants. It also publishes a magazine that promotes crafts.

Design Wales
PO Box 383
Cardiff CF5 2W2
tel: +44 (0)2920 41 7043
email: enquiries@designwales.org.uk
www.designwales.org.uk

Design Wales provides comprehensive advice and support services on all issues related to design.

Their services are provided free to all businesses in Wales.

The Department of Trade and Industry (DTI)
(Clothing, Textiles and Footwear Unit)
1 Victoria Street
London SW1H 0ET
tel: +44 (0)20 7215 5000
www.dti.gov.uk

A government department that advises UK businesses on legal issues, the DTI also provides information concerning export regulations.

Embroiderers' Guild
Apt 41, Hampton Court Palace,
Surrey KT8 9AU
tel: +44 (0)20 8943 1229
email: administrator@embroiderersguild.com
www.embroiderersguild.com

The Guild was set up in 1906 by 16 graduates of the Royal School of Needlework and is now the largest crafts association in the UK. The Embroiderers' Guild is a leading educational charity and registered museum, with a lively programme of exhibitions, events and workshops.

Fashion Awareness Direct (FAD)
10a Wellesley Terrace
London N1 7NA
tel: +44 (0)20 7490 3946
email: info@fad.org.uk
www.fad.org.uk

An organization committed to helping young designers succeed in their careers by bringing students and professionals together at introductory events.

The Prince's Youth Business Trust (PYBT)
18 Park Square East
London NW1 4LH
tel: +44 (0)20 7543 1234
www.princes-trust.org.uk

The Prince's Trust gives business advice and professional support and awards funding for young and unemployed people planning to set up a potentially successful new idea in business.

US

The Color Association of the US (CAUS)
315 West 39th Street, Studio 507
New York, NY 10018
tel: +1 212 947 7774
email: caus@colorassociation.com
www.colorassociation.com

Fashion Information
The Fashion Center Kiosk
249 West 39th St
New York, NY 10018
tel: +1 212 398 7943
email: info@fashioncenter.com
www.fashioncenter.com

National Art Education Association
1916 Association Drive
Reston
VA 20191-1590
tel: +1 703 860 8000
www.naea-reston.org

Fabric and resources.

National Network for Artist Placement
935 West Ave #37
Los Angeles, CA 90065
tel: +1 213 222 4035
www.artistplacement.com

New York Fashion Council
153 East 87th Street
New York, NY 10008
tel: +1 212 2890420

Pantone Color Institute
590 Commerce Boulevard
Carlstadt, NJ 07072-3098
tel: +1 201 935 5500
www.pantone.com

The Society of Illustrators
128 East 63rd Street
New York, NY 10021-7303
tel: +1 212 838 2560
www.societyillustrators.org

The Society of Illustrators can be joined via a membership scheme. It is home to a wonderful illustration museum and library. The website contains useful information for students, and there are annual competitions and bursaries.

United States Small Business Administration
26 Federal Plaza, Suite 3100
New York, NY 10278
tel: +1 212 264 4354

Museums, illustration and costume galleries

A number of museums offer reduced rates to students or free admission on certain days.

UK & Europe

Centro Internazionale delle Arti e del Costume

Palazzo Grassi
Campo San Samuele
San Marco 3231
20124 Venice
Italy
tel: +39 41 523 1680
www.palazzograssi.it

Galeria del Costume
Piazza Pitti
50125 Firenze
Italy
tel: +39 55 238 8615

Located in a wing of the Palazzo Pitti.

Kobe Fashion Museum
Rokko Island
Kobe
Japan
te: +81 (0)78 858 0050
www.fashionmuseum.or.jp

Kostümforschungs Institut
Kemnatenstrasse 50
8 Munich 19
Germany

Lipperheidesche Kostümbibliothek
Kunstbibliothek
Staatliche Museen zu Berlin
Matthaikirchplatz 6
10785 Berlin
Germany

MoMu
Antwerp Fashion ModeMuseum
Nationalestraat 28
B – 2000 Antwerpen
Belgium
tel: + 32 (0)3 470 2770
email: info@momu.be

Musée des Arts de la Mode et du Textile
Palais du Louvre
107 Rue de Rivoli
75001 Paris
France
tel: +33 1 44 5557 5750
www.ucad.fr

Musée de la Mode et du Costume
10 Avenue Pierre 1er de Serbie
75016 Paris
France
tel: +33 1 5652 8600

Musée des Tissus et des Arts Décoratifs
34 Rue de la Charité
F-69002 Lyon
France
tel: +33 (4)78 3842 00
email: info@musee-des-tissus.com
www.musee-des-tissus.com

Museum of Costume
Assembly Rooms
Bennett Street
Bath BA1 2QH
UK
tel: +44 (0)1225 477 173
fax: +44 (0) 1225 477 743
www.museumofcostume.co.uk

Museum Salvatore Ferragamo
Palazzo Spini Feroni
Via Tornabuoni 2
Florence 50123
Italy
tel: + 39 055 336 0456

Victoria and Albert Museum (V&A)
Cromwell Road
South Kensington
London SW7 2RL
UK
tel: +44 (0)20 7942 2000
www.vam.ac.uk

US

Costume Gallery
Los Angeles County Museum of Art
5905 Wilshire Boulevard
Los Angeles , CA 90036
tel: +1 323 857 6000
www.lacma.org

Costume Institute
Metropolitan Museum of Art
1000 Fifth Avenue at 82nd Street
New York, NY 10028-0198
tel: +1 212 535 7710
www.metmuseum.org

The Museum of American Illustration
Society of Illustrators and Norman Price Library
128 East 63rd Street
New York, NY 10021
tel: +1 212 838 2560
www.societyillustrators.org

**Museum at the Fashion Institute
of Technology**
Seventh Avenue at 27th Street
New York, NY 10001-5992
tel: +1 212 217 5970
email: museuminfo@fitnyc.edu

**The National Museum of American
Illustration (NMAI)**
Vernon Court
492 Bellevue Avenue
Newport
Rhode Island 02840
tel: +1 401 851 8949
fax: +1 401 851 8974
email: art@americanillustration.org

Illustration agents

Agent 002
Contact: Michel Lagarde
70 Rue de la Folie
Méricourt
75011 Paris
France
tel: +33 (0)1 40 21 03 48
fax: +33 (0)1 40 21 03 49
email: michel@agent002.com
www.agent002.com

Art Department
Contact: Stephanie Pesakoff (see p.217)
420 West 24th Street, #1F
New York, NY 10011
US
tel: +1 212 243 2103
fax: +1 212 243 2104
email: stephaniep@art-dept.com
www.art-dept.com

Big Active
Warehouse D4, Metropolitan Wharf,
Wapping Wall
London E1W 3SS
UK
tel: +44 (0)20 7702 9365
fax: +44 (0)20 7702 9366
email: contact@bigactive.com
www.bigactive.com

The Central Illustration Agency
1st Floor
29 Heddon Street
London W1B 4BL
UK
tel: +44 (0)20 7734 7187
fax: +44 (0)20 7434 0974
email: info@centralillustration.com

CWC International, INC
Contact: Koko Nakano
296 Elizabeth St 1F
New York City, NY 10012
US
tel: +1 646 486 6586
fax: +1 646 486 7633
email agent@cwc-i.com
www.cwc-i-com

Illustration Web
Illustration Ltd
2 Brooks Court
Cringle Street
London SW8 5BX
UK
tel: +44 (0)20 7720 5202
email: team@illustrationweb.com
www.illustrationweb.com

Traffic Creative Management
136, East 74th St
New York, NY 10021
UK
tel: +1 212 734 0041
fax: +1 212 734 0118
email: info@trafficnyc.com
www.trafficnyc.com

Annuals

The Society of Artists
www.illustratoragents.co.uk

The Black Book
www.blackbook.com

Le Book
www.lebook.com

American Illustration
www.ai-ap.com

Websites

www.adobe.com
The home page for all Adobe software packages.

www.collezionionline.com
View shows, videos and magazines online.

www.computerarts.co.uk
Offers creative suggestions, tutorials and the latest
news from the world of computer illustration.

www.costumes.org
Links to many other sites covering all aspects
of costume.

www.daviddownton.com
Website of fashion illustrator David Downton.
(see pp.218–21).

www.fashion-enterprise.com
Website of the Centre of Fashion Enterprise,
London College of Fashion.

www.fashionoffice.org
Online magazine covering fashion, beauty,
and lifestyle.

www.ideasfactory.com
Online 'Art and Design' zone.

www.jeffreyfulvimari.com
Website of commercial fashion illustrator
Jeffrey Fulvimari (see pp.224–26).

www.marquise.de
A site all about period costume, from the Middle
Ages to the early twentieth century.

www.promostyl.com
Website of the trend forecasting agency
(see pp.222–23).

www.vogue.co.uk
With links to the websites of all other Vogue
international editions.

Glossary

Adobe Illustrator An object-orientated (or vector) digital computer package.

Adobe Photoshop A bitmap (or raster) digital computer package.

Advertising The promotion through public announcements in newspapers or on radio, television, or the internet of a product, service, event, or vacancy in order to attract or increase interest in it.

Avant-garde A fashion or concept that is ahead of its time.

Bespoke Individual made-to-measure tailoring for men's suits.

Boutique French word for an independent, usually small, shop with unique stock and atmosphere.

Brainstorming Open discussion among colleagues or peers to introduce new ideas and concepts.

Brand A name or trademark used to identify a product and denote quality, value or a particular ethos.

Buyer The person responsible for planning and managing the buying and selling of merchandise.

CAD/CAM Computer-aided design and computer-aided manufacturing.

Canvas A strong, heavy, closely woven fabric that is stretched around wood to create a surface for painting.

Capsule collection A small range of related styles with a special purpose or impact.

Classic A term for a style that remains constantly popular and changes very little in detail, e.g. men's shirts, the cardigan, jeans.

Clothed life-drawing or fashion-life The act of drawing the clothed human figure from life.

CMYK palette A shortened term for cyan, magenta, yellow and black (the last "k" abbreviation used to avoid confusion with blue), the ink colours used for printing.

Collage The art of making pictures by sticking cloth, pieces of paper, photographs, and other objects onto a surface.

Collection The term used for fashion clothes that have related features or are designated for a specific season. "The Collections" is a colloquial description used for the Paris fashion shows.

Colour forecasting The prediction of future colour trends by analyzing data from trade shows, etc.

Colour palette/gamme A limited selection of linked colours used in fashion design and illustration.

Colourway The limited range of colours that a style of garment, or a collection, may be offered in; also the term for the choice of colours in which a printed textile is available.

Composition The way in which the parts of something are arranged, especially the elements in a visual image.

Contemporary Distinctly modern and in existence now.

Coordinates Fabrics or items of clothing that relate in colouring or style and which can be worn together.

Costing The base price of the garment, determined by the materials, trimmings, labour and transportation. An illustration might accompany a costing.

Couturier French word for fashion designer.

Critique/Crit Discussion and evaluation of work, often held as a group session at the end of a project or assignment.

CV (curriculum vitae) A chronological personal summary detailing educational and employment achievements and attributes. (Known in the US as a résumé.)

Degree show The exhibition of work which is assessed to ascertain a student's degree classification.

Design board A visual presentation board in a portfolio that represents a final design.

Design developments Drawings that progress through desirable or successful elements within a design theme.

Design roughs First-stage drawings for designs, usually made quickly in pencil and without extraneous detail.

Diffusion line A secondary, usually lower-priced garment line that allows consumers on a budget to buy into the designer look.

Digital imagery The process of transforming or altering a digital image by manipulating it on the computer.

Digital portfolio Examples of artwork saved digitally to be e-mailed or put on compact disks to post to prospective employers.

Draping A method of making a fashion style or pattern by manipulating fabric on a body or dress form.

Editorial Newspaper or magazine article that expresses the opinion of its editor or publisher. If the article is on fashion, it will often feature fashion illustrations.

Embellishment The addition of ornament or decoration to a garment, bag or item of footwear, to make it more interesting.

Embroidery Decorative stitching that may be produced by hand or machine, in a range of different types of thread.

Exhibition A public display, usually for a limited period, of a collection of works of art, illustrations or objects of special interest.

Fabric rendering The artistic, and perhaps accurate, representation of fabric using various media.

Fad A very short-lived fashion.

Fashion cycle The calendar by which a company will plan, design, make and market its ranges.

Fashion designer A person who devises and executes designs for clothes.

Fashion illustration An artistic image produced to promote a particular fashion.

Freelancer Self-employed person working, or available to work, for a number of employers, rather than being committed to one, and usually hired for a specific project or limited period.

Final collection The last college collection before graduation.

Flapper A young woman of the 1920s who disdained prior conventions of decorum and fashion.

Flats Diagrammatic drawings (see Specification drawings).

Glossies The high-quality magazines.

Graduation The completion of a course of academic study.

Graduate exhibition A display of graduates' work visited by potential employers.

Grain The direction of a fabric's threads. Fabric may be cut along a straight grain or 'on the bias', which gives it a draping, figure-hugging quality that may be emphasized in a drawing.

Handwriting, signature A personal design style, design features or way of drawing.

Haute couture French term for the highest quality of dressmaking. A designer or company cannot call themselves *haute couture* unless they have passed the stringent criteria of the Chambre Syndical of the Fédération Française de la Couture.

Illustration agent A company or an individual that can represent and promote the work of an illustrator.

Internship (also known as a placement) A period of study, usually between two weeks and nine months, spent within a business to gain work experience.

Label This term is sometimes used synonymously with logo, but is also used to describe the tag which identifies the designer or manufacturer and the origin, fibre contents and wash care of the product.

Layout pad A sketchbook with sheets of thin paper that can be traced through.

Light box A device with an illuminated surface that can be used for tracing an image.

Life-drawing The act of drawing the nude human figure.

Line-up A preview of *toiles* (*see* below) or finished garments on models to determine the balance, range and order of a collection. A line-up can also be illustrated and presented in a portfolio.

Logo A brand name or symbol used to identify a product or designer.

Mac A shortened term for an Apple Macintosh computer.

Manga A Japanese style of comic books or animated cartoons.

Mannequin A model of the human body, usually life-size, used to display or fit clothes. Smaller wooden mannequins are used to draw body proportions and poses.

Masking fluid A liquid that acts as a resist to paint.

Memorabilia Objects collected as souvenirs of important personal events or experiences. Sometimes such objects are considered to be collectors' items.

Mood board A presentation board that shows the overall concept and direction of a design collection. It captures the style and theme for a set of designs by displaying defining images, fabrics and colours that are influential in the design process.

Objective or observational drawing The act of creating an image to represent what is seen during direct observation.

Outline The edge or outer shape of something.

Palette In illustration, this refers to the range of colours used in an artwork.

Pantone A worldwide colour referencing system.

PC Abbreviation for personal computer.

Photomontage The technique of combining a number of photographs, or parts of photographs, to form a composite picture. Photomontage is popularly used in art and advertising.

Pixel Tiny, individual dot of light that is the basic unit from which images on a computer or television screen are made. In digital imaging it is the smallest unit from which the image is made.

Pochoir Line drawings that are highlighted with watercolour applied through finely cut stencils. The technique originated in Japan and was a popular form of fashion illustration in the early 1900s.

Portfolio A large, portable holder for flat artwork and press cuttings that should give a potential client a comprehensive view of the illustrator's or designer's capabilities.

Pose A particular physical posture or stance. The pose of the figure is a vital component of a fashion illustration, giving it impact and mood.

Postgraduate study The opportunity for a student to continue to learn, or carry out research, in an academic environment following graduation.

Première vision (PV)
French for "first look" and the name of the major fabric trade fair held twice a year in Paris.

Prêt-à-porter French for 'ready-to-wear', a term used for better quality and designer separates; it is also the name of a major fashion exhibition.

Price point Different ranges of price indicate quality and market level, e.g. budget, designer and luxury. An illustrator's specification drawings (see below) assist in establishing a price point.

Primary colours Colours that cannot be made by mixing other colours, but from which other colours are mixed.

Promotion Any means by which something is marketed to become better known and more popular. Promotional fashion illustration is mainly used in advertising to encourage the sale of clothing.

Proportion The relationship and balance between one aspect of a design and another. A principle of fashion design, in fashion illustration it also relates to the comparative size and shape of different elements of the human body.

Psychedelic A term often used to describe distorted or wildy colourful artwork that resembles images that may be experienced by somebody under the influence of a halluconogenic drug.

Range building The process of building a series of connected ideas that are realized in a clothing range.

Ready-to-wear Also known as off-the-peg, prêt-à-porter and clothing separates.

Research A methodical investigation into a subject or theme in order to discover facts and visual data.

Retail The selling of goods from a business to an individual consumer.

Scanner A device used to convert an image into digital form for storage, retrieval and transmission.

Secondary colours Colours produced by mixing two primary colours.

Shade The result of mixing a colour with black.

Silhouette The overall shape of a garment or person, without detail.

Sketchbook A visual notebook or diary used to create a personal response to the world and inspire ideas for finished works.

Snapshot A record or view of a particular moment in a sequence of events, or in a continuing process.

Specification drawings (also known as specs) A design drawing annotated with measurements and manufacturing details, such as the stitching and trimmings that are to be used in manufacturing a garment.

Stories Design themes comprising fabric, colour or style associations that are used within a particular collection.

Storyboard Also known as a theme board, this is a presentation of the concept for a collection with a detailed breakdown of styles and co-ordinates.

Stylist A fashion expert who prepares fashion items for photographs or presentations.

Tear sheets Also known as swipes, these are pictures lifted from magazines etc. that are used as initial inspiration or corroboration for a concept, not to copy.

Template A master, or pattern, that serves as a guide from which other, similar shapes can be made. A figure template is used as a guide in fashion design and can also be used for illustration.

Tertiary colours Colours made by mixing a primary colour with its adjacent secondary colour.

Theme A unifying image or concept that, in fashion design or illustration, appears repeatedly in a collection or throughout a series of sketches or illustrations.

Tint The result of mixing colour with white.

Toile French for a lightweight muslin, used to describe a sample or test garment.

Tone The result of mixing grey with a colour.

Tracing A copy of an image made by laying a sheet of translucent paper on top of the original.

Trend A current fashion or mode

Trend book A colour publication that outlines the predicted future trends up to two years ahead.

Trimming A term used in fashion illustration to describe the decorative detail on a garment, but which is also used for the finishing and cutting of loose threads.

Tutor In British universities, an academic who is responsible for teaching and advising an allocated group of students.

Tutorial A meeting with a tutor to discuss a student's progress.

Vector A mathematically defined object or group of objects that in computing can be a range of lengths, but which appear only in one dimension.

Viewfinder A simple device that helps to select how much of a figure's surroundings to include within the confines of a picture. This allows the selection of the view that works best.

INDEX

Page numbers in *italics* refer to captions

A

accent colour 80
acrylics *70, 71*
adhesives 62–63
Adobe Illustrator 63, 77
    tutorial 98, *99–101*
Adobe Photoshop 63, 77
    tutorial 113, *113–16*
agents 8, 215, 217
airhostess uniform *122*
American Vogue 225
anatomy 7, 30–31
Armani, Giorgio *13*
Art Deco 140, 142
Art Department 217
art materials 62–77, *62*
Art Nouveau 140, 141, 142
artistic techniques 8, 62–92

B

backgrounds 33
Bagshaw, Tom 8, 38, *39, 51*
    interview 158
    Photoshop tutorial 113, *113–16*
Bakkum, Vincent *11, 51,* 70, *70*
    interview 152
Bakst, Leon 141
Ball, Victoria
    interview 180
Ballets Russes 141
ballpoint pens 67, *67*
bangles 12, *12*
Barbier, Georges 142
beach huts *11*
beads 89
Beardsley, Aubrey 142
Beaton, Cecil 144
Bellows, George 10
Benito, Eduardo Garcia 143
Bérard, Christian 145
Berning, Tina 8, 26, *26,* 28, 67, *67,* 71, *71*
    interview 188
    mixed media tutorial 94, *94-6*
Berthold, François 150
bitmapped tools 76
Blackwell, Su 28
body proportions 7, 30, 33, 40-3, *40, 41, 42*
Bolin, Guillermo 143
Bolongaro Trevor 8, *86,* 130, *130, 131,* 132
books 12–13
Botero, Fernando 149
Bouché, René 145, *145,* 218, 221
Bouët-Willaumez, René 144, 145, *145*

brainstorming 14
Brissaud, Pierre 142
Brooks, Jason 146, *146,* 150, *150,* 221
buildings: structure *11*
butterfly theme 14, *14, 15*
buyers 133

C

Caballero, Paula Sanz 73, *73*
    interview 157
CAD/CAM systems 132, *132*
cameras 10, 76
Campbell, Stephen 143, *143*
card 64
careers 8, 214-26
Carlstedt, Cecilia 8, 16, *17,* 22, *55,* 69, 77, *83, 84, 86, 88, 91, 92*
    interview 186
Carosia, Ed *51,* 67
    interview 164
cartridge paper 64
Chanel, Coco 143
charcoal 62
checks 83, *83*
chicken theme 19, *19*
chiffon 86
Chin, Marcos 8, 142, *142, 151*
    Illustrator tutorial 98, *99–101*
    interview 162
Clark, Ossie *37*
Clark, Peter 12, *64,* 65
clothing: construction *32,* 33
collage 64, *64,* 65
    mixed media 74–75, *74*
collecting inspirational items 12–13
collections 124
    presenting 128, *208, 209*
colour 78–81
    accent 80
    complementary 79
    in fashion illustration 80–81, *80, 81*
    forecasting 80
    mixing 79
    in mood boards 122
    primary *78,* 79
    secondary *78,* 79
    tertiary *78,* 79
    warm and cool 79
colour palettes: fashion 80–81, *80, 81*
colour wheel *78,* 79
colour-prediction agencies 80
coloured backing papers 64
coloured pencils 66
commercial fashion illustrator 224–26
complementary colours 79
computers 63
    collage 74, 75
    linked to sewing machine 62
    templates 47
concept boards *see* mood boards

continuous-line exercise 37, *37*
'conversation pieces' 209
cool colours 79
costing 132
Cubism 142
curriculum vitae (CV) 216
customer profile 124
cutting mats 62

D

Dagmar 146
Dalí, Salvador 140
Davidsen, Cathrine Raben 22–24, *23*
Degas, Edgar 140
Delhomme, Jean-Philippe 150
denim 85, *85,* 87
design roughs 8, 124–28, *124, 127, 133*
Diesbach, Danielle de 222
digital illustration 76–77, *76, 77,* 150, 151
digital portfolios 74, *211*
Dignan, James
    interview 204
Dior, Christian 145
'don't-look-back' exercise 36, *36*
Dover, Poppy *208, 209, 210*
Downton, David 144, *144,* 150, 218-21, *218, 220*
drape 92, *92*
drawing 7
    design details 131
    exercises 36–37, *36, 37*
    human figure 30–60
    materials 66–67
    observational *35,* 36
    tutorial 109, *109–12*
dress for interview 214
Dryden, Helen 143
Dufkova, Petra
    interview 206

E

Einstein, Albert 14
embellished fabrics 87
embroidered fabrics 87
embroidery
    machine 62
    threads 73
    tutorial 102, *102, 104*
Emin, Tracy 12
English Roses (Madonna) 226, *226*
equipment 62
Eric (Carl Erikson) 144, *144, 145,* 221
Erté 142
exaggeration 131, 143
    of human features 40, 43, *43, 44*
exhibitions *13*
    graduate 214
Expressionism 145
eyebrows *53*

eyelashes 52
eyes *53*

F

fabrics 73
  checks 83, *83*
  denim 85, *85*
  design roughs 126, *127*
  drape 92, *92*
  embellished 87
  embroidered 87
  knitted *84*, 85, *85*
  on mood boards 122
  patterns 91, *91*
  prints 91, *91*
  rendering 83–92
  ribbing 84
  sheer 86–87, *86*
  shiny *88*, 89
  sourcing 126
  stripes 83
  textures and weaves 84
  woollen 84, *84*
  woven 85, *85*
faces 50–52, *50*, *51*, *53*
fashion design
  presentation 133
  range-building 126–28
fashion illustration 8
  colour palettes 80–81, *80*, *81*
  contemporary 151–206
  history 140–50
fashion illustrator 218–21
  commercial 224–26
feathers 89, *89*
feet 58, *58*
Fellows, Craig 8, 19, *19*, 136–37, *136*, *137*, *138*
figure *see* human figure
films 142
fineliner pens 67, 131
flannel 84
'flappers' 143
flats 8, 131–32
fleece 84
Folies Bergères 142
Forbes, Montana
  interview 196
found objects 12, 74
Fraser, Vince *211*
  interview 166
freelancing 215
Fulvimari, Jeffrey 224–26, *224*, *225*, *226*
fur 89, *89*
further education 8, 212–14
  portfolios 210–11

G

gabardine 84
galleries 11
Gardiner, Louise 8, 73, *73*, *80*, 81
  embroidery tutorial 102, *102*, *104*
  interview 194
Gazette du Bon Ton 142
georgette 86
Gibb, Kate 77, *77*
  interview 176
Gibson, Charles Dana *140*, 141
Goetz, Silja 66, *67*, 74
  interview 174
gouache 71
graduates
  exhibitions 214
  Fashion Week *215*
  portfolios 136, *136*, *137*, *138*, 210–11
Grafstrom, Ruth 144
graphics tablet 76
graphite sticks 66
Gregor, Max 45, *45*, 55, *80*, 81, *81*
  interview 184
Gruau, René 145, 218, 221
Gustafson, Mats 142, 146, 150, 221

H

hair 55, *55*
hand embroidery 102
  threads 73
hands 56, *57*
Harper's Bazaar 141, 142, 144
heads 50-2, *50*, *51*, *53*
Hegardt, Amelie 8, 69, *69*
  ink tutorial 118, *118–19*
  interview 190
Held, John, Jr 143, *143*
herringbone 84
highlights 89
history 8, 140–50
Høj, Iben 22–28, *22*, *23*, *24*, *26*, *84*, 92, 133, *133*, *134*, *134*, *135*
Hollar, Wenceslaus 140
hue 79
Hulme, Sophie 8, *88*, 124–28, *124*, *127*, *128*
human figure
  clothed 33, 83, 92
  drawing 30–60
    exercises 36–37, *36*, *37*
    from life 30–38, *32*, *34*, *35*
    observational *35*, 36–37
  exaggerating features 40, 43, *43*, *44*
  faces 50–52, *50*, *51*, *53*
  feet 58, *58*
  hands 56, *57*
  heads 50–52, *50*, *51*, *53*
  height 42, *42*
  measuring 33, *33*, 42, *42*
  nude 30–33, *31*

  poses 41, *41*, 45
  proportions 7, 30, 33, 40–43, *40*, *41*, *42*
  scale 33
  silhouette 60, *60*
  templates 47, *47*
humour *43*, 60, 143

I

ideas-bank 12
illustration agents 8, 215, 217
Illustrator (Adobe) 63, 77
  tutorial 98, *99–101*
Indian ink 68
ink 68
  tutorial 118, *118–19*
inspiration 7, 10-19
  collecting items 12–13
  sources of 10–13
  themes 16–18
interviews 8, 213–14
Iribe, Paul 141

J K

jobs: finding 214–16
journals 13
Keogh, Tom 145
Kiraz 146, *146*
knitted fabrics *84*, 85, *85*
knives 62

L

lace 86, 87
Lady's Magazine 140
Laine, Laura 26, 92, 133, *135*
lamé 89
Larocca, Alma
  interview 168
layout pad 126, *128*
layout paper 64
lead pencils 66
leather 89
legs: elongating 43, *43*, *44*
Leonardo da Vinci 31
Lepape, Georges 141, *141*
life drawing 34, *34*, *35*
Life magazine 141
light box 46, 62
lips 53
location
  sketching on 33
lookbooks 133
Lopez, Antonio 146, *146*, 149, 218

M

McCartney, Stella 148
machine embroidery 102, *102*, *104*
  threads 73

Madonna 226, *226*
magazines 13
mail-out folders 22–28, *22, 23, 24, 26,*
   133, *134, 135*
markers 67
Marshall, Francis 34, *35*, 144
Martin, Charles 142
Marval, Jacqueline 28
masking tape 63
Matisse, Henri 37, 140, 145
Mattotti, Lorenzo 142, 146
measuring methods
   human figure 33, *33*, 42, *42*
medium: finding 62
Michelangelo Buonarroti 31
mind-mapping 14, *15*
mixed media *31*
   collage 74–75, *74*
   tutorial 94, *94–96*
mohair 84
mood boards 122, *122*
movies 142
Mucha, Alphonse 141
museums 11

N

net 86, 87
Nishinaka, Jeff 64, *64*
   interview 172
non-waterproof ink 68
noses 53
nostalgia 11–12
nude figure 30–33, *31*, 34

O

O'Connor, Erin 218, 220, *220*
oil pastels 62
oils 71
organdie 86, 87
organza 86, 98
Orientalism 141
outline drawing exercise 37, *37*

P

packaging 12, 64
paints 62, 68–69, 71
Palmer, Gladys Perint 149
paper 64, *64*
paper sculpture 64, *64*
Parrish, Maxfield 225
past
   nostalgia for 11–12
pastel paper 64
pastels 62
patterned fabrics 91, *91*
pencils 62, 66
pens 62, 67
personality: depicting 43, *43*

Persson, Stina 24–26, *24*, 55, 58
   interview 154
Pesakoff, Stephanie 216, 217
photocopiers 63
photographs 10, *10*, 46, *46*, 47
photomontage: tutorial 108, *108–09*
Photoshop (Adobe) 63, 77
   tutorial 113, *113–16*
Picasso, Pablo 10, 16, 31–33, *31*, 145
pinstripes 84
plaids 83
Plank, George 143
Plovmand, Wendy
   interview 200
pochoir 141
Poiret, Paul 141
Pollard, Douglas 143
Pop Art 146
portfolios 8, 133
   arranging work in 209-10
   cases for 209
   digital 74, *211*
   further education 210
   graduate 136, *136, 137, 138*, 210–11
   presentation 122, 208–11, *208, 209, 210*
   professional 211
   size 208
poses 41, *41*, 45, *45*
postcards 13, *13*
postgraduate study 215
postgraduate travel 216
Pourquois Pas? 220, 221
presentation 8, 122-37
   fashion design 133
   portfolios 122, 208–11, *208, 209, 210*
presentation boards 19
primary colours 78, 79
printed fabrics 91, *91*
professional portfolio 211
Promostyl 80, 222–23, *222*
psychedelia 146
:puntoos *58, 60*, 192

R

range-building 126–28
Realism 148
Remfrey, David 148
researching themes 13–14
residencies 215
ribbing 84
Rounthwaite, Graham 150, *150*
Royère, Lysiane de 222
rulers 62
Ryo, Masaki
   interview 160

S

satin 89
saturation 79

scale of human figure 33
scalpels 62
scanner 76
schematic drawing 131, 132
Schiaparelli, Elsa 144, *144*
Schulz, Charles M. 225
secondary colours 78, *79*
self-employment 215
selling yourself 216
sequins *88*, 89
set design 10
settings 33
sewing machines 62
   computer programs 62
shades 79
sheer fabrics 86–87, *86*
Shimizu, Yuko 38, *39*, 58, *81*, 81
   interview 202
shiny fabrics *88*, 89
shoes 58, *58*
silhouette 60, *60*
Singh, Sara 38, *38*, 53, 57, 68, *68*
   interview 170
sketchbooks 7, 10, 16–19
   buying 18
   quick studies 34, *34*, 35
   research material 17
skin-tone markers 67
Smith, Kiki 28
Smith, Lewis 43, *43*
Smith, Sir Paul 10
snow theme 16, *17*
software 63, 77
specification drawings 8, 131, *132*, 132
spray adhesive 62–63
spray paint 71
steel rulers 62
stencilling 141, *141*
story boards *see* mood boards
style 221
Surrealism 140, *144*
sweet wrappers 64

T

taffeta 89
target market 124
technical drawings 131
teeth 52
templates 10, 45, *45*, 46–47, *47*, 126
tertiary colours 78, *79*
textures 84
theatrical costume 10
themes:
   butterfly 14, *14, 15*
   chicken 19, *19*
   inspiration 16–18
   researching 13–14
   winter 16, *17*
Time magazine 141
tints 79

tissue paper 64

tones 79

Tonge, Sophia Bentley *122*

Topshop 145, *145*, *220*

Toulouse-Lautrec, Henri 140

tracing 46

travel 10–11, 216

Trend Book 222, *222*

trend forecasting 222

tulle 86

tutorials 8, 94–119

tweeds 84

U

university

    courses 212

    interviews 213–14

    visiting 212–13

V

value (colour) 79

Vanity Fair 144

vector tools 76, 77

velour 89

velvet 89

Verlaine 226

Vertes, Marcel 144

viewfinder 33, *33*

Vionnet, Madame 143

Viramontes, Tony 146, *148*

Vogue 142, 143, 144, 145, 146

voile 86

W X Y Z

Wagt, Robert 8, 43, *43*

    photomontage tutorial 108, *108–09*

    interview 178

wallpaper 10, *11*, 64

warm colours 79

water-soluble art materials 66

watercolour paints 68–69

watercolour papers 64

weaves 84

websites 211

Wester, Annika: interview 182

White, Edwina 8, *55*, 67

    drawing tutorial 109, *109–12*

    interview 198

winter theme 16, *17*

woollen fabrics 84, *84*

working drawings 131

wrapping paper 64

Xerox machines 63

Zoltan 149, *149*

Picture sources and credits

Every effort has been made to contact the copyright holders, but should there be any errors or omissions, Laurence King Publishing would be pleased to insert the appropriate acknowledgement in any subsequent printing of this publication.

Illustrators, artists and photographers are listed alphabetically: numbers listed refer to the pages on which the work appears.

Antoniou, Rebecca 7
c/o Art Department – Illustration Division,
stephaniep@art-dept.com

Bakkum, Vincent 11, 51 (bottom), 70, 152–53
www.saintjustine.com, vincent@saintjustine.com,
www.pekkafinland.fi, pekka@pekkafinland.fi

Bagshaw, Tom 39, 51 (top right), 113–17, 158–59
www.mostlywanted.com, tom@mostlywanted.com

Ball, Victoria 139, 180–81
www.illustrationweb.com,
team@illustrationweb.com

Berning, Tina 27, 67 (bottom), 71, 93–97, 188–89
www.tinaberning.de, www.cwc-i.com,
agent@cwc-i.com

Bolongaro Trevor 86, 91 (left), 130–32
www.bolongarotrevor.com
info@bolongarotrevor.com

Bouché, René 145 (right) ©Condé Nast Archive

Bouët-Willaumez, René 145 (left)
©Condé Nast Archive

Brandreth, Louise 36 (bottom right)
looeb@yahoo.co.uk

Brooks, Jason 146 (below), 150 (left)
Courtesy the artist

Caballero, Paula Sanz 73, 157
www.paulasanzcaballero.com,
nairobiflat@paulasanzcaballero.com

Campbell, Stephen 143 (right)
c/o Art Department – Illustration Division,
stephaniep@art-dept.com

Carlstedt, Cecilia 17, 54 (top right), 61, 69 (top),
75, 82 (right), 83, 84 (right), 85, 86 (right), 87, 88
(right), 89, 90, 91 (column right), 92, 186–87
www.ceciliacarlstedt.com,
info@ceciliacarlstedt.com, www.art-dept.com

Carosia, Edgardo 51 (above left), 67 (top), 164–65
ed-press.blogspot.com, ed-book.blogspot.com,
ed.carosia@gmail.com, www.agent002.com.
www.bravofactory.com

Chin, Marcos 98–101, 142, 151, 163
www.marcoschin.com, marcos@marcoschin.com

Clark, Ossie 37 (right) Courtesy of Celia Birtwell

Clark, Peter 65 www.peterclarkcollage.com
peterclark2000@hotmail.com

Collison, Lindsey 47

Davidsen, Cathrine Raben 23 (right)
www.cathrinerabendavidsen.com

Dignan, James 204–05
www.jamesdignan.com, james@jamesdignan.com

Dover, Poppy 208–10
poppydover@yahoo.com

Downton, David 144 (bottom), 218–21
www.daviddownton.com
dd@daviddownton.com

Dufkova, Petra 206
www.illustrationweb.com

Erikson, Eric Carl 144 (top) ©Condé Nast Archive

Fellows, Craig 9, 18–21, 136–38
www.craigfellows.co.uk, info@craigfellows.co.uk

Forbes, Montana 50, 196–97
www.montanaforbes.com,
me@montanaforbes.com

Fraser, Vince 76, 166–67, 211, 227
www.vincefraser.com, vince@vincefraser.com

Fulvimari, Jeffrey 224–26, 226 (*The English Roses*,
published by Callaway Editions, Inc.
©2003 Madonna. All rights reserved.)
www.jeffreyfulvimari.com

Gardiner, Louise 72, 80 (right column),
102–05, 194–95
www.lougardiner.co.uk,
loulougardiner@hotmail.com

Gibb, Kate 77, 177
kategibb.blogspot.com, www.bigactive.com,
info@thisisanoriginalscreenprint.com,

Gibson, Charles Dana 140
Private Collection, London

Glynn, Chris 32 (top left and top right)
glynngraphics@hotmail.com

Goetz, Silja 66 (bottom), 74, 174–75
www.siljagoetz.com, silja@siljagoetz.com,
www.art-dept.com, stephaniep@art-dept.com

Gregor, Max 45, 54 (bottom left), 80 (bottom),
81, 184–85
www.illustrationweb.com,
team@illustrationweb.com

Hegardt, Amelie 69, (bottom), 118–20, 190–91
www.ameliehegardt.com,
info@ameliehegardt.com, www.trafficnyc.com,
www.darlingmanagement.com

Held, John, Jr 143 (left) Private Collection, London

Høj, Iben 22, 23 (left), 24, 26, 27, 84, 133–34
www.ibenhoej.com, info@ibenhoej.com

Huerta, Carmen García 44 (right) c/o CWC
International, Inc., agent@cwc-i.com;
www.cghuerta.com, cghuerta2@yahoo.es

Huish, Megan 10
meganhuish@mac.com; model: Hannah Warren

Hulme, Sophie 88, 125, 127, 128–29
www.sophiehulme.com, info@sophiehulme.com

James, Marcus 35 (right column)
marcus@marcusjames.co.uk

Kiraz 146 (top) Private Collection, London

Laine, Laura 121, 135 www.lauralaine.net,
laura@lauralaine.net,
malin@darlingmanagement.com

Larroca, Alma 168–69
www.almalarroca.com, www.almalarroca.blogspot.
com, alma.larroca@gmail.com

Le Pape, Georges 141 Art Archive/©ADAGP,
Paris and DACS, London 2010

Lindbergh, Peter (photographer) 13 (right)

Lökholm, Fredrika and Slivka, Martin
(photographers) 63 (all images)
© Laurence King Publishing Ltd

Lopez, Antonio 147
© The Estate of Antonio Lopez

Lovegrove, Gilly 12 (top), 13 (left), 32 (bottom),
33, 40–41, 42 (top), 46 (centre and bottom),
48–49, 50 (bottom), 52 (bottom), 55, 56, 58
© Laurence King Publishing;
gilly@love-grove.fsnet.co.uk

Marshall, Francis 35 (left) Francis Marshall
Archive/Victoria & Albert Museum/The Archive
of Art & Design/©ADAGP, Paris and DACS
London, 2010

Matisse, Henri 37 (left)
©Succession H Matisse/DACS 2010

Morris, Bethan 10, 11 (right and bottom),
12 (bottom), 14, 34 (centre), 36 (top), 46 (top left)
Bethanmorris1@yahoo.co.uk

Nishinaka, Jeff 64, 172–73
www.jeffnishinaka.com, paperart@earthlink.net

Nottingham Trent University 213, 215
www.ntu.ac.uk

Nsirim, Jacqueline 15 (below)
jnsirim@hotmail.com

O'Reilly, Rosie 36 (bottom left)
rosieoreilly@hotmail.com

Palser, Marega 34 (left and right)
marega@ntlworld.com

Persson, Stina 25, 54 (top left),
59 (bottom left), 154–55, back cover
www.stinapersson.com, www.cwc-i.com,
agent@cwc-i.com

Picasso, Pablo 31 (above) [Museu Picasso,
Barcelona/"AHCB-ARXIU Fotogràfic – J.Calafell/
©Succession Picasso/DACS 2010]; 31 (below)
[Musée Picasso, Paris/Photo RMN "Gérard Blot/
©Succession Picasso/DACS 2010]

Plovmand, Wendy 200–01
www.wendyplovmand.com, mail@
wendyplovmand.com, www.centralillustration.com,
info@centralillustration.com, www.trafficnyc.com,
info@trafficnyc.com

Promostyl 222–23 www.promostyl.com

:puntoos 2, 29, 59 (top left and right), 60, 192–93
www.trafficnyc.com, info@trafficnyc.com

Rounthwaite, Graham 150 (right)
www.grahamrounthwaite.com,
studio@grahamrounthwaite.com

Ryo, Masaki 160-61
www.masakiryo.com, www.cwc-i.com,
agent@cwc-i.com

Shimizu, Yuko 39, 59 (bottom right), 81, 202–03
www.yukoart.com, yuko@yukoart.com

Singh, Sara 38, 53, 57, 68, 170–71, front cover
www.sarasingh.com, mail@sarasingh.com,
stephaniep@art-dept.com, www.art-dept.com

Smith, Lewis 43 (bottom) lewis205@hotmail.co.uk

Tonge, Sophia Bentley 123
sophiabentleytonge@yahoo.co.uk

Viramontes, Tony 148
© The Estate of Tony Viramontes

Wagt, Robert 43 (top), 106–08, 178–79
www.lindgrensmith.com,
www.margarethe-illustration.com

Wester, Annika 182–83
www.annikawester.com, www.cwc-i.com,
agent@cwc-i.com

White, Edwina 5, 54 (bottom right), 66 (top),
109–112, 198–99
www.edwinawhite.com, fiftytwopickup@gmail.com

Zoltan 149 Courtesy the artist

p. 63
Art materials supplied by
London Graphic Centre,
16–18 Shelton St, London WC2
www.londongraphics.co.uk

p.208
photographer: www.richardstow.com
model: Chloe Pridham
pridhampster@gmail.com

Acknowledgements

I wish to thank the professional illustrators whose contributions make this second edition a success. Thank you for understanding that by sharing your talents you can inspire students all over the world to improve their fashion illustrations and portfolios.

This edition has been greatly enhanced by the work of fashion designers Iben Høj, Sophie Hulme and Bolongaro Trevor. The fabric renderings of Cecilia Carlstedt are an excellent addition, as are the motivating tutorials by Tina Berning, Marcos Chin, Louise Gardiner, Robert Wagt, Edwina White, Tom Bagshaw and Amelie Hegardt. A special mention to Sara Singh and Stina Persson for your beautiful cover images.

Three recent graduates also grace the pages of Fashion Illustrator. Craig Fellows, Sophia Bentley Tonge and Poppy Dover, I know you will all do very well in your chosen fields. Best wishes and thanks from me.

I must also thank the art and design academics who have influenced my own education. As a lecturer myself, I truly value and appreciate their input into my career. I thank Elizabeth Ashton, Gillian St John, Dave Gould, Julie Pinches, Jane Davison and Steve Thompson. In particular I wish Professor John Miles to know that it was his unwavering belief that I should write a book that led me down this path. Thank you John for all those motivational chats and tellings off!

Once again, the Laurence King team have made this publishing process run smoothly. My sincere thanks go to Jo Lightfoot, Lizzie Ballantyne and Peter Kent. It has been an absolute pleasure working with my brilliant editors Anne Townley and Peter Jones. Thanks both for understanding that chicken pox, Monkey Music classes and making a play-dough cake always had to come before finishing that chapter!

Finally, a very special thank you to Gaffa, my mum, Wendy and Hugh for being the finest family an author/mother could ask for. I don't think I could have completed this edition without your constant support, love and encouragement.

Dedication

To my gorgeous little girls, Matilda and Pollyanna. Being your mummy is the best job in the world! Yes, even better than being a fashion illustrator!!

My mum taught me to believe I can do anything in life, and I hope to do the same for you always.